Dynamics of International Relations

Moving from International to Global

Theory and Issues

Dynamics of International Relations

Moving from International to Global

Theory and Issues

Parmjit Kaur Gill
Sheveta Sehgal

ATLANTIC
PUBLISHERS & DISTRIBUTORS (P) LTD

Published by
ATLANTIC
PUBLISHERS & DISTRIBUTORS (P) LTD
7/22, Ansari Road, Darya Ganj,
New Delhi-110002
Phones : +91-11-40775252, 23273880, 23275880, 23280451
Fax : +91-11-23285873
Web : www.atlanticbooks.com
E-mail : orders@atlanticbooks.com

Branch Office
5, Nallathambi Street, Wallajah Road,
Chennai-600002
Phones : +91-44-64611085, 32413319
E-mail : chennai@atlanticbooks.com

Printed in India at Nice Printing Press, A-33/3A, Site-IV, **Industrial** Area, Sahibabad, Ghaziabad, U.P.

Contents

Preface.....v

List of Maps, Figures and Tables.....x

1. An Introduction to International Relations—From International to Global.....1

Part - I—History

2. History of International Relations: An Overview.....27

Part - II—Theory

3. Idealism or Liberal Internationalism.....73
4. Realism/Neo-realism.....87
5. Liberalism/Neo-liberalism and Interdependence.....109
6. Dependency Theory and World System Analysis.....127
7. The Alternative Approach: International/Global Political Economy.....144
8. Post Positivism.....162

Part - III—Issues

9. Human Security.....187
10. Gender Sensitization of World Politics.....198
11. Environment: Contrasting Conceptions and Global Responsibility.....217
12. Globalization.....246
13. Role of State and Non State Actors in Global Politics.....259

Bibliography.....286

List of Maps, Figures and Tables

List of Maps

Map I	World Political	xi
Map II	Cold War Europe	41
Map III	Rising Asia	66
Map IV	One World—Peaceful and Prosperous	83
Map V	World Physical with Soft Borders	120
Map VI	Environmental Degradation	220

List of Figures

Fig. 6.1	Centre-Periphery Model	129
Fig. 6.2	Galtung's Model: The Structure of Imperialism	134
Fig. 6.3	Interrelationships in the World Economy as Described by Wallerstein	139
Fig. 10.1	Women Woes	200
Fig. 11.1	Human Activity and Ocean Imbalances	219

List of Tables

Table 1.1	Four Major Debates in IR	8-9
Table. 6.1	Galtung's Five Types of Imperialism	134

Map I: World Political

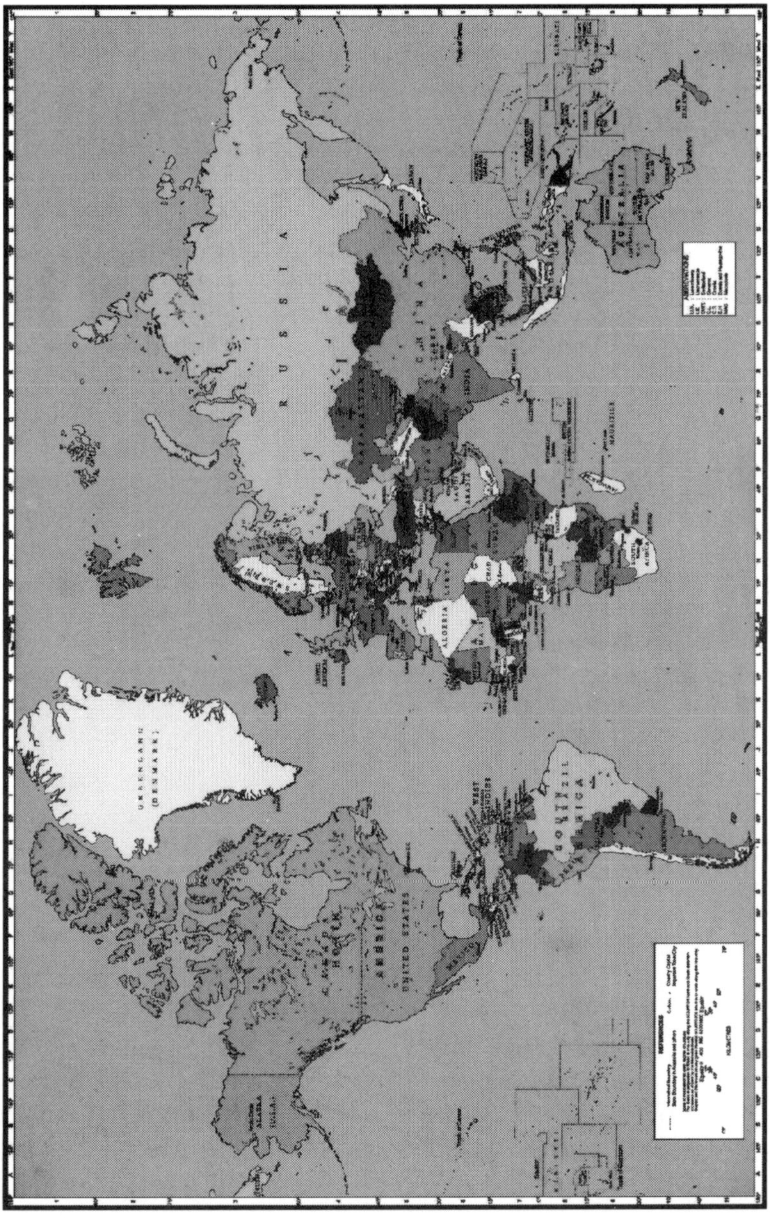

1

An Introduction to International Relations—From International to Global

Change is the law of nature. So are the international relations, moving from simple to complex. Over the time, relations among the international community are becoming a web of connectivity and interdependence. International relations are highly imperfect and consequent of it, same is the study of international relations (IR).

The world has not always been organized the way it is today, it makes more sense to speak historically of international system—the systems that were limited in geographic scope and hence cannot accurately be described as global or world systems.[1] Jeremy Bentham was the first political philosopher who used the term 'international' at the end of the eighteenth century at a time when national states were becoming both the principal actors in world affairs and the major secular objects of popular loyalties.[2] He used this term in order to distinguish between domestic and international law. Benthem's term has proved (flexible) resilient. But it now no longer refers only to relations between states, but covers any relationship that extends across state boundaries and the study of international relations has become an independent field. The term international has both political and sociological overtones. It can therefore embrace both interstate and transnational relations.[3]

International politics has become an unpredictable realm of relations of international community. Theories that study international relations/world or global politics failed to predict the major events that occurred in the past decades. The dissolution of erstwhile USSR or the incident of Sep. 11 were out of the preview of scholars' intellectuality, still it is an important subject to study. According to Little and Smith (2006), "World politics as an area of academic inquiry and practical activity holds at the one and the same time immense promise and immense potential difficulty. Its promise and a major reason for its attractiveness to students at all levels as well as to politicians and practitioners—lies in its focus on phenomena which are heavy with implications for the continued existence and flourishing of human kind. Questions of security and prosperity, order and justice, war and peace, and ultimately life and death, have always formed a major preoccupation of those engaged in the field".[4]

The study of international politics has largely concerned the study of states and their effects of anarchy on their foreign policies, the pattern of their interactions, and the organization of world politics. The study of international politics itself, that is, with relations between states, has been relatively neglected, and before the First World War most research took place in the traditional schools of history and international law. This academic framework reinforced the general view that inter-state relations were the products of the state themselves, and of a particular kind of politics, known as real politik (as of realists). The field of international relations emerged from this tradition and with the desire to develop a scientific and rigorous study of war in order to help pacify a violent world. International politics was conceived of as power politics in which the central problem for the state was the achievement of local and global hegemony.[5] The subject of international relations conservatively dates back to the early modern era (sixteenth and seventeenth centuries) in Europe, when sovereign states based on contiguous territories were initially established. It is deep-seated assumption in IR that the Westphalia (Treaty among the European countries which founded the sovereign nation states) system epitomizes (a perfect example) the international system. The assumption necessarily gives a strong Eurocentric bias to the discipline. Europe, it is argued, gave birth to the modern sovereign state and so the international system defined in terms of sovereign states must be viewed as a European product. The image of international system as an interstate system is now so deeply embedded that the two concepts are treated as synonymous. A whole network of terminology has grown up to reinforce this usage. So as for example, the multinational companies are identified as transnational rather than international actors. At the same time these transnational actors function within the existing international (means interstate) system. Although the international system has sometimes been acknowledged in terms of all the transactions that take place across state boundaries, this conception still privileges states as the defining unit of the system. Ever since the eighteenth century the relations between such independent states have been labeled 'international relations'. As states increasingly took the form of nation-states, people came to refer to 'international' as well as inter-state relations and so the Westphalia order became 'the international system'. Put another way, states came to participation the entire globe into separate polities with 'the international' being constituted only in the relations between sovereign states and with no empty space between them.[6] Today IR is the study of the global state system from various scholarly perspective.[7] However, issues of war are still valid and important but they are not confined to states, while a whole range of new questions now requires attention. Governments seem as concerned with economic issues as they are with security issues. Non-state actors, international organizations, etc. on international scene have grown remarkably in number, size and significance. It would seem foolish to try to analyze the interaction of states without bringing them in.

World politics has been facing the profound and unsetting change. The end of Cold War, the disintegration of USSR and end of communism in Eastern Europe, erosion of old axes of conflict and emergence of new axes of conflict and alignments and development of regionalism in the international arena are certain important dimensions surfaced in world politics. IR (study of international relations or shorthand name for the academic subject of international relations) has been certainly a dynamic discipline since its inception at the dawn of 20th century. Even the theory development of IR throughout this period has been a dynamic process. Due to methodological or theoretical shifts in international relations, we can see the emergence of various new global issues. World politics is an unpredictable realm of turbulent processes and events that catch the experts and masses by surprise. Basically, it is a rather practical discipline. It can be said that both theory and events or issues of world politics are complementary and supplementary to each other. The occurrence of global events at the beginning of 21st century implies a revolutionary restructuring of world politics.

It is worth recalling that in Morgenthau's views, IR as an autonomous field of study in political science is a twentieth century invention that began on the margins of the broader study of politics.[8] It is both an academic and public policy field, and can be either positive or normative as it both seeks to analyze as well as formulate the foreign policy of particular states. It is often considered a branch of political science. Political science studies states as political systems that are characterized by community, consensus, and a monopoly of the legitimate means of violence. As a result of these conditions, states are believed to be characteristically in a condition of peace; and domestic stillness serves as the unique feature of the national political order.

IR means the diplomatic—strategic relations of states, and the characteristic focus of IR is on issues of war and peace, conflict and cooperation. It is also the study about cross border transactions of all kinds: political, economic and social. And IR is likely to study trade negotiations or the operation of non-state institutions such as Amnesty International as it also covers conventional peace talks and the workings of the United Nations. Broadly, international relations concerns human relationships and interactions which cannot be looked at purely in the context of one state such as Britain or China. Centrally, international relations studies social interaction in contexts where there is no higher authority to encroach or arbitrate and which is outside any single governmental jurisdiction.[9]

The study of international politics is (was) overwhelmed by state-centrism and conception of politics as an autonomous process. As a result, the field is poorly prepared to deal with issues like globalization, political and economic crisis, systemic instability, or alternating change.[10] When we use the term international relations, we are principally referring to relations among states, as it is believed that it is necessary to emphasize that states continue to be the primary actors on the world stage. Furthermore, various types of states historically have dominated international politics.[11] International relations is the study of states. In state-centrism's extreme form, the territorial trap, international relations carves up the world into mutually exclusive territorial states and the study of international relations becomes the study of relations between these units. States are assumed to have authority over their political space. State territory and authority became tightly coupled in international relations theory.[12] States are important in international relations. The traditional view of international relations has been that the discipline's primary concern is the behavior of states and their interactions with each other. These interactions were characterized by the fact that they took place in a situation of anarchy where there is no government to oversee and control them. Thus, war becomes a common feature of the system and security the dominant goal of foreign policy. States are regarded as sovereign in the territories under their jurisdiction. There is no superseding body in the world which rules over the states and their governments. All states are fully sovereign in that no authority takes precedence over them in their territories. No doubt states are equal in terms of their claims to sovereignty, though they obviously differ in their capabilities and power. The rising power had become as a threat to the independence of other states. Resulting in the formulation of a counterweight or countervailing coalition or alliance. The rising power is constrained by the actions of the others, just as a member of the alliance will witness some degree of limitation on their freedom of maneuver by agreeing to work together to deter or defeat the ambitious state and maintain balance of power.[13] Realists tend to feel most comfortable with this use of the term international relations. But however, states are not the only important actors.[14] However, in the late twentieth century, to reduce everything to state behavior would seem to leave out too much. Even a part from the United Nations, the whole growth of the multinational cooperation's vitiates (make less good or effective) this position. The growing significance of international trade has seriously limited the states' economic sovereignty.[15]

The legacy of traditional international politics is not a healthy one. This is well illustrated by the difficulties that new issue areas are posing to the field. International politics is struggling to tackle with globalization. Although little agreement exists about a specific definition, the term generally refers to an increase in the amount and speed of inter-state phenomena. Activities in one part of the world are difficult to isolate, filter, or control in other parts of the world.[16] The fact of social change raises more fundamental questions. For example, the process of the economic globalization continues and makes the world one single market place and one single production site. There are number of emerging international organizations, transnational entities, speedy emergence of regional organizations, etc., which might bypass states. The ever increasing international trade and investment, expanding multinational business activity, enlarged NGO (non-governmental organization) activities, increasing regional and global communications, the growth of internet, expanding and ever extending transportation networks, exploding travel and tourism, massive human migration, increasing environmental pollution, growing regional integration, the growth of trading communities, the global expansion of science and technology, increasing privatization, and other activities have the effect of increasing interdependence across borders. The economic globalization continues and makes the world one single market place and one single production site.[17]

It is generally viewed that the ending of the Cold War and the demise of the Soviet Union brought a decisive change close to the era of the bipolarity, and in the process generated a challenge to the whole process of thinking in terms of polarity. Bipolarity was clearly over and what remained unclear was how to designate the polarity of the post-Cold War system.[18] The discipline of the IR has been state-centric which mainly takes into account state as a major player, and international relations revolving around the actions of states. The field of IR concerns the relationship among the world's governments (states). But these relationships cannot be understood in isolation. They are closely connected with other actors called non-state actors like international organizations, multinational corporations, international terrorism and individuals; other social structures including economics, culture, and domestic politics; and geographical and historical influences.[19] Therefore, there are several dimensions of investigating world politics. There is a challenge of organization and ordering of world politics. The challenge of theory is equally important. How is it possible to formulate viable and testable theories about an area of such complexity and diversity.[20]

Therefore, IR study is, generally, of social interactions and transcending the single government jurisdiction. It also includes actions and interactions between various other non-state actors. There has been a methodological and practical shift from International Politics (IP) and International Relations (IR) to world politics and global politics. Using the term world politics is more inclusive than either of the alternative terms. It is meant to denote the fact that our interest is in the politics and political patterns in the world, and not only between nation-states as the term IP implies. Thus, we are interested in relations between organizations or actors that may or may not be states. Thereafter, contemporary IR is concerned not only with political relations between states but also with a host of other subjects: economic interdependence, human rights, transnational corporations, international organizations, the environment, gender inequalities, development, international terrorism and so forth. Even some scholars prefer the label 'international studies' or 'world politics'. There are so many recent theoretical perspectives apart from Realism, Liberalism, Marxism, Neo-liberalism, Neo-Realism such as International Society approach, Social Constructivism and Post-Positivist Approaches like Post Modern Theories and Feminism to study the contemporary patterns of IR or global politics.[21] Generally, there are four major debates in the study of international relations, as it is shown by Table 1.1, in the due process of advancement of the theory of international relations. Majority of these theories/approaches are studied in the following chapters.

Table 1.1: Four Major Debates in IR

First Major Debate		
Idealism (of 1920s)	←→	**Realism (of 1940s)**
Emphasis		Emphasis
• International Cooperation		• Power Politics
• Peace, Progress		• State and its Security
• Collective Security		• War and Conflict
• International Organizations		• Balance of Power
Second Major Debate (Methodological)		
Traditional Approaches	←→	**Behavioralism**
Based on		Based on
• Values and Norms		• Facts, Scientific knowledge
• Understanding		• Explanation
• Subjectivity		• Objectivity
Third Major Debate		
Realism/ Neo-Liberalism ↕ **Liberalism/ Neo-Liberalism**	←→	Neo-Marxism
• Western-oriented		• Also Third World-oriented
• State as Dominant Actor		• Core-Periphery Relations
• Bipolar Power Structure		• Capitalist World Economy System
• European Interdependency		• Development and Undevelopment

Fourth Major Debate (Methodological)	
Positivism ◄──►	**Post-Positivism**
Consisted of	Consisted of
All Established Traditions	Post-Modernism
• Realism/Neo-Realism	• Critical theory
• Liberalism/Neo-Liberalism	• Constructivism
• International Society Approach	• Normative
• International Political Economy	• Gender and Environment

In the post-war period the growth of the welfare state and the intensification of patterns of international cooperation was intimately related. Moreover, the revolution in communications and transport technologies has facilitated greatly the global interplay of cultures, values, ideas, knowledge, peoples, social network, elites and social movements.[22] Due to the methodological shifts, there are drastic changes in the issues of world politics, especially in the globalized post-Cold War era that transferred world politics into global politics of twenty-first century. Mansbach and Rhodes (2006) viewed that this is the perfect time to study global politics. We remain in a period of turbulent transition. We are witnessing the evolution of war and the global security agenda, rapid changes in world's political institutions, and the emergence of increasingly divergent, competing and sometimes dangerous conceptions of identity.[23] In today's world, issues like terrorism and crime, nuclear proliferation, human rights, human security and development, and environment protection and sustainable development compete for attention in global negotiations along with more traditional issues of war and peace; concerns are mounting about the ability of nation-states and international institutions like UN to manage to solve the problems generated by non-state actors, may be to some extent along with nation states.[24]

It is widely accepted that the discipline of international relations has undergone something of a sea change. The growing self-awareness and interdependence of mankind provide the social and public conditions for the growth of a theory that is strong enough to survive the swings of public fashion, as well as periods of high political tension. There is a need to challenge the ruling model of the nation state system in order to organize world society. The time is now ripe for enlarging the small area that has housed international relations, and for reconstructing it so as to accommodate within it larger and more spacious conceptions. The first step is such an undertaking would be to give it a new name 'world politics'. Within the study of world politics, international relations is a subfield, concerned with world systems that are still characterized by the dominance of interstate relations. The general field of world politics may be defined as the study of the politics of world society. The study of the politics of world societies thus has a future dimension as well, in relation to which the application of principles of world politics assumes special importance. World politics is the set of activities that is concerned with the achievement of order and justice for world society.[25] The term 'world politics' was better to use for advanced international relations and studies during the second half of twentieth century. It was the time when international institutions and international law were growing; functionalist, neofunctionalist and interdependence theories put forward the idea of European cooperation. During the early 1970s, the identity and importance of Third World gained ground in the international relations. Then, the scope of IP (study of international politics) was not as suitable to cover all these issues, as the term world politics.

The evolution of world politics singles out for analysis some features of contemporary world. These features are liberalization, interdependence (especially in economic terms), nationalization of the state, etc. The structure of world politics is, at every point in time, susceptible to some modification and change. The closing years of the twentieth century were a time of significant change for world politics. The 1990s alone saw the collapse of Soviet communism and long-standing Cold War rivalries, a dramatic increase in the number and political influence of non-state actors and unprecedented advances in computer technology, such changes, which continue to characterize world politics in the twenty-first century.[26] These changes are being produced by related positive and negative causes. The chief positive cause consists of rapidly and radically improving technology, especially of transportation and communication. The chief negative cause of the growing awareness of the existence of the world-wide community of mankind is the expanding scope of the destructiveness of weapons.[27] World politics today, includes the international institutions and organisations as important actors. It is, thus, seen as no more than a stage on which various actors appear, act their roles, and make their existence. The term international relations seems too exclusive, it does not represent a widening concern beyond the state, and still restricts the focus on state dominated international relations. But there is need to think beyond "international" relations

The word 'world politics' is broader than the 'international politics' on other grounds too. World politics is more inclusive than either of the alternative terms. It is meant to denote the fact that the interest is in the politics and political patterns in the world, and not only those between nation-states (as the term international politics implies). Thus, it shows the relations between organizations that may or may not be states, for example, multinational companies, terrorist groups, or human rights non-governmental organizations (NGOs); these are all known as transnational actors.[28] Similarly, the term 'international relations' seems too exclusive of course, it does represent a widening concern simply from the political relations between nation-states, but it still restricts the focus to international relations, whereas the relations between, say, cities and other governments or international organizations can be equally important.

The second half of the twentieth century is witnessing a new upsurge of transnationalism on a wide variety of fronts. In fact, it would be difficult to avoid such an upsurge of transnational activities in the contemporary period given the rapid growth of interdependencies in the world system associated with far-reaching developments. The rapid and continuing developments in a variety of areas such as communications, transportation and technology have caused an effective shrinking of the world and have led to a situation in which the state, nation-state, and states system are increasingly obsolescent and ineffective structures for the achievement of human security and welfare.[29] The international system in these conditions 'explodes'. A system of 'mixed actors' creates the potential for a multitude of coalitions and balances, corresponding to the intersection of novel and existing issues and the absence of a clear or unified global hierarchy.[30] In recent years, the dynamics and processes of global politics have been increasingly influenced by non-state actors such as international non-governmental organizations such as Greenpeace, etc. and multinational corporations, regional cooperations, etc. The world has grown smaller and more interconnected. The world has extended the idea beyond national boundaries and posited the existence of an emerging global civil society. Now the civil society is becoming a transnational phenomena that it is effectively spreading across borders and being transposed from national to the international level, with implications for world politics. Yet conventional (and largely state-centric) theoretical frameworks used in the study of international relations have been hard pressed to explain many of these developments. Feminism, constructivism and other new perspectives that have made inroads into international relations in recent years have contributed considerably to our understanding of world politics.[31] The transformation of world politics manifests itself in these complex, interdependent relationships among diverse national and transnational actors. This by no means indicates that the nation-state is dead, however. Governments still retain the capacity to influence, indeed to shape transnational interactions. Thus, it is important not to exaggerate the impact of non-state actors on world politics. Nation-states retain a (near) monopoly on the use of coercive force in the international system, and they retain enormous capacity to shape global and national welfare. The nation-state cannot be lightly dismissed, therefore; it still molds the activities of non-state actors more than its behavior is molded by them.[32] World politics has become simultaneously more diffuse, penetrating new regions and activities, and more interconnected with linkages between varieties of actors. The resulting conditions of interdependence—between actors and states—increase both the mutual sensitivity of those engaged in world politics and, in many cases, their mutual vulnerability to new forces.[33] The shift to an increasingly interdependent and global world system, and the emergence of a large number of new states in the twentieth century have created a situation in which the core meanings of the concepts state and nation state are much less clear than they were when applied primarily to the European arena. The growth of interdependencies and, therefore, of interpretations among the units of world politics in the contemporary period is producing a wide range of developments.[34] For many analysts this means that interdependence between national societies has been supplanted by processes of globalization, in which activities are increasingly de-linked from territory of national authorities, and in which there are new forms of unpredictability and potential instability. The contemporary world society is global. The process by which number of historical societies were brought together into one global system might be referred to as globalization.[35]

The world regularly throws up for processing a variety of problems not all of which require or deserve attention at the global level. The issues that do need and do receive attention at the global level become the substance of world politics. In other words, world politics has to do with both global level politics and the structure of the entire world society.

No doubt that the state remains an important unit in world politics or even that it is increasingly important in some parts of the world and with respect to some purposes or functions. The only change is in the role of state boundaries in marking a simultaneous shift in the status of most important human activities. The growing assortment (a varied collection) of transnational organizations whose purposes are political, economic, cultural, and so forth and whose membership is based on some criterion other than statehood or nationality. There are the international and regional organizations that are composed of states and fundamentally oriented toward political activities. The growing importance of these types of organizations in the twenty-first century has witnessed expansions of such striking proportions that it deserves to be designated as one of the great ages of organization at levels other than that of the state.[36]

The tentative inference can be taken that at the onset of a new century, world politics has developed the potential to become truly globalized politics, soon, called global politics. The concept of 'globalization' has become seriously overworked over the last few years and its use often conveys very little of significance. It provides a rhetorical flourish to suggest that the world we are living in momentous times.[37]

The last half of the twentieth century—the concept of global interdependence and globalization, the worldwide expansion of markets, technology, transportation, and communication—has given birth to the concept of global politics. Over the last two decades, though, there has been a terminological shift from the study of international politics to the study of global politics. Whereas international politics has focused or studied on how states have established norms, laws and institutions to help them engage in collective action and create order, the study of global politics does not focus only on the interests of the states but also comprise other actors and issues (which sometimes go unnoticed in the study of international politics), including international organizations, regional organizations, transnational organizations, non-government organizations, etc. and issues such as gender, terrorism, environment, transnationalization of economy, etc. finally got the attention they deserved. Thus global politics represents relations among different kinds of actors having different kind of authority and power.[38]

When we think about the concept 'global politics', generally, it confines that global politics transcends the traditional distinction between the international and domestic in the study of politics. Global political system and global political process embraces a world-wide network of interactions and relationships between 'not only states but also other political actors, both above and below it. In post Cold War world politics we have seen the survival of only one 'superpower'—USA. The immediate post-Cold War era had become uni-polar with the rapid spread of the US sponsored politics and strategic system across the world. But in the present scenario there is weakening hold of US hegemony relative to the growing multipolarity in the world system. Geopolitics, as a paradigm to acquire 'space and power', continues to sustain conflicts and wars particularly in the peripheries[39]. It also seems that global politics is diminishing the role of geopolitics or geostrategic issues in international relations although the Third World Countries (TWCs) are still entangled into such conflicts.

In much social-scientific as well as everyday usage, global is used interchangeably with world and international simply to indicate areas of social life beyond the national level.[40] Global means to that extent people effectively do not have a territorial location, apart from the broad sense of being situated on the planet earth. The discipline is moving away from the study of international politics or international relations towards the study of global politics. Thus global refers to—non, extra, post, supra territorial aspect of the world system. In the global domain, territorial boundaries distance is covered at present with no particular impendent and effectively in no time. Large number of ordinary people is being affected by world affairs as never before. This weak, vague usage clearly reflects the thought which has hardly begun to grapple with the distinctiveness of global relations. In this way of thinking, the difference between global and international cannot really be indicated, and a 'global world' is a tautology (saying same thing over different words).[41] The use of the word global rather than other terms is little more than homage to intellectual fusion. Global means connected with the natural habitat of humankind, our global planet, and earth.[42]

The emerging field of global politics is increasingly focused on the study of global governance. Global governance offers a systematic concept to consider various efforts at the global level to come to terms with the loss of control and to balance the unrestrained processes of globalization. The word *global governance* means various developments and institutions surpassing the state which try to adjust and manage the new forces of globalization. The jurisdiction of global governance is enhanced over the time concerning human rights, environment and terrorism as well.

To talk about global issues—those which are issues of global politics, Snarr (1998) questioned what is global issue? He used this term to refer to two types of phenomena. First, these are those issues that cross political boundaries (country borders) and, therefore, affect individuals in more that one country. A clear example is air pollution produced by a factory in the US and blown into Canada. Second, there are problems and issues that do not necessarily cross borders but affect a large number of individuals throughout the world. Ethnic rivalries and human rights violations may occur within a single country but have a far wider impact.[43]

The process of globalization is making the world a different place. It may be reducing the powers of governments and role of the state both internally and externally, particularly over economic matters. The international economic system is very interdependent so the distribution of wealth, at least partially, is a global problem.[44] The significance of globalization itself is open to dispute. The broader range of topics considered as international relations is in part because of a broader view and the explanations under the narrow view is proved inadequate.[45]

The post-Cold War world had now to be seen as being multi-dimensional. First, the fact of single surviving super power, the military strength of the United States and its continuing economic importance. The other side is a relative decline of the United States, particularly its economic clout, and the various constraints on the application of its power. The vision of a new world order and new international security systems raised by the Bush (Sr.) Clinton administrations were soon enough lost in the midst of the post-Cold War chaotic situation. United States' old concentration of military and economic strength has at least in the present era of history lost its universal characteristic. The United States remains lone superpower in military terms but no longer enjoys a commanding role in international economy. Germany (in

Europe) and Japan have risen as new economic powerhouses with incommensurate military power. Yet, they have not assumed the crushing military burdens and global policing responsibilities[46].

The concept of global politics also includes the deregulation of finance capital, the expansion of foreign direct investment, and the intensified deployment of information technologies. The newly emergent forms of collective identity, political consciousness, and diaspora that appear to have unsettled the principal of nationality as a locus of everyday social relations, as well as new forms of technologically mediated socio-cultural interaction that seem oblivious to national territorial boundaries. Thus global politics refers to the process through which interdependencies among geographically distant localities, places, and territories are at once extended, deepened and intensified.[47] More recently, Stephen-Kobrin has argued persuasively that the declining relevance of 'the idea of geography as a basis for the organization of politics and economics' is one of several changes in global political economy that auger such as new medievalism.[48] The other changes he mentions are equally compelling departure from interstate politics: 'space, geography and borders', 'the ambiguity of authority', 'multiple loyalties', 'transnational elites', 'distinctions between public and private property', and 'unifying belief systems and supranational centralization'.[49]

In global politics in which the traditional distinction between domestic and international affairs is no longer valid. No doubt old issues remain on the agenda, they increasingly share space with some new topics which obtain global importance, such as environmental politics, human security, terrorism, the sources of international change, gender, etc. The ecology of international politics is no longer dominated by states and increasingly includes non-state actors such as non-governmental organizations, transnational corporations, international organizations, regional organizations, transnational networks of all kinds operating alongside state in a reconstituted global political domain. Under these conditions, 'politics everywhere, it would seem, are related to politics everywhere else'. Where the functioning of any political unit was once constant by structures within its boundaries, now the roots of its political life can be traced to remote corners of the globe.[50]

As the Cold War era of conflict and rivalry fades, it is being replaced with an expanding awareness of global independence. No modern society can isolate itself from the vagaries (an unpredictable change) of the world market, or transnational movements of capital, ideas, beliefs, crime, knowledge and news, seems evidence enough of the emergence of a truly global society.[51] As McLuhan remarked many years ago, one of the defining characteristics of the modern age is the developing realization that we live in a 'global village'. The events happen in one country have one thing is common (for example, 9/11 terrorist attack) it reflect the increasing complex and transnational character of global politics. The line that once so neatly divided domestic from foreign affairs and foreign from global affairs is now much harder to find. Issues that once were the privilege of governments, such as air and water pollution, are now matters of international diplomacy. All viewpoints agree that global politics is highly interdependent. The term global assume, at the minimum degree of interdependence. Interdependence is shorthand for the transnationalization of global politics not just events but also ideas, institutions and decisions. It is a phenomena that draws societies closer together, with both positive and negative consequences. For example, today we see the integration of world economy into a single unit, global threats such as terrorism, ecological imbalances and disasters make the countries interdependent. Now the domestic issues become transnational ones.

The role of the finance corporations is becoming more significant to global politics. The size, scope and unregulated nature of the financial sector heralds the 'end of geography', that is the demise of the territorial state. However, the impacts of financial globalization upon governmental decision-making are likely to vary considerably with the strength of the domestic economy and, once again, to vary according to region.[52]

In this era, the world was fundamentally changed. Concurrent integration and fragmentation of political authority are taking place at a dramatic pace, as the old breaks down and new arrangements are made. Events since the end of the Cold War have made clear that the modern system of global politics based on independent sovereign states is eroding and evolving, and new political processes and institutions are acquiring importance. [53]

Politics can no longer be understood as a purely local or national social activity but must be conceived as a social activity with a global dimension. This invites elimination of the traditional distinction between domestic and international politics, between the foreign and the domestic. It also demands a certain abstract readjustment: thinking of politics as a motion which stretches across space rather than as a social activity which is confined within the boundaries of the nation-state, or at the international level as an activity confined to interactions between governments. Such a readjustment is realized in the concept of global politics.[54]

Thus, global politics defines in terms of plural forms of governance based at the international and civil society as well as state levels. International are, however, generally inter-state forms, and the politics of civil society cannot be defined without reference to state forms. This is as true of global as of national civil societies. Global politics does not develop merely through state institutions, but the forms of state are essential to any reconceptualisation of global society and politics.[55]

In the twenty-first century, therefore, there is a need of global politics which aims to construct a new relationship between the emergent global society and culture and state institutions. The new global politics will be based, as many have argued, partly in the developing global civil society. But it will also be based partly in, and have the aim of transforming, state power as well as social relations.[56] In global relations people are connected with one another pretty much irrespective of their territorial position.

Thus, the global revolution is therefore a revolution in a new sense not simply a political rather than a social revolution, or a national and international revolution, but a set of changes in which these terms are themselves recast. The global revolution involves new relations of politics, economics and society, as well as of the national and international aspects of all these relations.[57]

Elizabeth Dowdeswell, then Executive Director, UN Environment Programme (May 1994) viewed, "The global village. The New world order. The Peace dividend. These are all buzzwords of the 1990s that reflected an optimistic outlook for the dawning of the next century. Each idea brought a sense that finally we could progress from the dysfunction caused by failing to understand that we are one family". These words express feelings of disappointment and frustration common to liberal internationalists in the mid-1990s. The end of Cold War brought hopes for enhanced international cooperation and a fresh commitment to strengthening the role of international organizations which would, in turn, facilitate attempts to address a range of global issues—economic inequality, social injustice, armed conflict, environmental change and degradation.[58]

We can conclude here that the subject of IR is continuously advancing as it is proved by the developments in IR theories. From the issue of war and peace the study has incorporated gender and environment, role of information technology in global politics and globalization, human security and state sovereignty as well. Conventional theories, particularly realism, of IR deny to give serious attention to issues such as gender, environment or human security.

REFERENCES

1. Pual Viotti, R. and Mark V. Kauppi (2007). *International Relations and World Politics Security, Economy, Identity*. New Delhi: Pearson Education. p. 42.
2. Richard W. Mansbach and Edward Rhodes (2006). *Global Politics in a Changing World: A Reader*. New York: Houghton Mifflin Company. p. 7.
3. *Ibid.*

4. Richard Little and Michael Smith (eds., 2006). *Perspectives on World Politics*. London, NewYork: Routledge. p. 1.
5. Charles Reynold (1975). *Theory and Explanation in International Politics*. London: Martin Press. p. 6.
6. Stephine Lawson (2004). *International Relations*. UK: Polity Press. p. 210.
7. Robert Jackson and George Sorenson (2003). *Introduction to International Relations Theories and Approaches*. New York: Oxford University Press. p. 2.
8. Martin Griffith (ed., 2007). *International Relations Theory for the Twenty First Century*. New York: Routledge. p. 5.
9. Michael Nicholson (1997). *International Relations a Concise Introduction*. New York: Palgrave. p. 2.
10. Robert A. Denmark (1999). "World System History: From Traditional International Politics to the Study of Global Relations", *International Studies Review*. Vol. 1. p. 43.
11. Pual Viotti, R. and Mark V. Kauppi. *Op. cit.* p. 27.
12. Michael Barnett and Kathryn Sikkink (2008), "From International Relation to Global Society" in Christian Reus Smith and Duncan Jindal (eds.,). *Handbook of International Relations*. New York: Oxford University Press. p. 64.
13. Stephine Lawson. *Op. cit.* p. 44.
14. Pual Viotti, R. and Mark V. Kauppi. *Op cit.* p. 27.
15. Michael Nicholson. *Op. cit.* p. 16.
16. Robert A. Denmark. *Op. cit.* p. 49.
17. Robert Jackson and George Sorenson. *Op. cit.*, p. 28.
18. Barry Buzan (2004). *The United States and the Great Powers*. London: Polity Press. p. 34.
19. Joshua S. Goldstein (2003). *International Relations*. New York: Longman. p. 3.
20. Richard Little. *Op. cit.* p. 2.
21. Robert Jackson and Georg Sorenson. *Op. cit.* pp. 30-54.
22. Anthony G. McGrew and Paul G. Lewis (eds., 1992). *Global Politics: Globalization and the Nation-State*. London: New York. p. 2.
23. Richard W. Mansbach and Edward Rhodes. *Op. cit.* p. xiii.

24. Charles W. Kegley and Eugene R. Wittkopf (1999). *World Politics-Trend and Transformation.* London: MacMillan. p. 204.
25. George Modelski (1987). *Principles Of World politics.* New York: The Free Press. p. 8.
26. Craig Walkentin (1998). *Reshaping World Politic. the Internet and Global Civil Society.* New York: Rowman and Little Field Publication. p. 1.
27. Herbert J. Spiro (1966). *World Politics the Global System.* Illinois: The Dorsey Press. p. 1.
28. John Baylis and Steve Smith (eds., 2007). *The Globalization of World Politics: An Introduction to International Relations.* New York: Oxford Press. p. 3.
29. K.J. Holsti (2006). "States and Statehood", in Richard Little and Michael Smith (eds,). *Perspective on World Politics.* New York: Routledge. p. 21.
30. *Ibid.*
31. Charles W. Kegley and Eugene R. Wittkopf. *Op. cit.* p. 204.
32. *Ibid.*
33. Richard Little. *Op. cit.* p. 6.
34. George Modelski. *Op. cit.* p. 41.
35. James N. Rosenau (1990). *Turbulence in World Politics: A Theory of Change and Continuity.* Great Britain: Harvester Wheatsheaf. p. 132.
36. Roger Tooze (1988). "The Unwritten Preface: International Political Economy and Epistemology". *Journal of International Studies.* Vol. 17. p. 287.
37. George Modelski. *Op. cit.* p. 19.
38. Michael Barnett and Kathryn Sikkink. *Op. cit.* p. 64.
39. Sudeepta Adhikari (1999). "A New Dimension to Post Cold War Geopolitics". *Geographical Review of India.* Vol. 61. No. 1. pp. 35-36.
40. Martin Shaw (2000). *Theory of Global State: Globalist as Unfinished Revolution.* UK Cambridge University Press. p. 9.
41. *Ibid.*
42. Yale H. Ferguson and Richard W. Mansbach (2008). *A World of Polities Essays on Global Politics.* New York: Routledge. p. 7.

43. Michal T. Snarr and D. Neil Snarr (eds., 1998). *Global Issues.* Boulder, London: Lynne Reinne. p. 2.
44. Michael Nicholson. *Op. cit.* p. 4.
45. Stephine Lawson. *Op. cit.* p. 61.
46. V.P. Dutt (1997). "Post Cold War Scenario", *World Focus.* pp. 7-8.
47. Neil Brenner (1999). "Beyond State-centrism? Space, Territoriality, and Geographical Scale in Globalization Studies", *Theory and Society.* Vol. 28. p. 8.
48. Yale H. Ferguson and Richard W. Mansbach. *Op. cit.* pp. 168-69.
49. *Ibid.*
50. *Ibid.* p. 22.
51. Anthony Mcgrew (1992). *Global Politics Globalization and the Nation State.* Cambridge: Polity Press. p. 325.
52. Charlotte Bretherton and Geoffrey Ponton (eds., 1996). *Global Politics: An Introduction.* UK: Blackwell Publishers. p. 7.
53. Richard W. Mansbach and Edward Rhodes. *Op. cit.* p. xiii.
54. Anthony Mcgrew. *Op. cit.* p. 3.
55. Stephen Chan and Jarrod Wiener (1999). *Twentieth Century International* A Reader. New York: I.B. Tarus. p. 3.
56. *Ibid.* p. 210.
57. Martin Shaw. *Op. cit.* p. 18.
58. Charlotte Bretherton and Geoffrey Ponton. *Op. cit.* p. 1.

PART – I

HISTORY

2

History of International Relations: An Overview

International relations need to understand the events of the past. The core concepts of IR as state, sovereignty, balance of power, war and peace, dominance and security are related with the past history of international trends. We will study here the major events of past history. The commercial revolution beginning in the thirteenth and fourteenth centuries Europe began its slow emergence from the stagnation that prevailed since the fall of Rome 700 years earlier. Part of this resurgence was the revival of commerce and the growth of a new commercial class whose livelihood lay not in the production of goods but rather trading. This commercial class faced a problem because conditions in medieval Europe were not conducive to trade. A Europe fragmented into so many small political units was unable to provide many of the prerequisites for commerce. Law enforcement was weak, making the transport of valuable commodities over large distances very risky indeed. The infrastructure was in a terrible state of disrepair, roads, ports and marketplaces had all deteriorated since the fall of Rome, and the small size of political units inhibited any rebuilding. Individual fiefdoms did not possess the resources to build the infrastructure, and political fragmentation made coordination very difficult. Finally, systems of measurement and currency were unreliable.[1] Modern history of international relations is dominated by Europe till 1900 and so on.

Great civilizations thrived in other parts of the world too, of course: India and China, among others, had extensive, vibrant civilizations long before the historical events covered below. But the European emphasis is justified on the basis that contemporary international relations, in both theory and practice, is rooted in the European experience, for better or worse. The year of 1648 is very important for the students of international relations, as it is known for the birth of European nation-state system and decline of empires.

The purpose of this historical overview is to trace important trends over time—the emergence of the state and the notion of sovereignty, the development of the international state system, and the changes in the distribution of power among key states. These trends have a direct impact on international relations theory and practice today.[2]

The great revolutions in human history are the American and French Revolutions. The American Revolution of 1776 and the French Revolution of 1789 signaled the introduction of a new idea that would in time unravel the political order of European societies. Before these revolutions, the rulers of Europe claimed divine sources (divine rights theory which advocates king's rule is Gods' will) as the basis for their legitimacy. As Louis XIV ruled over the people of France not because the people wanted him to rule but because it was supposedly God's will. At the core of the American and French revolutions was in order to be legitimate governments needed to derive their authority from the people over whom they ruled.

American Revolution was against the European rule by the people of thirteen colonies of North America and they won it in 1776. After the span of eleven years, these thirteen colonies formed United States of America, The French Revolution did not start out as a revolution but merely as resistance to Louis XVI's attempts to raise taxes (largely to pay off debts incurred when the French sided with American colonists in their war for independence). The resistance rapidly snowballed into a revolt against the monarchy itself, resulting in the overthrow of Louis XVI in 1792 and the establishment of the French Republic. A

Reign of Terror eventually ensued in which thousands of nobles and supposed enemies of the revolution met with a gruesome end, usually via the infamous guillotine. Even Louis XVI and his queen, Marie Antoinette, were not spared.[3] American and French revolutions set the path for modern democracy in Europe in particular and in the world in general. These revolutions are always the shining stars in international relations. After the treaty of Vienna and defeat of Napoleon in 1815, there was change in international power structure.

Europe was thrown into balance of power politics when the medieval dream of universal empire collapsed and a host of states of more or less equal strength arose from the ashes of that ancient aspiration. When a group of states so constituted are obliged to deal with one another there are only two possible outcomes: Either one state becomes so strong that it dominates all the others and creates an empire, or no state is ever quite powerful enough to achieve that goal. In the latter case, the pretensions of the most aggressive member of the international community are kept in check by a combination of the others; in other words, by the operation of a balance of power.

The new world order, the balance of power system did not purport to avoid crises or even wars. When working properly, it was meant to limit both the ability of states to dominate others and the scope of conflicts. Its goal was not peace so much as stability and moderation. By definition, a balance of power arrangement cannot satisfy every member of the international system completely; it works best when it keeps dissatisfaction below the level at which the aggrieved party will seek to overthrow the international order. Theorists of the balance of power often leave the impression that it is a natural form of international relations.[4] In the history of international politics has there been changing power position of states time to time. Modern nation state system took birth due to rising nationalism in Europe. When we study the history of international politics it revolves around Europe and its imperial instincts for the past five to six centuries. In this very period sometimes major powers were reduced to secondary status, and secondary powers emerged as major powers. Spain, Portugal, England, France, Germany, Russia, Japan, and Austria-Hungary Empire remained major powers from time to time in the past five centuries.

The modern state system is characterized by a small number of relatively large sovereign political units. It gradually took shape as Europe began to emerge from the medieval period around 1300. The economic pressures of the commercial revolution and the military dynamics of the gunpowder revolution contributed to the creation of larger and larger political units. The Protestant Reformation and the Thirty Years War (1618-48) brought the origins of the modern conception of sovereignty as embodied in the Peace of Westphalia (1648). The period between the Peace of Westphalia and the French Revolution of 1789 was a period of relative calm in which wars and conflicts tended to be limited, modest affairs. This calm was rooted in the nature of European societies and politics, particularly absolutist monarchism, the lack of any strong sense of loyalty or connection between people and their rulers, and the absence of ideological conflict. The American and the French revolutions marked the beginning of modern nationalism and its doctrine of popular sovereignty. With time, this idea contributed to the erosion of absolutist monarchism and the international order to sustain. Similarly, the industrial revolution of the 1800s transformed European societies in ways that had a profound effect on international politics. Increasing wealth and advances in technology solidified European dominance of the globe. Nationalism and the industrial revolutions combined to create the total war of World Wars I and II.[5]

Twentieth century is the witness of two world wars which drastically changed the power equations in international politics. In the beginning of 20th century Prussia, Japan and Russia were considered great powers. After the First World War Britain, France, Austria-Hungary came to be reckoned as great powers. Along with them, United States emerged very slowly as a strong power in international politics. Besides, between the World Wars, the Soviet Union (USSR) consolidated the Bolshevik Revolution. With the result, there was tremendous industrial progress in Soviet Union.

Kissinger viewed that almost as if according to some natural law, in every century, there seems to emerge a country with the power, the will, and the intellectual and moral impetus to shape the entire international system in accordance with its own values. In the seventeenth century, France under Cardinal Richelieu introduced the modern approach to international relations, based on the nation-state and motivated by national interest as its ultimate purpose. In the eighteenth century, Great Britain elaborated the concept of the balance of power, which dominated European diplomacy for the next 200 years. In the nineteenth century, Metternich's Austria reconstructed the Concert of Europe and Bismarck's Germany dismantled reshaping European diplomacy into cold-blooded game of power politics.[6]

First World War: After the assassination of Franz Ferdinand in June 1914 Austro-Hungary threatened Russia's fellow Slavs in Siberia. This sparked a total war in Europe. The complicated alliance system built up over the previous two decades rapidly ensured that Austria-Hungary and Germany, on side, confronted Britain, France, and Russia on the other. The ensuing war lasted for four years. US too entered the war indirectly in 1917, and European empires used colonial forces. When the First World War was over there was establishment of first international organization called 'The League of Nations' by the Treaty of Versailles, 1919. The main purpose of the League was to maintain world peace through the 'Collective Security System'.

Despite the general reputation of the League as a dismal failure in maintaining peace, the statistical record tells a different story. Plano and Riggs said that the league was successful in solving more than half of the disputes that came to its attention. The League failed decisively in major instances.[7]

The League failed to prevent Ethiopian crisis of 1935-36 when it was invaded by Fascist Italy. Then, Germany daringly violated the League when it reoccupied Rhineland in 1936 and annexed Austria in 1938 and similarly Czechoslovakia (1939) and then attacked Poland in 1939. During the interwar period 1919-39 the European powers reverted to the old policy of alliances, secret diplomacy, conflict and competition. Therefore, the League of Nations could not prevent the belligerents from opting such policies.

European states whose empires encompassed much of the globe by 1945 had been replaced by one in which the major arbiters of international affairs were the two new 'superpowers'—the USA and the Soviet Union. Europe was in a temporary state of ruin and indebtness, with Eastern and Central Europe lying under Soviet occupation. Second World War 1939-45 further intensified European disintegration. This war was fought between the Axis powers Japan, Italy and Germany on the one side and the allied forces France, USA, UK and USSR on the other. US declared war on Japan when the latter destroyed US war fleet in Pearl Harbour of the Pacific in 1942. After three years US prepared atom bomb and dropped these bombs on Hiroshima and Nagasaki of Japan in 1945 and that was the formal end of this war. The second war also saved peace treaties. All this culminated into the creation of the UNO.

The Allies in 1945 faced a completely new set of circumstances shaped by the course of the war. Similarly, the period after 1945 was influenced by the consequences of the war. Many of them helped to define international relations in the post-war world. The times of European preponderance in world politics came to a close, as European nations were overshadowed by the flanking powers—the United States and the Soviet Union. In the course of the war, this pair had outmatched their European counterparts militarily as well as economically. The Axis onslaught had taxed the last of the great powers of Europe-namely, the British Empire and France—to the limits. The winners filled the position of vanquished Germany, the third great power of Europe, in the arena of world politics. This led to American supremacy.

Economically, the United States had done well. Militarily, US forces had prevailed over the armies of the Axis in Europe,

Africa, and Asia. The United States abandoned its former isolationist reticence to assume the leading role in shaping a new world order. The Soviet Union having changed alliances during the war was on the winning side in 1945. Although the Soviet Union had sustained unimaginable losses by all accounts. Soviets wanted to consolidate their sphere of influence and become a player in the new international arena.[8]

Diverging interests over the shaping of the postwar European order were expressed by Soviet dictator Joseph Stalin and US President Roosevelt. This initiated a growing divide that, in turn, set the stage for the Cold War and the bipolar international system. The nuclear age set in when the United States dropped the first atomic bombs on Japan in August 1945. The failure of US-Soviet cooperation subsequent to the war, and the resulting distrust between the two superpowers created the basis for the arms race. Independence movements were on the rise throughout Asia, the Middle East, and later Africa against their own masters.

The destruction wrought by German hegemonic aspirations during the war resulted in allied consensus to forestall the possibility of repetition. Built on the foundations of the League of Nations, the Allied hopes to institute collective security were placed with the United Nations (UN), created soon after the end of the war.[9]

The Second World War (1939-45) significantly altered the international scene. Important scene was that USA and USSR (Union of Soviet Socialist Republics) emerged two powerful states. For the first time in the history of international relations—a non-European country—the USA became a decisive factor in international politics. The Axis powers (Germany, Italy) of Western Europe were shattered after their defeat. The condition was not much better of allied (The Successors—Britain, France). They all lost largely in terms of men and material. This phenomena created the power vacuum in international order. The weakening of European states was instantly covered up by USA and USSR. Though these two states incurred heavy losses but they were able to retain their military, economic and industrial supremacy. Even during the

Second World War, the leadership of Roosevelt (the then US President) and Stalin (then USSR President) played a vital role to lead and direct the war politics. Tensions between the Soviet Union and the United States had always been present since the Communist Revolution in 1917 in USSR. Communist Russia throughout evoked hostility or a non-friendly response in the capitalist world. The presence of free economic enterprise in capitalist countries was in direct contrast to the state ownership of means of production in Soviet Union. But these differences submerged during the Second World War against common threat of Nazism. These differences surfaced again after the end of the war.

In the summer of 1945, it was known both in Washington and Moscow that Japan was ready to acknowledge defeat and abandon the war which it had begun by the attack on Pearl Harbor. In July the Americans experimentally exploded the first nuclear weapon in the history of mankind and in August, they dropped two bombs on Hiroshima and Nagasaki. Japan surrendered forthwith and this clinching of the imminent American victory deprived the Russians of all but a token share in the post-war settlement in the Far East. The Second World War ended with an act which contained the two central elements in the Cold War: The advent of nuclear weapons and Russo-American rivalry.[10]

USA was the only combatant not to have experienced fighting on its own soil during the world wars. Europe, Japan and even Soviet Union were devasted and impoverished. Despite the enormous costs of fighting the war, and the distortions imposed on it by a high level of military production, the US economy was in good shape. The Soviet Union, in contrast, was badly damaged and struggling to be a superpower. USA had the atomic bomb by 1945 whereas the Soviet Union did not. But this did not stop the Soviet Union from retaining large armed forces and keeping a firm military control over Eastern Europe.

How can we define the term 'superpower'? It is not very easy and simple as it seems to be. The term superpower was first coined by William Fox in 1944. Recalling that at the time,

Germany, Italy and Japan (the Axis powers) were all but defeated. Most of Europe was in tatters and China was in the midst of a civil war. Fox defined a superpower as a state that possessed great power plus great mobility of power. He argued that only the great United States, the Soviet Union and Britain deserved to be called superpowers because these three states would be responsible for shaping the post-1945 world. But it would be a mistake to think that they were three states of equal power. After 1949 nuclear explosion by USSR, USA and USSR both emerged superpowers. Even Britain was almost bankrupt by the end of the Second World War and was being dictated by USA. The term superpower implies that there is hierarchy of power among states. It is a state that plays a crucial leadership role in the international system and is able to gain the allegiance of other states. Within its sphere of influence, a superpower can impose its political will on smaller or weaker states with relative impunity. Not only does a superpower have the capacity to project effective military power far from its territory but it also has enormous military resources at its disposal. Besides, a superpower has special duties with respect to the maintenance of international order and holds a privileged status in international forums and organizations. Fox defined a superpower as a "great power whose armed forces is so mobile that it can deploy in any strategic theatre, as opposed to a great power whose interests and influences are confined to single regional theatre. The possession of two military characteristics by the superpower: one, the full range of strategic nuclear armoury, and two, the capacity to deploy its forces, whether armed conventionally or with nuclear weapons, in any strategic theatre of the world". Therefore, the superpowers has the capacity to intervene, interfere and move in any part of the world without affecting its own power, prestige and popularity in any substantial way.[11]

According to *Oxford Dictionary of Politics*, "In its generic use, the term (superpower) refers to those few states with powers (defined by combining a series of variables together—e.g. economic wealth, population, size, and above all, military strength, especially in the possession of sophisticated nuclear armaments) far transcending that of the rest of the states in the international arena. More specifically, the term refers to the two states, the United States and the Soviet Union, in the time of the Cold War. Both competed against each other for influence in the global politics of the Cold War."[12]

A nation could be described as a major power, as different from a superpower, when she is able to assert or dictate her position beyond her region. A country could be described as a major power when she possesses all the concomitants of power along with nuclear capability and also a capacity to maintain balance of power within a given region. However, nuclear capability does not make a nation a major power. It is the capacity to maintain or upset the balance of power in a region which is more important. For example, before the First World War Britain, Germany, Russia, France, etc. had been major powers during late 19th and early 20th centuries. These states maintained European balance of power system from time to time. Fox argued that there was a qualitative difference between the superpowers of the post-1945 era and the European great powers of the eighteenth and nineteenth centuries. Even though they were significant international actors, they never had the global reach and influence as of USA and Soviet Union after the Second World War. The superpowers phenomena during the Cold War period engulfed the whole world relations in its lap. US and USSR both were increasing their spheres of influences not only in Europe but also in other areas of the world. Superpowers seem to be powerful in respect of dictating their terms to their bloc partners in regard to foreign policy.

According to Wenger and Zimmermann, "Following the end of World War II, hopes abounded that the future world order would be informed by the vision of 'One world' and that law and order would replace the anarchy of international relations. Instead, the antagonism between East and West, between communism and liberal democracy, between a socio-economic command economy and capitalism—in short, between two fundamentally divergent social and value systems (ideologies) largely determined international politics. The post-war world was organized into two distinct bolcs, with the United States and the Soviet Union at the two centers. The process leading up to the bipolar international system of the Cold War".[13]

The rise of the United States as a world power after 1945 was of paramount importance in international politics. Its conflict with the Soviet Union provided one of the crucial dynamics in world affairs, and one which affected—directly—every part of the globe. In the West, historians have debated, with vigour and acrimony, who was responsible for the collapse of the wartime relationship between the United States and the Soviet Union. The rise of the Soviet Union as a global power after 1945 is equally crucial in understanding international affairs in this period. Relations between the Union of the Soviet Socialist Republics (USSR) and its Eastern European 'allies' with the people's Republic of China (PRC) and with various revolutionary movements and governments in the Third World have been vital issues in world politics as well as key factors in Soviet-American affairs.[14]

The Cold War

The Cold War between the two post-war superpowers was not an episode like other wars of modern times. The term 'Cold war' was invented to describe a state of affairs. The principal ingredient in this state of affairs was the mutual hostility and fears of the protagonists. These emotions were rooted in their several historical and political differences and were powerfully stimulated the myths which at times turned hostility into hatred. The Cold War dominated world affairs for a generation and more.[15]

The term 'Cold War' was coined by Walter. Lippman to describe the tension and conflict in the bilateral relationship of the US and USSR after World War II. As a concept in international relations, it denotes a state of constant conflict and strife, maintained and perpetuated without a direct armed conflict between the antagonists. Every expression of hostility and tension is used without a direct use of arms. Cold War, "a state of intensive competition, political, economic and ideological, which yet falls below the threshold of armed conflict between states".[16]

The most popular view about Cold War was 'an intense struggle for power between the superpowers'. The word 'War' implies tension, armed conflict, and a zero-sum relationship between the superpowers. The word 'Cold' refers to the presence of factors that allegedly restrained the confrontation and prevented a 'hot' war. Conventional meaning is based on a definition of the Cold War that assumes a high level of East-West tension with the threat of escalation to nuclear conflict. According to the orthodox argument, the Cold War was a struggle between conflicting universal values. In the West, the concepts of a market economy and a multi-party democracy were cherished. In the East, single party system and a command administrative economy were highly valued. The obvious conflict of ideas and obstinate nature of those who defended them were the driving forces behind the conflict.[17]

The policies of containment followed by the United States were defensive reactions to an inherently aggressive and expansionist enemy. It was a period of American dominance whose legitimacy was based on a mythical Soviet 'threat'. In contrast to the view that Cold War was inherently antagonistic, regardless of who was the main instigator. In fact, Cold War was very useful to both sides. For the United States, it solved problem of what to do about Germany and Japan, both of whom were key states on bringing about the Second World War. For the Soviet Union and United States, the Cold War permitted a *de facto* solution of the German problem by freezing the social/political contours of Europe, both East and West. [18]

Therefore, the name 'Cold War' is normally given to the period of intense conflict between the United States and Soviet Union after World War II. After the war Soviet Union effectively began occupying the countries of Eastern Europe and the United States became a liberator of the countries of Western Europe. In Germany these two superpowers along with France and Britain, established zones of occupation and a framework for four power control. During Yalta and Postdam (both 1945) conferences about post-war settlement, serious differences emerged. Shortly, we can say that Cold War was phenomena of opposite interests and ideologies between US and USSR. They were competing and conflicting with each other without direct 'hot war'. But mutual hostilities, arms race, nuclear arms race, zones of influences were prevalent during this period.

Origin and Bases of Cold War

After the war was over, Japan and no other axis power was capable to compete USA's nuclear bomb. Along with it, there was the end of common enemy of the allied powers. Then the western alliance turned towards post-war international order and security system. As the war drew to a conclusion, the fundamental disagreements among allies (USA, France, Britain and USSR) resurfaced. The increasing conflict between the new superpowers posed insurmountable problems in constructing a viable post-war security system. A number of contentious issues soon surfaced. These contentious issues were: The Atom Bomb—The sudden invention of atomic bomb by USA created Soviet Union suspicious of USA hegemony. USA earlier never shared its secret of nuclear bomb. Even USA believed that USSR would never be capable to produce the bomb in the coming 10 years. This will help US to check Soviet aggression. But USSR created nuclear bomb in four years. Secondly, Churchill's (then British PM) Fulton speech of 5th March, 1946 made differences more deep, "if the Western democracies stand together in strict adherence to the principles of UN Charter, their influence for furthering those principles will be immense and no one is likely to molest them. If, however, they become divided or fail in their duty and if these all important years are allowed to slip away, then indeed catastrophe may overwhelm us all". This speech specially targeted USSR and it was sign of coming closeness of Western democracies of Britain, France and US, etc. Soviet Union regarded it as a unilateral attack by 'Capitalism' and 'Imperialism' over socialist countries. Conflict was not only limited up to Central Europe; it had reached beyond Europe on the issues of Iran,

Turkey, Greece and Truman Doctrine. Truman Doctrine constituted a call to resist outside forces and was clearly directed against international communism or Soviet Union. Truman's address to Congress in March 1947 had a significant impact on the future of superpowers relations. He said, "I believe that we must assist free peoples to work out their own destinies in their own way". President Truman's proposal for an interventionist foreign policy can be understood as prelude to the Cold War. The Truman Doctrine and the associated policy of containment expressed the self-image of the United States as inherently defensive, and were underpinned by the Marshall Plan for European economic recovery, proclaimed in June 1947, which was essential to the economic rebuilding of Western Europe. In Eastern Europe, democratic or other anti-communist forces were systematically undermined or eliminated and being replaced by Marxist-Leninist regimes loyal to Moscow. Moscow understood that, the Western world was inspired by capitalist values which demanded the destruction of USSR and the extirpation of communism by any means available, but above all by force or the threat of irresistible force. The major factors which led to a Cold War atmosphere between the two superpowers became identifiable during post-war conferences. The famous Iron Curtin speech made by Churchill led to permanent wedge between the superpowers.

Important bases of Cold War:

- Ideological differences: Communist ideology led by USSR was against capitalism. Communist ideology advocates state control on means of production and advocates socialist governments which America (capitalist) considered largely totalitarian and anti-democratic. Communist ideology was intent upon converting the entire world. Therefore, it posed a real threat to freedom and liberty throughout the world. On the other side, communist Soviet Union blamed capitalism for the exploitation of resources in all over the world.

Map II: Cold War Europe

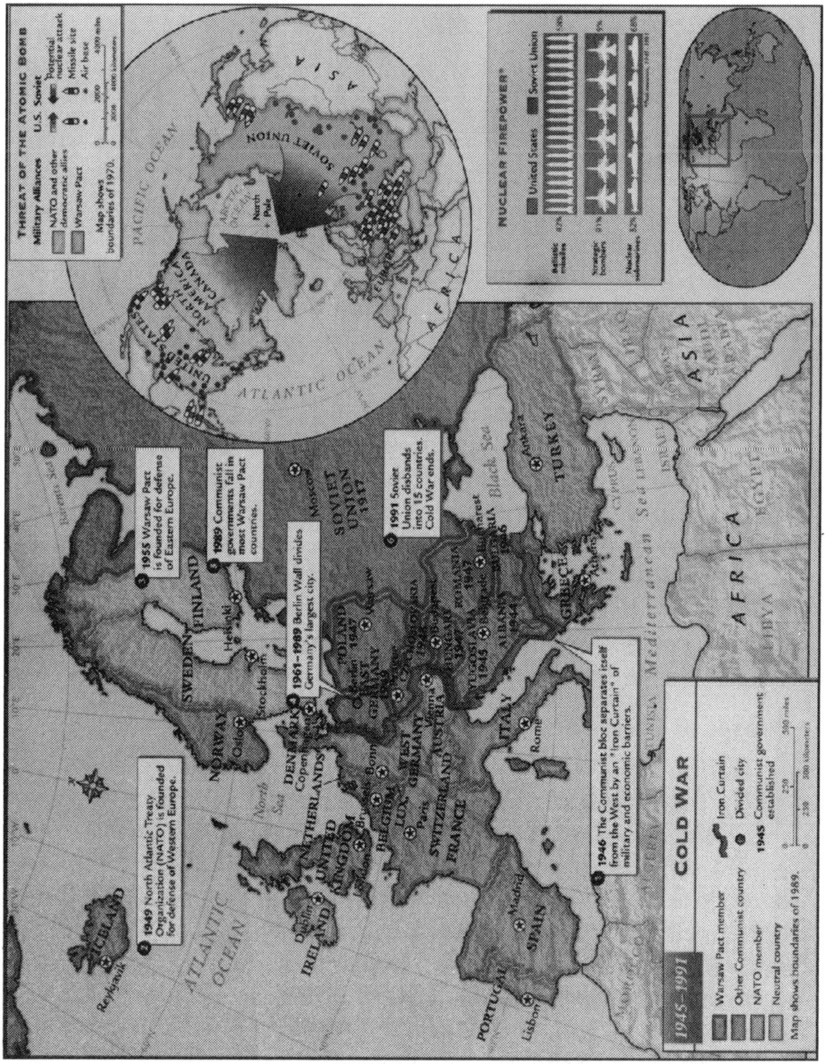

• Historical background: Soviet distrust of American intentions was based on historical record of hostility: As America's intervention in Russia in 1918-19; Former's refusal to establish diplomatic relations till

1933; US nourished hostility towards Soviet Union due to growing Soviet belligerence; Russia's unwillingness to permit democratic elections in countries liberated from Nazis; and Soviet Union's disagreements in post-war resettlements.

- German issue: The Cold War mainly originated from the German issue, and remained confined mostly to Europe for a long time. The Western powers were against the division of Germany and wanted to keep joint control of France, England, US and USSR. But USSR was interested to keep the Germany fully under its sphere of influence. Later on, under this conflict resulted in division of Germany.
- Mutual misunderstanding and antagonism: According to some scholars, the mistrust and consequent fears were the basis of Cold War. Mutual fear and suspicion produced hostile interaction between the two parties. The diplomacy of co-existence failed. Both the capitalists and the communists developed mutual suspicion. Soviet expansion in East Europe played greater role for erosion of diplomacy of co-existence.

Phases of Cold War

From the onset of Cold War till the demise of USSR in 1991, there had been different phases of Cold War. During this long period of 45 years, sometimes there was arms race, period of deterrence and increased hostilities, conflict and competition. At other time there was some understanding developed between the two superpowers, specifically regarding nuclear arms or the era of detente, reduced hostilities or controlled competition and conflict. On the basis of this we can divide the Cold War period into three important phases:

1945 to 1962—First Cold War

1962 to 1978—Detente Era

1978 to 1986—Known as Second or New Cold War

A. Phase I—1945 to 1962

During this period the polarization of two blocs occurred. US, a capitalist, led the Western or democratic states—Britain, France, Greece, Italy, West Germany, Japan and Australia. She also increased its influence in South East Asia, Central Asia, Australia and New Zealand. There was formation of defense alliances on US side known as NATO, SEATO, CENTO, ANZUS, etc. On the other hand, Soviet Union established its supremacy and zone of influence in Eastern Europe which included the countries: Poland, Hungary, Bulgaria, Romania, Czechoslovakia and East Germany alike. During this first phase of Cold War, major important international controversial issues were The German Division, Korean War (1950), the Suez Crisis (1956), Vietnam War, Cuban Missile Crisis (1962), the Berlin War Crisis (1961) and Hungarian Civil War (1956). Germany was divided into two parts. Federal Republic of Germany (West Germany) brought under control of joint forces of USA, France and England. German Democratic Republic (East Germany) fell under the influence of USSR or Communist Bloc. The popular East-West divide was division of Europe and particularly division of mighty Germany, which remained an aggressive power throughout the half of 20th century. German division fulfills the purpose of weakening its power for a long time. The Korean War (1950) ushered in an era of the third party projections of bipolar rivalry. The emergence of People's Republic of China (communist China—1949) as the second biggest communist state perfected the capitalist vs. communist dimension of the Cold War crisis. Cold War brought conflict in Korea, divided it between communist Korea (under the influence of China and USSR) and non-communist South Korea. US extended help to South Korea as a part of its containment policy. Then war seemed between communism and US. With the direct help of China, the UN troops (led by US) were pushed back by North Koreans across the 38th parallel. This 38th parallel divided the Korea into North Korea and South Korea. Cuban Missile Crisis (1962) is considered the greatest of all Cold War crisis. Cuba, an American continent Island country, where the Castro regime was increasing dependence upon the Soviet Union for economic aid, assistance and the placement of Soviet missiles and troops on Cuban territory. Castro was extremely against US hegemony over whole American continent. He strengthened Cuba for its independence in international relations. Then President Kennedy of US imposed a naval blockade on Cuba until the missiles were removed. Consequently, The Kennedy-Khurchev (USSR) communication during the Cuban Crisis not only prevented a hot-war but it led to an era of *detente*. This important doctrine and most of the defense and power alliance came into existence during this period.

Truman Doctrine: To combat the communist danger, the first important step taken by US President Truman was in 1947. Truman doctrine advocated US intervention in any part of world to contain communism. Truman declared to help to "free people to maintain their free institutions and their national integrity against aggressive movements". Truman doctrine was endorsed by US Congress in defence of Greece and Turkey where communist threat was eminent due to civil war.

Marshall Plan: US Secretary of State George Marshal formed a plan known as Marshall Plan. It envisaged that United States should do whatever it is able to assist in return of normal economic health in the world, without which there can be no political stability and no assured peace. USSR considered Marshall Plan as to control USSR's increasing popularity and influence. USSR rejected the plan and decided that communist countries will not take any advantage of the capitalist design of interference. Therefore, this plan contributed to strengthen the economies of Western Europe and to make their dependence on US.

North Atlantic Treaty organization (NATO)—1949: The formation of NATO, its structure and sophistication, reflected the Western alliance's new purpose and the seriousness of the West's perception of East's aggressive tendencies and growing military power. This treaty was signed by 12 nations in Washington for the purpose of safeguarding the freedom, common heritage and civilization of their people founded on the principles of democracy, individual liberty and rule of law.

The twelve original members were—US, United Kingdom, France, Canada, Belgium, Denmark, Italy, Iceland, Luxemburg, Netherlands, Norway, Portugal, Greece and Turkey joined in 1952 and West Germany in 1955.

Although, NATO's formation was under the rules and regulations of UN Charter but practically it was not according in the spirit of these rules. There was tremendous criticism of NATO all over the world particularly from communist world which called it formation of military alliance and will disturb the pace of world and will increase international tension. The formation of NATO undoubtedly, had given rise to the opponent alliance called Warsaw Pact. Besides, the dominant position in NATO was being enjoyed by US and UK which undermined the sovereignty of other partners. Despite numerous shortcomings NATO had promoted political, social and military co-operation among member states and encouraged them to settle their mutual disputes and differences amicably.

Central Treaty Organization (CENTO): US increased its influence up to West Asia. In 1954 an alliance between a NATO member Turkey formed an alliance with Pakistan in 1955. Earlier Turkey and Iraq joined an alliance known as Baghdad Pact. Later on Baghdad Pact was joined by Britain, Pakistan and Iran, renamed as CENTO. However USA never joined this pact but it was under auspices of USA. In March 1979, Iraq, Pakistan and Turkey left CENTO. By September 1979 CENTO was officially ceased to an existence. The purpose of Baghdad pact was to counter communist danger in the region. US was providing economic and military aid to member countries.

South-East Asian Treaty Organization (SEATO): Also known as Manila Pact. USA, UK, France, Australia, New Zealand, Pakistan, Thailand and Philippines signed a pact at Manila in 1954. US bloc's concern here was Korean issue and if South Korea fell into communist zone then there will no stop for communist bloc to reach one by one to South Asian states. Pakistan withdrew its membership in 1972. France was not taking keen interest in SEATO by 1974. Australia and New

Zealand decided not to participate in SEATO sessions. Finally SEATO was dissolved in 1977.

Australia, New Zealand and United States Pact (ANZUS): US pact with Australia and New Zealand with the purpose to secure pacific from communism.

Communist Information Bureau (Cominform): It was a communist bloc alliance, created in response to Marshall Plan. Communist parties of Yugoslavia, Bulgaria, Rumania, Hungary, Poland, USSR and Czechoslovakia participated in it. The proposal of Cominform was to coordinate the policies of communist parties and to discuss about mutual economic assistance for communist countries.

Sino-Soviet Treaty: Soviet Union made a treaty with China in 1950—a treaty of friendship, alliance and mutual assistance for thirty years duration. They promised to render military assistance in case of any threat by Japan and any other power.

Warsaw Pact: Communist bloc's Warsaw Pact was a bold response to NATO. In May 1955, Albania, Bulgaria, Hungary, East Germany, Poland, Romania, USSR and Czechoslovakia concluded a pact at Warsaw (Poland). Along with treaty of friendship, cooperation and mutual assistance. The proposal was also made to set up joint command of armed forces of the signatory states with its headquarters in Moscow, to be headed by Soviet Marshal I.S. Koniev and Deputy Commander in Chiefs also appointed from other partners. The contracting parties agreed to settle international disputes by peaceful means in accordance with the UN Charter and to develop economic and cultural ties.

All these doctrines, treaties and pacts certainly enhanced the tension between the two blocs and divided the international relationship into bipolar order. Through these pacts Soviet Union and US both were trying to bring more and more areas under their influence. All important alliances were occurred during this phase of Cold War.

B. The Detente Era—1962 to 1978

According to *Oxford Dictionary of Politics,* detente means literally 'loosening'. Detente was used to refer, the period of reduced tension in relations between the United States and Soviet Union during the Cold War. It was closely associated with the process of arms control, and the main period of detente ran from the Nuclear Partial Test Ban Treaty (1963) to the late 1970s. In brief we can say that detente means reduced hostilities, controlled conflict, competition and arms race. It was an era of more stability than arms race and deterrence.

According to Len Scot, "How far the arms race was the result of mutual misperceptions, how far the unavoidable outcome of irreconcilable political differences, are central questions. Some influential Americans believed that the Soviets were bent on world domination, which the communist rhetoric of world revolution certainly encouraged. What is clear is that nuclear weapons provided context and pretext for their more dangerous confrontations, most notably when the Soviets deployed nuclear weapons in Cuba in 1962. It is also clear that when political confrontation gave way to Soviets—American detente, agreements on nuclear weapons became the most tangible achievement of détente".[19] 1970s witnessed a shifting balance of power. There was Sino-US understanding by 1971. President Nixon of United States then referred early 1970s as an 'age of Negotiation'.

US-Soviet relations steadily improved with the US withdrawal from Vietnam. The ideological rift between USSR and China was a thaw to ideological alliances. Rising China's armed forces and nuclear arsenals added a new dimension to international relations. Besides, Willy Brandt, West German Chancellor (1969) enthusiastically pursued 'Ostopolitik'—aimed at reaching a series of constructive agreements between East and West. Poland tried to make comfortable relations with West Germany. The leading incidents towards East-West detente were:

- Nuclear Test Ban Treaty—1962
- NPT—1968
- Biological Weapons Conventions—1972
- Conference on Security and Cooperation in US, Canada and Europe in which 33 European countries

participated from both East and West Europe (CSCE) —1975

C. New Cold War—1979 to 1986

The new Cold War started in 1979. There was direct intervention of USSR forces in Afghanistan in 1979. This was the end of detente era and entrance of next face of Cold War. The Belgrade Conference on New Strategic Arms Limitation Talks (SALT) failed in 1977-78 due to US allegations that the Soviet Union was not honoring the pledges of human rights made in 1975. It was President Carter's aggressive policy but Brezhnev (USSR) accused US (Jimmy Carter) of West's interference in East's internal affairs. Carter also demanded concessions on immigration from Moscow.

USSR's direct military intervention in Afghanistan led to end of detente era. She was justifying its action that West was attempting to destabilize Afghanistan, a country bordering the USSR, a threat to USSR. Under the US President Ronald Reagan, NATO took a decision to deploy American made cruise missiles towards the close of 1979, and the advanced medium range Pershing II missiles in West Europe. America intervened in El Salvador, Soviets in Nicaragua, Vietnam, Angola and Mozambique. Reagan's Star War and Bomber B-20 programme further aggravated the tension.

In 1985, Mikhail Gorbachev became the President of USSR. He understood the actual hollowness of communist economies. He made several efforts to reduce the tension between US and USSR and loosened some pressure on East European countries. As a result, there was German unification in 1990 and disintegration of USSR by 1991. Ultimately it was the end of Cold War, and bipolarity emerged at international scene.

Impact of Cold War on World Politics

Bipolar World Order: Cold War power politics divided the world into two camps opposite to each other. All the world politics was being guided by bipolar world order. International organizations like UNO also became catapuller of bipolar world politics. UN Security Council members misused their veto power a number of times in favour of their bloc members or camp followers. Foreign policy of not only bloc members but of non-members had been dictated by bi-polar world structure. International order was maintained by bipolar balance of power. Notwithstanding, this bipolar balance of power saved the world from any large scale world war.

Impact on European Colonialism: US was against European colonialism in earlier period. Later on, to maintain the status quo US started favouring European colonialism. This US policy gave the advantage to USSR to become the 'Messiah' of Third World. USSR raised voice against colonialism at every platform. The Marxian leaders of TWCs were leaning more heavily towards communist camp.

Emergence of Non-Aligned Movement (NAM): Cold War had given impetus to formation of NAM—an organization of newly independent countries of Asia and Africa, or Latin America to keep their independence in international relations. These countries wanted to take more advantages from both blocs along with their autonomy. NAM was the movement which loosened the bipolar competitive international order upto great extent. This organization along with UN played an active role to diffuse the tension between the two blocs whenever it ripened.

Arms Race: Cold War's most dangerous impact was that most of the states indulged in arms race. They were developing more and more arms of mass destruction, especially by US and USSR. For example, in the period from 1945 to 1985 US developed from 2 to 11,200 bombs and warheads. Similarly, USSR made from 0 to 9900 nuclear arms in the same period. China, France, England also became nuclear powers.

Proxy Wars in Third World Countries: The highly advanced high-technology arms race encouraged both super-powers engaging in proxy wars in areas other than Europe. Korea, Vietnam, Egypt (Suez Crisis), Cuba, Cambodia, Afghanistan, etc. became victims of proxy wars. Cold War also destabilized the social, political, and economic development of TWCs.

Impact on Economy: Cold War affected the whole world economy. It increased the difficulties of superpowers by high defence spending which resulted in numerous economic problems. Developing countries were also following arms race and increased their defence budgets to maintain their security within the region. Bordering states were being aided by superpowers. India, Pakistan, Iran, Iraq, North Korea and South Korea are some examples.

In short, Cold War was one of most important happenings at international level, which engulfed the whole world into its influence. Almost half a century world relations have been dictated by bipolar world order. Two superpowers dominated and maintained their hegemony at international level.

Collapse of Soviet Bloc, End of Cold War and Post-Cold War Era

Disintegration of Union of Soviet Socialist Republics (USSR) and the Communist Bloc was one of the most important event in international politics in the 20th century. Soviet Union, which remained a superpower almost for four and half decades, had posed a deterrence to USA and its capitalist bloc failed to be equal of an opponent by 1985. Both USSR and USA respectively led their respective power blocs for half a century. Not only that, even world politics was largely controlled by this bipolar world order. Students of international relations spend a lot of time trying to understand things that actually did happen. Sometimes, however, it is just as interesting and equally important to ask about and understand those things that did not happen. The peace of Cold War provides a good example of just such a non-event. For more than forty years, two of the greatest military powers of the world had ever known divided by an intense ideological rivalry, struggled against each other across the globe. But despite the intensity of the conflict, they never actually went to war with each other. In many ways, this is a very curious outcome. It is unusual in international history for two great powers to compete against one another on such a scale and never fight. If any 'non-event' cries out for an explanation, it is the curious peace that was the Cold War.[20]

The events in 1989-91, from the collapse of the Iron Curtain (No connectivity between East and West Europe) to the dismantling of the Soviet Union in December 1991, represent a turning point in three distinct respects. First, they marked the end of the broadly bipolar structure, based on US-Soviet rivalry, which the international system had assumed since the late 1940s. A second set of important changes took place at the level of the nation-state. Former communist states experienced serious problems of transition ranging from economic collapse, which affected them all (most of the communist regions) to the disintegration of the state itself. Even those states which maintained communist systems, such as China, North Korea and Cuba, faced enormous challenges, since they had to accommodate themselves to the position of increased marginality. Yet those states not in the throes of post-communist transition were also forced to redefine their national interests and roles in the light of the radical change in the international balance of power. This applied as much to large states such as the United States, whose policies had been premised on the Soviet threat, as to small states in the Third World which had been to greater or lesser degree 'client' states of the superpowers.[21]

It is instructive to remember how grim international politics looked by the middle of the 1980s and how much changes occurred (mostly for the better) in the ensuring decade. By the end of 1988, the United States and the Soviet Union agreed for the first time to dismantle a whole category of nuclear weapons. The eight-year war between Iran and Iraq finally ended in 1988.[22] The Soviets pulled their troops out of Afghanistan. There was a little doubt that most dramatic political events in the late 1980s and the first half of 1990s took place in the communist world. A decade of reforms in China culminated in massive pre-democracy demonstrations in Beijing in 1989.

The demise and eventual dissolution of the Soviet Union was unquestionably a major event that transformed critical aspects of international relations, especially in Europe.[23] We are now over two decades into the post-Cold War world. The mere fact that almost everyone still describes the period since 1989 as the 'post-Cold War Era' is in itself telling. This is an era that remained defined by what it is not rather than what it is. Although all agree that we are no longer in the Cold War, there is no consensus about what sort of world has replaced it.

Debate about the end of Cold War is mired in as much ideological controversy as is debate about its origins. One version credits Ronald Reagan with having brought the Cold War to an end by instigating a renewed US military build-up in the early 1980s particularly in the form of Strategic Defense Initiative (SDI) (the star war initiative) of 1983, thereby sparking off the 'second Cold War'. The result was that the USSR was drawn into an arms race that its already fragile economy could not sustain. In a broader form, this explanation has been elaborated, by Fukuyama (1992) amongst others, into the triumphalist 'end of history' thesis. This thesis suggests that the West 'won' the Cold War ultimately because only US-style liberal democracy offered a viable economic and political system. Other versions place heavier stress on the structural weakness of the Soviet economy and the catastrophic mishandling of the reform process by Mikhail Gorbachev.[24]

Among the most striking features of communism's collapse was its suddenness, a surprise as much to most western experts on the Soviet Union and Eastern Europe as to political leaders and the public. It is true that revolutionary change by its nature contains a large element of the incalculable. Institutional inertia, social customs and psychological habit ensure that systems can maintain their outer shapes long after they have begun to decay internally. Perhaps the most useful general observation on the causes of revolution remains that of French political philosopher Alexis de Tocqueville that 'the most dangerous moment for a bad government is generally that in which it sets about reform'. This model, generalized as it is, is useful starting point for an understanding of Mikhail Gorbachev's revolutionary period in power.[25] Gorbachev's 'new thinking' laid the groundwork for even more radical reforms by undercutting the moral and intellectual basis of the Stalinist state. Soviet-style communism had displayed all the characteristics of totalitarian rule, including central control over the armed forces, the mass media, and the economy; a dominant monopoly party; an official ideology; and a systematic program of terror against suspected political opponents and the mass murder of innocents deemed unworthy by the regime.[26] The most important fact to keep in mind about the Soviet political and economic system before Gorbachev came to power in 1985 was that all power was centralized in the communist party, which governed the nation. Although separate government structures and institutions existed, they were mere reflections of the fundamental control the party exercised over Soviet political life. Furthermore, not only was the communist party the primary repository of political power, it was also the main source of social rank, power and privilege within the Soviet Union. The party was hierarchically organized, with sharp gradations in power and authority according to rank. All personnel matters, not only within the party but also in all other key Soviet institutions were tightly controlled by the party hierarchy.[27] It was not Gorbachev's intension to dismantle the Soviet Union. His widely read political credo, *Perestroika* (1987) was firmly anti-stalinist but not anti-socialist. Gorbachev advocated through *Perestroika* means "restructuring: The political and economic restructuring". It referred to the market oriented economic reforms, ending the leading role of the communist party. To emprise law, allowing state enterprises to sell part of their product in the open market and also allowing foreign companies to own Soviet enterprises. He also introduced *glasnost* which means greater openness and democratization: To promote principle of freedom to criticize; loosening of control on media and publications; and freedom of worship or religious freedom etc. Policy changes under the influence of Gorbachev's these concepts lifted the pressure people of different nationalities, resulting in seccession. The collapse of the Soviet Union was economic in nature. At the heart of the problem was the Soviet Union's command economy. Put simple, Soviet economic policy since its inception had been to increase inputs (e.g., labor, capital, raw material, and energy) to bolster production. Upto the 1960s, this formula resulted in an impressive growth rate, because Soviet planners before then were still in route to mobilizing the full potential of all available wasteful. By contrast, capitalist economies carefully consider the extent and type of inputs used and compensated by maximizing productivity, that is, efficient production of goods. In the 1970s as economic power rose to prominence, the Soviet input potential was employed to the limit productivity stagnated. Industrial plants overdue for overhauls simply continued to produce goods of questionable quality, lacking stimuli that exist in open-market economies. Consequently, it began to fall behind the standards set by international economy.[28]

During the Soviet occupation of Afghanistan (1979 to 1988), as a consequence, the 120,000 Soviet soldiers stationed in Afghanistan incurred heavy losses by the standards of the day. Some 15,000 men perished in fighting the Mujahideen between 1979 to 88. Till the Soviet withdrawal a decade later, 37000 wounded during the war. The politburo or political bureau justified intervention in Afghanistan by referring to the Soviet Union's internationalist duty to support a fellow communist government. With the rise of Mikhail Gorbachev in 1985, a significant change in the conduct of Soviet War took place. He realized that the war was imposing an unbearable financial and human toll on the strained Soviet economy. His conclusion was simple: All Soviet troops had to withdraw, and moreover, Gorbachev was under pressure to satisfy the West. In its bid to improve Soviet relations with the United States, peace in Afghanistan became imperative. Gorbachev finally agreed to withdraw all Soviet troops without any kind of settlement with Mujahideen. Conversely, he did seek a settlement with the United States. An agreement with Reagan—stipulating that both superpowers cease all direct or indirect support for their clients. Consequently, Afghanistan was plunged into a protracted civil war.[29]

The story in the rest of the communist world was virtually a mirror image of that in China. In Eastern Europe, and especially the Soviet Union, dramatic strides towards political liberalization and democracy coincided with equally dramatic economic deterioration. Gorbachev instituted an equally profound revolution in foreign policy, especially in Soviet relations with its erstwhile satellites in Eastern Europe. "In 1989", according to historian, Eugene Linden (1966), "While the nations of Western Europe celebrated the bicentenary of the French revolution, the nations of Eastern Europe re-enacted it". In that year, a long process of liberalization in Poland culminated in open parliamentary elections, and other states were soon to follow Poland's lead. As the *Los Angles Times* (December 17, 1989) observed in the wake of 1989 revolution in Eastern Europe, "It took 10 years in Poland, 10 months in Hungary, 10 weeks in East Germany, and 10 days in Czechoslovakia." (World Development Report 1992). By the end of the year the regime of Nicolae Ceausescu in Romania had also been overthrown. By 1991, even the long-isolated regime in Albania was liberalizing in various ways. In October 1990, East and West Germany were unified in one Federal Republic of Germany, and in 1991, the Warsaw Pact was officially disbanded and the Cold War was over.[30]

Moscow had good reason to fear that the 'nationality question' might sooner or later be the Soviet Union's undoing. Ironically, it was Gorbachev's reforms that created the climate in which the non-Russian nationalities could dare to strife for self-determination and independence. Gorbachev put his policies, known as 'Perestroika' and 'Glasnost' into effect as *Glasnost*, in particular, encouraged a climate of local criticism of the central government and the communist party. The immense psychological impact of this decision (to allow satellite states—Poland, East Germany, Czechoslovakia, Hungary, Bulgaria, Romania—to leave the Soviet fold) was increased by the geographical proximity of many of the republics to these East European nations. Independence became a political idea that was catching. With the demise of Soviet Union, independence for all the republics became a reality. Consequently, the independence movement surged in the Baltic States first, where Lithuania, Latvia, Estonia (which had been independent for a time before they were seized by Stalin under his infamous 1939 pact with Hitler) pushed the peace of reform further and faster than Gorbachev intended. In 1990, Lithuania led the way. On March 11, 1990, it formally declared its independence from Moscow followed by others. President Gorbachev attempted to stabilize the situation with a new Union Treaty that redefined the relationship between the central government and the republics. This treaty was heavily tilted in favor of the republics, so much so that some experts saw it as fundamental transformation of the very nature of Soviet state. For instance, the treaty permitted the republics to conduct their own diplomatic and commercial relations with other countries, reserved to them the right to secession, and permitted them to suspend national law. It was probably not coincidental that the attempt to remove Gorbachev from power took place on the eve of this treaty's signing. After the coup's failure, the treaty became moot as the floodgates were opened, and a majority of republics announced their intention to become independent. In December 1991, the Soviet Union ceased to exist.[31]

The collapse of communism in Eastern Europe marked most graphically by the destruction of the Berlin Wall in November 1989, was intimately related to events in Soviet Union but also had roots of its own. The nations of Eastern Europe (East Germany, Poland, Bulgaria, Romania, Albania, Hungary, etc.) had experienced only forty years of communist rule as opposed to the seventy years of the Soviet Union and in all cases except Yugoslavia had had communism imposed on them rather than choosing it themselves. The suddenness of communist collapse in Eastern Europe, and the relative ease with which citizens shed the habits of forty years, suggests that those habits were to a considerable extent a matter of form. One important force which had held them in place since the late 1940s was the threat of Soviet intervention to reimpose orthodoxy should Eastern Europeans stray from the path set down for them.[32] Gorbachev's top-down approach to reforming Soviet rule did have an impact on the member states of the Warsaw Pact. The introduction to *perestroika* and *glasnost* resulted in rapid delegitimization of communism in Eastern Europe. Gorbachev's reform policy was interpreted as an abnegation of traditional Soviet imperial claim. Between 1989 and 1991, there followed a chain reaction that resulted in the disengagement of communist Eastern Europe from Soviet domination. Poland was the first Soviet satellite to break away. Discontent with the communist leadership and the declining standard of living in Poland gave rise to *solidarnose* (solidarity) during the 1980s, a movement that had its roots in the heavy industry unions. In April 1989, *solidarnose* was legalized and free elections were negotiated with the government for June 1989. Following the elections in August 1989, Tadeusz Mazowiecki was confirmed as the first non-communist Prime Minister of Poland. During the same month, the regime of Janos Kadar was overthrown in Hungary; in October the single-party system was abolished and political opposition was legalized. By the end of 1989, East European states had successfully overthrown communist rule. Shortly, East Germany, Czechoslovakia, Bulgaria, Romania and Albania forced communist governments out of power.[33]

A new era of cooperation among European states emerged. West Germany and East Germany got united. Berlin Wall, the symbol and physical manifestation of Cold War in Europe got demolished. However, the wall was a propaganda disaster for East Germany and the Communist bloc. It became key symbol of what Western powers regarded as communist tyranny, particularly after the high profile shootings of would-be defectors. Political liberalization in the late 1980s, associated with the decline of Soviet Bloc, led East Germany to relax border restrictions, culminating in mass demonstrations and the fall of the East German government. The wall was destroyed by a euphoric public in the November 1989, and its fall was the first step towards the German unification, which was formally concluded on October 3, 1990.

Consequences of Collapse of Soviet Bloc

The demise of Soviet Union or Communist bloc was beginning of new era of independence not only for 15 republics that comprised old USSR, but also of Eastern communist countries. Soviet Republics became highly contentious about new negotiations proposed by Moscow. The Baltic States

(Latvia, Lithunia, Estonia) and Georgia refused to consider entering a new association with Russia on any terms. The order eleven republics eventually agreed to join the loose-knit federation, the Commonwealth of Independent States (CIS), but reserved the right to opt out at any time. Ukraine second only to Russia in territory, population and wealth has been particularly suspicious of Moscow's motives and truculent in its insistence on unimpeded freedom of action.

The dismantling of Soviet Bloc was taken by Left as the reaction, understandably more varied and complex, has been again along predictable lines. The collapse of a system which nurtured and sustained the hopes of generation after generation of socialists throughout the world is a dreadful event from the point of view of socialites everywhere—this is how Ralph Miliband put it at the very outset. It has been seen as a tragedy and a defeat not only for the 'faithful among them but for the critics too, who had criticized in the hope of a change for the better and had never even remotely visualized this change for the worst. It is a defeat not because the regimes in Eastern Europe and Soviet Union were models of the society the socialists want, but because they and the political movements influenced by them were the focus of the first world wide challenge to capitalist power, capitalist morality, capitalist exploitation and capitalist culture. And however flawed or deformed their actually existing socialism was, it was yet the symbol of the a possibility, the possibility of escape from the essentially predatory system, capitalism. Socialists who had no illusions about the Soviet Union, nevertheless, viewed it as a strategically significant entity. As G.A. Cohen has underlined it: The Soviet Union needed to be there as a defective model so that, with one eye on it, we could construct a better one. It created a non-capitalist space to think about socialism.[34] The collapse of Soviet Bloc was unquestionably extremely important event of 20th century international politics. Its impact was irreparable and immeasurable all over the world. We will discuss here its major consequences on other countries and international politics:

End of Cold War: Four decades old Cold War between two power blocs, which created the bipolar nuclear world, which dominated the world politics, was ended with the demise of Soviet Bloc and disintegration of USSR. There was East-West dichotomy, as Europe had been divided into two parts. Both the power blocs were conflicting on several international issues, particularly entangled at UN and UN Security Council. Security Council usually had been handwork of this bipolarism during Cold War period. Every international issue, problem, conflict had been engulfed and colored by Cold War politics. With elimination of one bloc (Communism), Cold War was over automatically.

East Europe: The demise of communism in Eastern Europe was welcomed with great enthusiasm in the West. In Poland, Czechoslovakia and Hungary, the new popularly elected governments moved quickly to solidify democratic reforms and dismantle the failed machinery of central planning.

(a) **German Unification:** Gorbachev allowed German reunification and declared to withdraw the Soviet Union's nearly 400,000 troops from Eastern Germany and to allow the reunited Germany to remain in NATO. No less significant was Moscow's acquiescence in the dissolution of the Warsaw Pact, which was formally accomplished in the spring of 1991.[35] The division of Germany and of Berlin were resented deeply by the German people. The demand for political and economic liberalization in East Europe received a great impetus from the changes in Soviet Union after Gorbachev came to power. In November 1989, East Germans were granted freedom to leave and cross over the west at any point along the country's borders, including the crossing points through the Berlin Wall. The Kremlin greeted the opening of the wall as 'wise' and 'positive'. Erich Honeker, the East German Party Chief, resigned and Egon Krenz Oho took over the pursuit of *Perestroika* in East Germany. The breaking of the Berlin Wall was welcomed by the people all over the world as a historic event. Once the wall was broken East and West Germany struck down the barriers between them and set on the path of unification. Free elections were held in East Germany on March 18, 1990, followed by economic union on July 1. In September 1990, the four allies of World War II signed an agreement to end their remaining occupation rights. On October 3, 1990, unified Germany's flag (Black, Red and Gold) was hoisted in front of the Reichstag in Berlin. The German merged with eleven states of Federal Republic of Germany (FRG). One thing that seems to emerge from the change in both East and West Europe is that the US and the USSR will no longer direct European affairs, much less exercise hegemony.[36]

(b) **The Breakup of Czechoslovakia:** After the fall of communism in Czechoslovakia, the Slovakian problem emerged. The Slovak question, which threatened the cohesion of the state. The Slovaks' penchand for independence was advanced in 1992. Slovaks were alienated by the Czechs' preponderance within the federation. The Czechs also reneged on promise to Slovaks a measure of autonomy. Another reoccurring problem that fueled resentment was questions over use of the Slovak language, which hitherto had not been recognized as the official language first in Slovakia. Thus following the decline of communism, the Slovak Prime Minister Vladimir Meciar seized the first possible opportunity to break away from the federation. At least, the separation occurred toward the end of 1992. The absence of violence during the difficult transition from the multinational federation to nation-state attests to the unusually high sagacity and foresight among the leader of two people.[37]

(c) **Yugoslavia:** By 1990, democracy and free elections had replaced communism. Accompanying the rise of democracy came unleashing of divisive ethnic fervor and the creation of numerous native parties among Yugoslavia's many peoples. Economic collapse accompanied the uprising of nationalistic feelings as production, trade and tourism all declined dramatically while bankruptcies and unemployment rose. By June 1991, Croatia and Slovakia, the two wealthiest, northern Yugoslav republics, declared independence. What followed was a bloody Civil War which claimed an estimated 10,000 casualties. The efforts of these republics proved largely successful and by January 1992 both were widely recognized as independent nation-states. In addition, the Yugoslav republics themselves had their own internal ethnic divisions and soon declared independence.[38] In Bosnia-Herzegovina, a referendum was held in 1992. Bosnian Muslims and Croats voted in favour of leaving Yugoslavia and forming a new state. Thereafter the most tragic of post-Cold War European conflicts unfolded with great speed and intensity exacting and appalling price in terms of lives lost, people displaced and property destroyed. Finally, on 22 December 1995, a US-brokered peace deal was signed by warring parties at Dayton. But states of Kosovo which remained under Serbian rule was finally resolved in 1999 after an extensive air war conducted by NATO against Serbia, following which Kosovo was made into formal protectorate under the protection of West.[39]

(d) **The Expansion of NATO:** Again US played the central role in solving the Balkans (Kosovo) problem of Europe. Then one of the most obvious is the extent to which Europe after the Cold War remained every bit as dependent on the USA for its security as it had been before. Then, among the most critical actions in Europe after 1989 was the American decision to expand NATO and to offer full membership to several former members of the Warsaw Pact including Poland, Czech Republic and Hungary—who joined in

1994. And Baltic Republics Bulgaria and Romania joined ten years later. USA under Clinton administration was convinced that there was no European answer to European problem. With some resentment American pressure remained in Europe.[40]

The South or the Third World: The affect of dismantling communism obviously was serious on the Third World countries. Firstly, although the East Europe disturbed the communist regimes in South, somehow Cuba and North Korea have become successful for persisting their communist political system till now with greater efforts. Tienamen Square Event (1989) in China was chain effect of withdrawal of communism in Eastern Europe. Gorbachev visited China in the same year and minimized the serious misunderstandings between the two. Secondly, the socialist model of economy came under pressure in Third World after demise of communism. There was imposition of market-oriented policies in these countries, e.g. Brazil, India, Mexico, etc. Thirdly, the concept of non-alignment and existence of NAM was being challenged. It has been considered that both these concepts related to bipolar world structure, where there was role to play for the South as the Third Force. Now the situation was changed. Fourthly, disintegration of USSR or whole Soviet bloc seriously affected the third world economies and trade, because East bloc was trading with the third world countries. The demise of it obviously caused serious problem for them. Fifthly, the ethnic or violent movements emerged in several third world countries which have been victims of US-USSR power politics, e.g. Iraq, Afghanistan, Cambodia, Libya, etc.

US Hegemony and Gulf War: With the Soviet withdrawal from a position of America's adversary, the nature of international relations is perceived as US domination over the rest of the world. A unipolar world was perceived in which the US will have the control of the working of UN as well as the power to shape or mould the international affairs at global level. This perception could be justified by first Gulf War and Kosovo crisis where US played a central role to establish its hegemony.

Globalization is another significant trend in the post-Cold War period with which states are struggling. Although the economies of the world have been very interdependent since the European powers began colonizing the globe and interdependence increased dramatically by the early 1970s. Free trade often clashes with other issues such as security, human rights, labor standards and environmental regulations.

According to Ian Clark, "There are still significant elements of continuity, especially in terms of the American influence in the world and the perpetuation of the institutions created under American tutelage during the Cold War". The ending of Cold War has not brought with it any fundamental alteration in the scope of American power and commitments throughout the world. US forces remain in Japan, Korea, and Europe, though in somewhat smaller numbers, just as they were at the height of the Cold War. The passing of the Soviet military alliance in Europe, the Warsaw Pact, has not been accompanied by the end of the American alliance, NATO. The Gulf War, considered at the time of possible harbinger of a "new world order", demonstrated the continuing centrality of the United States. A handful of other nations contributed military forces, money and military bases, but the outcome was determined by the military power of the United States. The 2003 war which toppled Saddam Hussein (and then executed), with the significant exception of Great Britain, was almost entirely an American undertaking. Even with the reductions in US military spending that accompanied the end of the cold war, no other nation possesses the necessary combination of capability and willingness to challenge the military power of the Unites States. Whether one wishes to refer to this as American 'hegemony', 'dominance', or 'unipolarity', the basic point remains the same. Ian Clark highlights this point again in remarking on the essential continuing in the role of American Power..... There are institutions that were created during Cold War, and which were almost defining attributes of it, that still endure into the post-Cold War era.[41]

The triumph of capitalism, therefore, did not lead to an improvement in the lives of billions of people, a point made not just by radicals critical of status quo, but also by those who insist that after the failure of planning (of communism socialist system), capitalism stands alone as the only feasible way rationally of organizing a modern economy. A well known Peruvian economist Hernando de Soto, admired by many rightists, viewed (The hour of Capitalism's Triumph 2001), 'its hour of crisis'. After ten years of reform, restructuring, and dancing to the 'economic turn' of the experts at the IMF (International Monetary Fund), the masses were still waiting. Communism has been seen off, he accepts, and possibly for good. But its demise has not for the most part seen a viable capitalism kick-started in those parts of the world where it was not already well established. The 'new world order' thus looks like the old one with North American, Europe and parts of Asia still in economic command. Everything has changed, or soon it seems, but the fundamentals remain the same.[42]

The retreat from socialism has inevitably meant a retreat from Marxism. In fact, in its entire history, no specific development has more single handedly opened the floodgates of attack on Marxism, its analytic categories and political project that the collapse of the degenerate and deformed regimes in the Soviet Union and East Europe which claimed to have successfully built socialism and to be on the road to communism. This world historic event, whose substantive origins lay in a series of developments in the post-Lenin Soviet Union, coupled with the stagnation, retreat or even defeats of the international revolutionary movements in recent years, has negatively conditioned, in its process and combination, so much of what is happening around and within Marxist theory today. 'Actually existing socialism' was born of revolutions primarily led by Marxists, had proclaimed Marxism as its official ideology and in its own way represented the first major and seemingly successful revolutionary wave against capitalism. It should not be difficult to understand, therefore, that its collapse is seen as defeat of Marxism itself by its opponents in their anti-communist perspective, which refuses to make any distinction at all between theory and practice.[43] Although the collapse of the Cold War provided further space for developments in thinking to flourish, reflective critical thought on the discipline, its purpose, methods and agenda. According to K.J. Holsti (The Dividing Discipline, 1987), from at least 1980s new ideas had been introduced into IR debates that departed from both realist and mainstream liberal ways of thinking as well as from orthodox Marxist analysis. By 1990s IR textbooks included largely about feminism, post-modernism, environmentalism or the role of culture in world politics. During the period from 1989 onwards some grand ideas in world politics emerged to fill at least part of the vacuum left by the collapse of the old world order. These ranged from Francis Fukuyama's announcement of the 'end of history' to Samuel Huntington's forebodings concerning a 'clash of civilizations'. The latter especially, has implications for post-Cold War development such as the incidence of deadly conflict that appears to revolve around issues of 'identity' politics, including culture, ethnicity or religion. In certain parts of the world, especially the Asia Pacific region, the concept of culture has also featured in casual theories relating to economic growth. Ideas about culture now play a significant role in some branches of security studies as well as normative theory.[44]

September 11, 2001 marked the end of the post-Cold War era. The key factors shaping world politics since 9/11 has been Islamic terrorism and the United States-led war on terror. US foreign policy has come under sustained attack after it decided to go to war against Iraq. The world is now a less stable place that it was before 9/11.[45] US adopted realist security formula and for almost ten years US was after Al-Qaida and its mastermind Osama Bin Laden. For this purpose US attacked Iraq, executed Suddam Hussain and killed thousands of people there. Next intervention of US was in Afghanistan where she uprooted Taliban rule and established its military bases. It all proves that realist theory is still very important in international relations.

Map III: Rising Asia

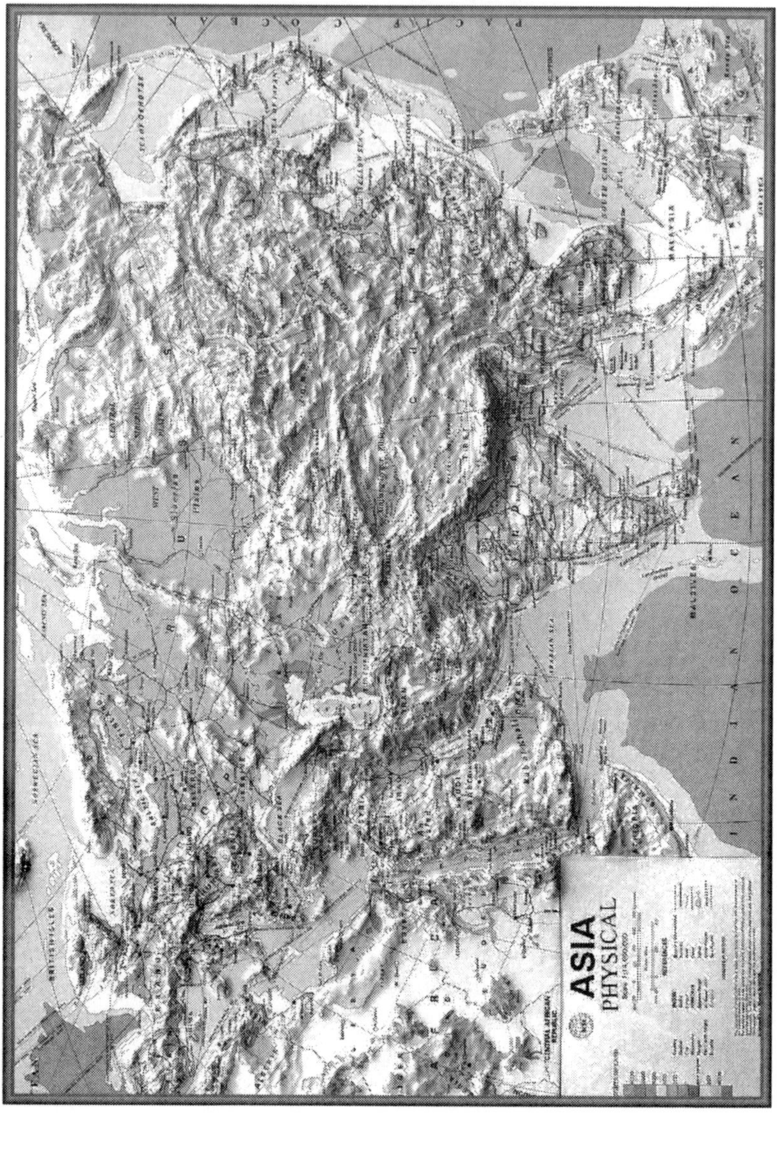

All the major political perspectives use different parts of the history of international relations in the second half of the twentieth century to advance their claims about global politics. Realism concentrates on the Cold War rivalry, liberalism on the rise of economic interdependence, and idealism on the value conflicts and growing concern over human rights. The world economic system perspective focuses on the continued division of the international capitalist system into a core and a periphery, constructivism on how the Cold War rivalry was socially constructed, and feminism on the masculine nature of the Cold War and the effects that the Cold War and its end has had on the ladies.[46]

Thus, history of international relations, generally start with European predominance till the end of Second World War. Subsequently, US left its isolation policy during the First World War and emerged the most powerful superpower after the end of Second World War. By the end of 1999s USSR, the only superpower that could challenge US, disintegrated along with its communist bloc. Then, US remained the lone superpower.

Twenty-first century is presumed as the Asian century considering rising China and India, both are nuclear powers. Besides South Africa and Brazil are equally putting forth their existence for their scenario. How far these third world countries could play their role in global politics only time would tell.

REFERENCES

1. Keith L. Shimko (2005). *International Relations Perspectives and Controversies*. Boston, New York: Houghton Mifflin Company. p. 15.
2. Karen Mingst A. (2004). *Essentials of International Relations*. New York: W.W. Norton and Company. p. 17.
3. Keith L. Shimko. *Op. cit.* p. 19.
4. Henr Kissinger (1994). *Diplomacy*. London: Simon and Schuster. p. 21.
5. Keith L. Shimko. *Op. cit.* p. 41.
6. Henry Kissinger. *Op. cit.* pp. 17-28.

7. Dhirendr Dwivedi (2005). *Collective Security Under United Nations Retrospect and Prospects*. New Delhi: Kanishka Publishers. pp. 19-20.
8. Andreas Wenger and Doron Zimmermann (2006). *International Relations from the Cold War to the Globalized World*. New Delhi: Viva Books Private Limited. pp. 11-12
9. Donald J. Puchala (2003). *Theory and History in International Relations*. New York: Routledge. p. 57.
10. Peter Calvocoressi (2004). *World Politics 1945-2000*. Delhi: Pearson. p. 2.
11. Martin Griffiths and Terry o' Callaghan (2004). *Key Concepts in International Relations*. London: Routledge. pp. 303-304.
12. Mclean, Iain and Alistair (2005). *Oxford Concise Dictionary of Politics*. US: Oxford University Press. p. 326.
13. Andreas Wenger and Doron Zimmermann. *Op. cit*. p. 13.
14. Len Scott (2005). "International History, 1945-1990" in John Baylis and Steve Smith (eds.). *The Globalisation of World Poltics. An Introduction to International Relations*. Oxford: Oxford University Press. p. 98.
15. Peter Calvocoressi. *Op cit*. p. 3.
16. Rama S. Melkote and A. Narshim Rao (1992). *International Relations*. New Delhi: Sterling. p. 231.
17. Martin Griffiths and Terry o' Callaghan. *Op. cit*. pp. 35-36.
18. *Ibid*. p. 37.
19. Len Scott. *Op. cit*. p. 101.
20. Keith L. Shimko. *Op. cit*. p. 32.
21. Richard Crockatt (2005). "The End of Cold War" in John Baylis and Steve Smith (eds.,), *The Globalisation of World Poltics. An Introduction to International Relations*. Oxford: Oxford University Press. p. 112.
22. James Lee Ray and Juliet Kaarbo (2002). *Global Politics*. Boston, New York: Houghton Mifflin Company. pp. 78-79.
23. Keith L. Shimko. *Op. cit*. p. 39.
24. Andrew Heywood (2002). *Politics*. New York: Hampshire: Palgrave. p. 133.
25. Richard Crockatt. *Op. cit*. p. 113.
26. Thomas Magstadt M. and Peter M. Schotten (1993). *Understanding Politics*. New York: St. Martin's Press.

27. *Ibid.*
28. Andreas Wenger and Doron Zimmermann. *Op. cit.* pp. 202-04.
29. *Ibid.*
30. James Lee Ray and Juliet Kaarbo. *Op. cit.* p. 80.
31. Thomas Magstsdt M. and Peter M. Schotten. *Op. cit.*
32. Richard Crockatt. *Op. cit.* p. 118.
33. Andreas Wenger and Doron Zimmermann. *Op. cit.* pp. 206-07.
34. Randhir Singh (2006). *Crisis of Socialism*. New Delhi: Ajanta. p. 19.
35. Thomas Magstadt M. and Peter M. Schotten. *Op. cit.*
36. Rama S. Melkote and A. Narshim Rao. *Op. cit.* p. 250.
37. Andreas Wenger and Doron Zimmermann. *Op. cit.* p. 214.
38. Thomas Magstadt M. and Peter M. Schotten. *Op. cit.*
39. Michel Cox (2005). "From the Cold war to the War on Terror", in John Baylis and Steve Smith (eds.). *The Globalisation of World Politics. An Introduction to International Relations*. Oxford: Oxford University Press. pp. 149-50.
40. *Ibid.*
41. Keith L. Shimko. *Op. cit.* p. 39.
42. Michel Cox. *Op. cit.* p. 14.
43. Randhir Singh. *Op. cit.* pp. 28-29.
44. Stephine Lawson (2004). *International Relations*. UK: Polity Press. p. 61.
45. Michel Cox. *Op. cit.* p. 152.
46. Van, Godfried, Benthem Van den Bergh (1993). "A World in Flux: Power Relations and Global Order" in Kanta Ahuja, Huub Cappens et al. (eds.). *Regime Transformations and Global Realignments Indo-European Dialogues on the Post-Cold War Period*. New Delhi: Sage. p. 105.

PART – II

THEORY

3

Idealism or Liberal Internationalism

Idealism is a doctrine which means that external world must be understood through consciousness. Generally, Idealism believes in that behavior which is shaped by the pursuit of an unattainable objective such as equality or justice. In a general sense, idealism was by those liberals who had sought to bring an end to war among the states through peaceful means. They were charged with having strong plea for system of international relations which would set the norms for justice for world peace.

Idealism/liberal internationalism emphasizes on the impact ideas have on the behavior, the equality, dignity, and liberty of the individual, and the need to protect people from excessive state regulation. It treats the individual as the seat of moral value and virtue and asserts that people should be treated as ends rather than means. It defines politics at the international level more as a struggle for consensus than a struggle for power and prestige.[1] The dominant alternatives to conservatives and realism as an approach to understanding social reality and international relations are liberalism and idealism. Idealism seems more unfair because it suggests that people who hold 'idealist' views are somehow woolly-headed dreamers devising fanciful plans for world peace. Generally, idealism is merely a different way of looking at the understanding of the world that grows out of different beliefs and assumptions than those who support realism. Theoretically, it is more called liberal internationalism which is an alternative to realism.[2]

Idealism allegedly dominated the study of international relations since the end of First World War until the late 1930s. It is also referred as utopianism. Idealism is in fact a variant of liberal internationalism. Notable liberal idealists are Immanuel Kant, Richard Cobden, John Hobson, Norman Angell, Alfred Zimmern, Woodrow Wilson and Mahatma Gandhi. These idealist thinkers were propagating a great variety of idealist doctrines which includes: pacifism, collective security system world federalism, humanitarianism, legal institutionalism, international law, and moralism.

Idealist thought concerning international politics in the United States has been much more conditioned by political heritage than by any specific philosophic strain. Thought has been significantly influenced by liberal idealism for which Woodrow Wilson was the principal proponent in thought and action. Idealism particularly conditioned American thinking about international politics between World Wars first and second. Idealism has significant underlain the approaches of an international system based on law and effective international organization. The flavor of this idealism pervades the preamble to the Charter of the United Nations. Idealism is not a structural system or theory and tends to stress judging of states and state action by the same standard that are applied to individuals in our society. Things are good and bad, or right and wrong, in contrast to the seeming impersonality and amorality of power politics. Idealism is more an approach to international politics as they ought to be rather than they are.[3]

Idealism is closely associated with a distinctly Anglo-American tendency to assume that statesmen enjoy broad freedom of choice in the making of foreign policy. The whole case of idealism is based on the general idea of evolutionary progress in society. This idea emerged in the eighteenth century and acknowledged as the major source of inspiration behind the American (1776) and French (1789) revolutions. Idealism envisaged a world order characterised by the absence of war, inequality, tyranny and marked by constant progress in human welfare brought about by the use of reason, education and science. The theoretical position of idealism in international relations is the offspring of the liberal outlook.

The decisive push to set up a separate academic subject of IR was occasioned by the First World War (1914-18), which produced millions of causalities; it was driven by a widely felt determination never to allow human suffering on such a scale to happen again. That desire not to repeat the same catastrophic mistake that inflicts mass destruction. According to Gilberth (1995), the war was a devastating experience for millions of people, and particularly for young soldiers who were conscripted into the armies and were slaughtered by millions, especially in the trench warfare on the western front. Some battles resulted in tens of thousands and sometimes 100,000 casualties or even more. On first learning of the war's devastation one man who had been isolated was quoted as follows: "Millions are being killed. Europe is mad. The world is mad."[4]

According to idealism, a state's foreign policy is not determined by the international system around it, but rather by its own internal order—democratic, communist, dictatorial, etc. In general, liberals have observed that the least aggressive states tend to be ones with democratic governments and capitalistic economies—the so called liberal democracies, most of which are industrialised countries. The controversial claim that no democracy has ever truly gone to war against another democracy lies at the heart of Democratic Peace Theory.[5]

Why was it that the war began in the first place? And why did Britain, France, Russia, Germany, Austria, Turkey and other powers persist in waging war in the face of such slaughter and with diminishing chances of gaining anything of real value from the conflict? These questions and others like them are not easy to answer. For liberal thinkers, the First World War was in no small measure attributable to the egoistic and short-sighted calculations and miscalculations of autocratic leaders in the heavily militarized countries involved, especially Germany and Austria. Why was early academic IR influenced by liberalism? The United States was eventually drawn into the war in 1917. Its military intervention decisively determined the outcome of the war: It guaranteed victory for the democratic allies (US, Britain, France) and defeat for the autocratic central powers (Germany, Austria, Turkey). At that time the United States had a President, Woodrow Wilson (his address to Congress asking for declaration of war in 1917 having the slogan 'Making the World Safe for Democracy'), who had been a university professor of political science and who saw it as his main mission to bring liberal democratic values to Europe and to rest of the world. Only in that way, he believed, could another great war be prevented. In short, the liberal way of thinking had solid political backing from the most powerful states in international system at the time.[6]

It is clear that idealism as an approach emerged in the very initial stage of IR discipline. In fact, early IR discipline of 20th century is motivated by strong forces of idealism. The main assumptions postulated by idealism in international relations are as follows:

Human nature includes a "good" or altruistic drive that makes people capable of compassion and collaboration through reason and ethically inspired education. Human concern for other's welfare makes progress possible. Sinful or wicked human behavior, such as violence is the product not just of flawed people but of evil institutions.[7]

Idealists would argue that politics and international politics too is the art of good governance. International relations should necessarily involve principles of justice, obedience to international law/rules which are derived from universal moral principles. A respect for fellow humans, both domestically and internationally.

Peace not war is normal state of affairs. In Kant's words (In his work 'Perpetual Peace'), peace can be perpetual. The laws of nature dictated harmony and co-operation between peoples. War is therefore unnatural and irrational: It is an artificial contrivance and not a product of imperfect social relations or some peculiarity of human nature. A common thread running through liberal thought, from Rousseau, Kant and Cobden, to Schumpeter and Doyle, is that wars were created by militaristic and undemocratic governments for their own vested interests. Wars were engineered by a 'warrior class' bent on extending their power and wealth through territorial conquest. According to Paine (in the 'Rights of Man') the 'War System' was contrived to preserve the power and the employment of princes, statesmen, soldiers, diplomats and armaments manufacturers, and to bind their tyranny ever more firmly upon the necks of people. Wars provided governments with excuses to raise taxes, expand their bureaucratic apparatus and thus increase their control over their citizens. The people, on the other hand, were peace loving by nature, and only plunged into conflict by the whims of their unrepresentative rulers. War was the product of aggressive instincts of authoritarian and unrepresentative elites. Both for Kant and Schumpeter, war was the outcome of minority rule. Immanuel Kant again viewed, "If, as inevitably the case under this constitution, the consent of the citizens is required to decide whether or not war was to be declared, it a very natural that they will have great hesitation in embarking on that dangerous an enterprise" (The Perpetual Peace).[8]

Idealists were profoundly suspicious of concentrated forms of power, especially state power. When they looked at the international system, they saw power being exercised in the interests of governing elites and against the wishes of masses. 'Secret diplomacy' was the name they gave to the way unrepresentative slites practised international relations in the pre-democratic era. They disputed the view that foreign policy was a specialised art which was best made by professional diplomats behind closed doors and away from the influences of national politics. If the democratization of domestic politics could produce important economic and social reforms, there would be a commensurate improvement in the conduct of foreign policy as a result of popular participation.[9]

Idealist regarded the balance of power (BoP) as the most pernicious aspect of secret diplomacy. BoP was 'a foul thing' which gave no credence to the common interests of humankind and the just claims of small nations seeking self-determination. The balance of power was the product of elite collusion which resulted in international relations being 'arranged' to suit the interests of those who ruled Great Powers.[10] Balance of Power was the veil behind which the armaments industries enriched themselves through state expenditure on weapons of war. It was also a smokescreen which concealed British imperial interests.

Idealism presents a picture of the future international society based on the notion of reformed international system free from power politics, immorality, and violence. The idealist approach to international relations has always held out the promise of bringing about a better world with the help of education and international organizations. Moral nations should try to follow moral principles in their international behaviour, abstain from all forms of traditional power politics, and adopt policies of non-partisanship. By adopting such a course the evil influence of power politics may be progressively minimised. The correct understanding of international society could be acquired through right reason, that the public opinion was prepared for being moulded in accordance with the demand of reason. Educational reforms bring the enlightenment which will create the enlightened international society disliking war and conflict. Idealism is based upon the values that are philosophically sound and are of primary importance. Even the concept of international morality is the reciprocity or mutuality of national interests.[11] Idealists refuse to accept 'power' as the determinant of relations between notions. For them, politics is the art of good government rather than the art of possible. International relations should necessarily involve principles of justice, obedience to legitimate law or rules which are derived from universal moral principles.

Idealism is against the notion that security can be established through 'balance of power' or 'power management' at international level. The First World War discredited the laws of both economics and politics. The self operating laws of (BoP System) had failed to prevent the most destructive conflict in human history. The experiences of 1914-18 brought to the fore liberal thinkers and politicians who 'considered the old assumptions and prescriptions of power politics to be totally discredited and who helped to give birth to new procedures and a firm system of international law and organisation preserving peace by a system of collective security. The commitment to collective security was designed to prevent this situation recurring by ensuring that in future, the aggressor would be confronted by all member states. Destructive forces of international anarchy could only be brought to an end if the international system was regulated in the same way as domestic society. Collective security system was, advocated by idealists, meaning that all the nations who are members of collective security system will defend their fellow nation from aggressive power. Collective security system will under an international organisation. So, idealists also advocated international or 'international law' or 'international legalism'. The collective security system has pursued 'open diplomacy' not secret diplomacy; international cooperation rather than conflict; peaceful solution of international disputes. The 'Covenant of League of Nations' was the first international organisation. It is also known as collective security system. The idea of 'League' was largely motivated by 'Idealists' after the end of 1st World War.

President Woodrow Wilson (1856-1924) was one of the main architects of the peace settlement negotiated in Paris after the First World War. Wilson's fourteen point formula was an attempt to incorporate US constitutional prescriptions globally. The League of Nations was designed as an overarching authority which would regulate the behaviour of states towards each other. Members would be required to submit their disputes to arbitration and, if necessary, use sanctions to compel aggressor state to conform to a peaceful method of conflict resolution. The League would in theory, be run by an alliance of major powers permanently committed to opposing aggression on the grounds of principle. According to President Wilson, "There must be not a balance of power but a community of power; not organised rivalries but an organised common peace".[12] Woodrow Wilson was prominent idealist who proposed 14-point formula for the Peace Treaty of 1919 (Versailles). As follows:

- Open covenant openly arrived at
- Freedom of the seas alike in peace and war
- The removal of all economic barriers to trade
- Reduction of national armaments
- A readjustment of all colonial claims
- The evacuation of Russian territory and to independent determination by Russia of her own political development and national policy
- The evacuation and restoration of Belgium
- The evacuation and restoration of France and return of Alsace-Lorraine
- A readjustment of frontiers of Italy along national lines
- Self-determination for the peoples of Austria-Hungary
- A redrawing of the boundaries of the Balkan States along historically established lines of nationality
- Self-determination for the peoples under Turkish rule
- The independence of Poland with free access to the sea guaranteed by international covenant
- The formation of a general association of nations under specific covenants for the purpose of affording mutual guarantees of political independence and territorial integrity to great and small states alike.

These 'fourteen points' contain many idealist principles. In particular, the importance of self-determination from colonial rule as well as the need for an international organisation to maintain peace and security.[13] Two major points in Woodrow Wilson's ideas for a more peaceful world deserve special emphasis. The first concern is his promotion of democracy and self-determination. Behind this point is the liberal conviction that democratic governments do not and will not go to war against each other. The second major concern was Wilson's program of creation of an international organisation that would put relations between states on a firmer institutional foundation than the realist notions of balance of power. Instead, international relations would be regulated by a set of common rules of international law. In essence that was Wilson's concept of international relations.

It is important and worth to discuss Gandhian thought of idealism. The reason is not only that he was contemporary of idealists of inter war period but his firm faith and confidence in world peace and non-violence. Mahatma Gandhi also professed his own kind of idealism regarding international relations. For him nationalism and internationalism are not opposite to each other (as dictated by realism and fascism). He was doubtful about the modern national states which encourages fanatic nationalism. He said in 1925:

> It is impossible for one to be internationalist without being a nationalist. Internationalism is possible only when nationalism becomes a fact, i.e., when peoples belonging to different countries have organized themselves and are able to act as one man. It is not nationalism that is evil, it is the narrowness, selfishness, exclusiveness which is the bane of modern nations which is evil. Each wants to profit at the expanse of, and rise on, the ruin of the other. Indian nationalism has, I hope, struck a different path. It wants to organize itself or to find full expression for the benefit and service of humanity at large.[14]

Gandhi was harshly against the nuke physical power of the state which brings bloodshed and violence. Speaking against atom bombs dropped by USA on Japan's two cities, he said:

> There have been cataclysmic changes in the world. Do I still adhere to my faith in truth and non-violence? Has not the atom bomb exploded that faith? Not only has it not done so, but it has clearly demonstrated to me that the twins constitute the mightiest force in the world. Before it the atom bomb is of no effect. The two opposing forces are wholly different in kind, the one moral and spiritual, the other physical and material.[15]

For him force of spirit is infinitely superior, ever progressive and endless. Again he said, "Man knows that only evil can come out of evil, as good out of good."[16]

Gandhi had floated the idea of world federation as early as in 1924. He was not in favour of isolated, self-centered fundamental nationalist world. He believed in peaceful, interconnected and interdependent states. In this perspective, he left behind him the other idealists of his time like Woodrow Wilson in constructing the liberal, utopian internationalism of world federation. His words:

> The better mind of the world desires today not absolutely independent states warring one against another, but a federation of friendly interdependent States. The consummation of that event may be far off. I want to make no grand claim for our country. But I see nothing grand or impossible about our expressing our readiness for universal interdependence rather than independence.[17]

He strongly advocated brotherhood and cooperative neighborhood and was against the hard borders. Instead he said:

> There is no limit to extending our service to our neighbors across our state-made frontiers. God never made those frontiers.[18]

He dreamed the structure of a world federation which can be raised only on foundation of non-violence, and violence will have to be totally given up in world affairs. Gandhi was staunch advocater of human liberty and was against colonialism. According to him:

> Nations have, in a sense, therefore, almost become gangs of robbers, whereas they should be a peaceful combination of men and women united for the common good of mankind. In the latter case, their strength will lie not in their skill in the use of gunpowder, but in the possession of superior moral fiber.[19]

Map IV: One World—Peaceful and Prosperous

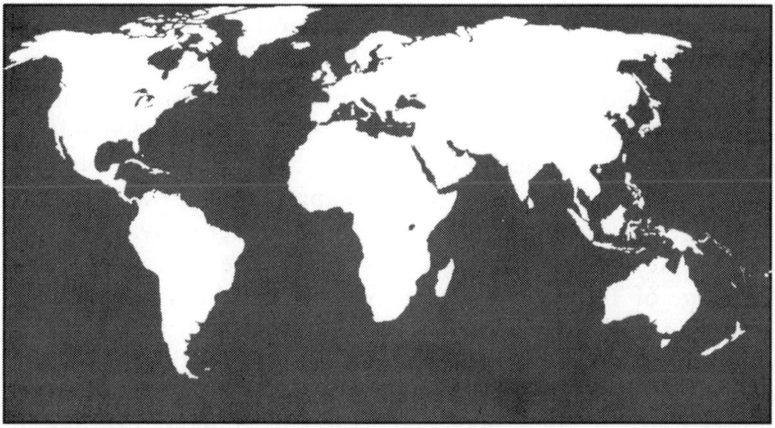

Idealism fell into disrepute with the collapse of the League of Nations and the outbreak of thc Second World War in 1939. Although the idealists had sought to use the League system to replace European real politics, in fact it simply became a forum that reflected the competing national interests of the great powers of the day. Instead, the League of Nations never became the strong international organisation that idealists imagined. Germany and Russia's strained relationship with League (Germany joined in 1926, left in 1933, Russia joined in 1934, and was expelled in 1940 because of its war with Finland). Under US isolationalist foreign policy orientation, senate did not pass US membership of League. Consequently, the strongest nation could not become the member of League. Gradually, league became defunct and could not fulfill the purpose for which it was formed.

Norman Angell's (The Great Illusion-1909) thinking was based on a liberal view of human beings of human society: Human beings are rational, and when they apply reason to international relations they can set up organizations for the benefit of all. Public opinion is a constructive force; removing secret diplomacy in dealings between states, and introduce opening diplomacy to public scrutiny assures that agreements will be sensible and fair. These ideas were prevailing in 1920s international environment. These ideas were dominated in the first phase of IR. But 1920s and 1930s developments of Fascism and Nazism gave serious setbacks to liberal ideas. Authoritarianism also increased in Central and Eastern Europe – Poland, Hungary, Romania and Yugoslavia.

Liberal idealism was not a good intellectual guide to international relations, particularly, in 1930s. Interdependence did not produce peaceful cooperation. The League of Nations was helpless in the face of the expansionist power politics conducted by the authoritarian regimes in Germany, Italy, and Japan. Academic IR began to speak the classical realist language of Thucydides, Machiavelli and Hobbes in which the grammar and vocabulary of power was central. The most comprehensive and penetrating critique of liberal idealism was that of E.H. Carr, a British IR scholar. In his 'The Twenty Year's Crisis' Carr argued that liberal IR thinkers profoundly missed the facts of history and misunderstood the nature of international relations. They erroneously believed that such relations could be based on a harmony of interest between countries and people. According to Carr, the correct starting point is the opposite one: We should assume that these are profound conflicts of interest both between countries and between people. International relations is in a basic sense about struggle between such conflicting interests and desires.[20]

Idealism ignores the elements of power in international relations. Idealism was called utopianism, because they are blamed to ignore the real power-politics in international politics. Their futuristic attitude undermined the past and present real state of affairs in international politics. Their imagination about the 'ideal world' or ideal international society could not bring the desired fruits. There was an optimistic view of the possibilities for peaceful relations among humans. For some liberals this derives from a more positive assessment of human nature, at least to the extent that they can learn from their mistakes, but also confidence in the capacity of individual humans to choose rational courses of action in politics, as in other fields such as economics.[21] He here argued that idealism was an expression of the political philosophy of satisfied great powers. It was simply the product of a particular set of social, political, and historical circumstances rather than a timeless moral code devoted to universal ends. When it came to a concrete political problem, it could not find an absolute and disinterested standard for the conduct of international politics. Not all the states keep interest in peace. Those who dominated the international system were more likely to pursue peace because it was in their interests to maintain the international status quo.[22]

Even the neo-liberals (contemporary theory of liberal IR) recognize that cooperation may be harder to achieve in areas where leaders perceive they have no mutual interests. They also believe that states cooperate to achieve absolute gains and greatest obstacle to cooperation is 'cheating' or 'non-compliance'. It means that states are not naturally bound to cooperate. Personal gains are predominant.

In the end, we can say that although inter-war idealism was seriously challenged with the breakout of Second World War and, therefore, by the realists, idealism contributed lot to the IR. It provided the element of morality to international relations. Realists were too much obsessed by the power factor and they fail to realize the importance of moral values altogether. How it can be said idealism was a total failure—when we see that internal society attained its ground through moral values. The continuous growing value of international law, institution is being recognised by the international community. Notwithstanding, without moral principles where is the way and objective for international community to achieve.

REFERENCES

1. Charles W. Kegley (2007). *World Politics Trends and Transformation*. Belmont: Thomson and Wadsworth. p. 25.
2. Keith. L Shimko (2005). *International Relations Perspectives and Controversies*. Boston, New York: Houghton Mifflin Company. p. 51.
3. Norman J. Padelford, et al. (1976). *The Dynamics of International Politics*. New York, London: Macmillan. p. 42.
4. Robert Jackson and Georg Sorensen (2003). *Introduction to International Relations*. New Delhi: Oxford. pp. 35-36.

5. Andrew Vogt (August 15, 2010). "Idealism and Liberalism: International Relations Theory in Brief", http//www.bukisa.com
6. Robert Jackson. *Op. cit.* pp. 36-37.
7. Charles W. Kegley. *Op. cit.* p. 26.
8. Scott Burchill (1995). "Liberal Internationalism" in Scott Burchill and Andrew Linklater (ed.). *Theories of International Relations*. Hampshire and London: Macmillan. pp. 31-32.
9. Ian Clark (1999). *The Hierarchy of States: Reform and Resistance in International Order*. Cambridge: Cambridge University Press. p. 52.
10. M. Howard (1978). *War and Liberal Conscience.* Oxford: OUP. p. 89.
11. Mahindra Kumar. *Theoretical Aspects of International Politics.* Agra-3: Shiva Lal Agarwalas and Co. p. 52.
12. R.D. Makinlay and R. Little (1986). *Global Problems and World Order*. London. p. 56.
13. Tim Dunne (2005). "Liberalism" in John Baylis and Steve Smith (eds.). *The Globalisation of World Politics—An Introduction to International Relations*. Oxford and New Delhi: Oxford University Press. p. 191.
14. *Young India* (18-6-1925). Ahmedabad: Navajivan Publishing House. p. 211.
15. *Harijan* (10-2-1946). Ahmedabad: Navajivan Publishing House. p. 8.
16. *Ibid.* (29-9-1946). p. 335.
17. *Young India*, *Op. cit.* (26-12-1924). p. 425.
18. *Ibid. (*31-12-1931). p. 427.
19. *Ibid.* (21-10-1926). p. 366.
20. Robert Jackson. *Op. cit.* pp. 38-39.
21. Lymen Tower Sargent (1999). *Contemporary Political Ideologies: A Comparative Analysis.* Fort Worth: Harcourt Brace.
22. Edward Hallett Carr (1948). *The Twenty Years' Crisis 1919-1939—An Introduction to the Study of International Relations*. London: Macmillan. pp. 86-88.

4

Realism/Neo-realism

Although realists were not the first to think and write about international relations, they were the first to offer a comprehensive account of the international system in practice—'codifies practice'. They stressed upon to develop generalizations about patterns of behaviour in international relations, and to emphasize recurring phenomena rather than unique events. In the US, Hans Morgenthau, Arnold Wolfers, Klaus Knorr and Henry Kissinger were European émigrés who suffered, at first hand, the operations of unchecked power operating in support of an alien value system. These realists also viewed that states are primary actors in international relations because they retain monopoly on the legitimate use of violence.[1] Realism is the dominant theory of international politics—once upon a time (in 1940s) when the international politics was considered realist only.

We associate realism with thinkers from Thucidides, Niccolo Machiavelli to twentieth century scholars like Hans Morgenthau and Kenneth waltz (a neo-realist) and policymakers like Henry Kissinger. Realists insist that a person should look at world affairs as they really are and not as he or she might want them to be. Doing so, realists understand that the principal players in the international arena are nation-states, usually with significantly different cultural traditions and each acting in its rational self-interest within an environment of international anarchy. As no sovereign authority over nations exists to control their activities, states must develop their interactions with other states on their own.

International or multinational organizations may be useful but are not of primary consequence. A struggle for power is ongoing in world politics, and in pursuing the national interest above all, policymakers use various tools, including diplomacy, economic power, and ultimately, military force, to try to attain their aims. A country's relative level of power, including economic and military power, determines its relations with other states.[2] On the basis of these prominent tenants of international politics theory, realist construct the laws of international relations.

Classical political realism is a pessimistic view of human nature. It was critical element of a conservative social and political philosophy which holds the view that human nature is a mix of good and bad features, and the latter can never be completely eliminated. More secular versions of conservatism emphasize that even though people are capable of rational, thoughtful, and ethical behaviour, they are also motivated, perhaps even more so, by the basic impulses of lust, passion and greed. Realism presents us with one way of looking and understanding the world, one that grows out of conservative assumptions about the nature of people and human societies. It is a vision of world politics in which states must interact and deal with their conflicts without the benefits of a central authority to do for them what governments do for their citizens. It is a world in which some states benefit from the existing world order, and these nations inevitably find themselves in conflict with others who would benefit from changing the existing order. Though conflicts of interests are common, violent conflict among nations (war) remains relatively rare. Nevertheless, the anarchic nature of international politics derives nations to prepare for and occasionally fight wars.[3]

Realism is said as the first theoretical perspective for understanding international relations that we consider because it has historically been the dominant lens through which world leaders and scholars alike have understood international politics. Indeed, realism can be traced back to Thucydides' account of the Peloponnesian Wars between the Greek city states Athens and Sparta in 431-04 B.C. Thucydides, a historian, described and explained the relations between these actors with the realist propositions. Realism was also the dominant way leaders in Europe in the seventeenth through early twentieth century understood international relations. It was during this period that the modern international system was created, largely based on realist notions. After World War II, scholars of international relations embraced realism as the dominant perspective for explaining international politics. The chief advocate of the realist theory of international politics was Hans J. Morgenthau, considered the father of modern realist thought. His classic text, *Politics Among Nations*, was first published shortly after World War II and carefully defined the realist theoretical perspective that most scholars would then adopt. Because of this dominant position in many ways, all of the other theoretical perspectives for understanding global politics are reactions to and criticisms of realism.[4]

Realism involved commitment to a set of propositions about international politics which were essentially extrapolations from the diplomatic history of nineteenth century Europe. They were propositions which the generation of statesmen in Europe after 1919 either had lost or misunderstood: Re-education in the 'perennials' was clearly necessary. The catechism was simple. All states sought, or would seek, power, given the opportunity. It was an essential prerequisite for the achievement of any other goals. Today's enemy could be tomorrow's ally. The use of any means was acceptable or at least possible, though only one or two might be appropriate at any single moment. The best operator was the man who possessed 'traditional wisdom' and the man who possessed 'traditional wisdom' was the best operator.[5]

Advocates of the new, ascendant paradigm known as realism or *realpolitik* as a specific philosophy, emerged to frame an intellectual movement, whose message reads like the antithesis of idealism. Among the principal prophets of this new world view were E.H. Carr (1939), George F. Kennan (1951, 1954), Hans, J. Morgenthau (1948), Reinhold Niepuhr (1947) and Kenneth W. Thompson (1960). Here the name of ancient Indian philosopher Kautilya can also be included. Realism deserves careful scrutiny because its socially constructed world view continues to guide much thought about world politics.

Realism, as applied to contemporary world politics, views the state, which should answer to no higher political authority, as the most important actor on the world stage. Moreover, conflicts of interests among states are assumed to be inevitable. Realism also emphasizes the ways in which the anarchical nature of international politics dictate the choices that foreign policy makes as rational problem solvers who must calculate their interest in terms of power.[6] Twentieth century realism was emerged as opponent of international liberalism or idealism. It had been considered as first major debate in the theory of international relations between idealists and realists which was won by realism.

The most comprehensive and penetrating critique of liberal idealism was that of E.H. Carr, a British, IR scholar. In *The Twenty Years' Crisis* (1939, 1964), Carr argued that liberal IR thinkers profoundly misread the facts of history and misunderstood the nature of international relations. They erroneously believed that such relations could be based on a harmony of interest between countries and people. According to Carr, the correct starting point is the opposite one we should assume that there are profound conflicts of interest both between countries and between people. Some people and some countries are better off than others. They will attempt to preserve and defend their privileged position. The underdogs, the 'have not's' will struggle to change that situation. International relations is in a basic sense about the struggle between such conflicting interests and desires.[7] Within the realist paradigm, the purpose of statecraft is national survival in a hostile environment. To this end, no means are more important than the acquisition of power, and no principle is more important than self-help. In this conception, state sovereignty, a cornerstone that realists in the seventeenth century wrote into international law, gives heads of state the freedom and responsibility to do whatever is necessary to advance the state's interests and survival.

To the hardcore realist, respect for moral principles is a wasteful and dangerous interference in the rational pursuit of national self-advantage. To these proponents of power politics, questions about the relative virtues of the values, within this or that ideological or religious system cannot be allowed to interfere with sound policymaking. A state's philosophical or ethical preferences are neither good nor bad—what matters is whether they serve its self-interest. Thus, the game of international politics revolves around the pursuit of power: Acquiring it, increasing it, projecting it, and using it to bend others to one's will.[8] At the basic realist ideas and assumptions are: A pessimistic view of human nature; a conviction that international relations are necessarily conflictual and that international conflicts are ultimately resolved by war; a high regard for the values of national security and state survival; a basic skepticism that there can be progress in international politics that is comparable to that in domestic political life.[9]

Realism emphasises on balance of power system which is the most successful international system to manage the power. Then President Nixon (US) states once in an interview with *Time* magazine. "We must remember the only time in the history of the world that we have had any extended periods of peace is when there has been balance of power." It is when one nation becomes infinitely more powerful in relation to its potential competitors of that the danger of war arsis. So, I believe in a world in which the United States is powerful. I think it will be a safer world and a better world if we have a strong, healthy United States, Europe, Soviet Union, China, Japan, each balancing the other not playing one against the other an even balance.[10]

The basic assumptions of realism are:

- Sovereign nation-state system is the most successful administrative system in the world affairs and balance of power is the only international system to manage the power and establish stability, where all the states aspire to maximize their power.

- Supreme political reality is national sovereignty, national freedom or independence.
- There is constant law of human nature, which is narrowly selfish and is not free from sinful acts and desire for self-advantage and power.
- There is anarchy in the international system and biological rules of 'survival of the fittest' (Darwin) and a 'war of all against all' (Hobbes) prevail.
- To eliminate the instinct for power from international politics is a utopian thinking.
- National security is the most important task of foreign policy of a state. Moral values, international law are not superior and important to national security.

The western thinkers have ignored to incorporate Kautilyan philosophy as a part of classical political philosophy as of Thucydides, Machiavelli or Hobbes.

E.H. Carr and Hans Morgenthau are modern classical realist thinkers of 1940s. They are founders of twentieth century realism.

E.H. Carr's *The Twenty Years' Crisis* (1939) is not a textbook of international theory, but a critique of the prevailing wisdom of its day. Published on the eve of the Second World War, it is a devastating attack on liberal 'utopianism' which had inspired the post–Great War political arrangements in Europe, most particularly the idea of collective security as it was enshrined in the institution of the League of Nations. In response to the horrors of the First World War, liberal internationalists, or 'utopians' as Carr called them, sought to abolish war as an instrument of statecraft. Liberals were convinced that the forms of international diplomacy could be restructured to make them more peaceful. Self-determination and statehood would be available to all national groups. Secret diplomacy would be abolished and replaced by public consent in the conduct of foreign policy. The balance of power principle would give conduct of foreign policy. The balance of power principle would give way to a system of collective security, where individual acts of aggression would be met by the collective force of world opinion and military power.[11]

Carr wanted to establish the science of international politics and to rescue this study from wishful thinking. (of utopian idealists). He professes that power is the centre of international system and every nation had an identical interest in peace and in war. Carr's *Twenty Years' Crisis 1919-39* denies accepting the idealist idea which advocates that there is harmony of interests. According to Carr, "just as the ruling class in a community prays for domestic peace, which guarantees its own security and predominance, and denounces class war, which might threaten them, so international peace becomes a vested interest of predominant power".[12] Thus Carr discarded the view of liberals that good for one state is good for all. Instead, nation states are engaged in the protection of their own security. Therefore, they do not accept international organizations at the cost of their own state's security and interest.

Hans J. Morgenthau created a realist text book *Politics Among Nations* in the aftermath of Second World War. Actually he has been considered more systematic and enlightened classical realist thinker and is also called as father of classical realism. From the tone and style of the book it is possible to sense the extent to which the US academic community was influenced, if not enthralled by developments in the natural sciences during this period. Morgenthau took up Carr's challenge to create a science of international politics by applying the positivist methodology of the 'hard' or natural sciences to the study of international relations. The intellectual rigour of this approach would reveal the underlying 'reality' of world politics, from which certainties and predictions could be deduced. His definition of theory, for example, is explicitly borrowed—from the natural sciences. Theories, according to Morgenthau, should be judged not by some preconceived abstract principle or concept unrelated to reality, but by their purpose which is to bring order and meaning to a mass of phenomena which without it would remain disconnected and unintelligible. They must be consistent with the facts and within itself. In other words, theories must be factual, independent and retrospective. Theories must also satisfy strict empirical and logical criteria: Do the fact as they actually are lend themselves to the interpretation the theory has put on them, and do the conclusion at which the theory arrives follow with logical necessity from its premises?[13]. Human nature is self centered, power seeking and self-interested and all these tenets of human nature are constant. Morgenthau's realist theory is generally known as six principles of political realism which are:

- Politics, like society in general is governed by objective laws that have their roots in human nature. Therefore, realism is rational.
- Political realism is the concept of interest that is defined in terms of power where all the states are struggling for power. All people prefer their security and survival first and therefore, the states.
- Ethics or moral ideas are not applicable in international politics. They could be possible in private sphere. A state's interest cannot be sacrifice for the cause of moral ideas. Because a political leader owns heavy responsibility of security and welfare of people.
- The imposition of any ideology (like democracy) by any powerful state (as of US) on other will be dangerous for international peace and stability. Secondly, the moral ideas of democracy, respect for international organizations, etc. are suitable to the states for whom they are beneficial.
- Statecraft is a sober and uninspiring activity that needs deep knowledge, intelligence and integrity.
- Politics is an autonomous sphere of action. It cannot be reduced to Kant's moral ideas of international peace or Marxian economics. Politics is independent of all of it.[14]

However, we would like to mention here about the work of famous Ancient Indian philosopher Kautilya, who had produced the important example of realism in his classic text *Arthashastra*. The war like temper finally saw its culmination in the ideas of the *Arthashastra*, a handiwork of Kautilya. He held power as the basis of the state. An ideal king, he said, was possessed of valour, powerful resolute mind, quick in his decisions and actions and intelligent enough to take advantage of the weakness of his enemies for the enlargement of his kingdom. For him, territory was more valuable than men and materials.

For the first time, it was Kautilya who developed a systematic and comprehensive theory of inter-state relations (Mandala Theory) in *Arthashastra*. The pivotal point in the Mandala Theory is the national king, who intends expanding his power at the cost of neighboring states. He accepted the age old doctrine that war was an extension of diplomacy. Actual armed clash was sought to be avoided as much as possible. In his opinion a good ally was that who had long standing, submissive, easy to roused, relations, powerful and never of contradictory nature. He sought total dictation and dictatorship for the friendly state. He advocated "Forms of treacherous fights;...Secret means to injure an enemy; wonderful and delusive contrivences;...."[15] These views of Kautilya match with secret alliances of realist balance of power.

The genius thinker also mentioned the term neutrality in his Mandala Theory. For Kautilya the conqueror (*viji gishu*) should make peace when he thought that he was weaker than the enemy. He further says, "conqueror should adopt neutrality when he thinks that either of them can overcome each other. But the conqueror should march against the enemy when he is certain that he is equipped with great strength whether he had been concluded a neutral treaty earlier with enemy". Kautilya said in his sixfold policy:

> Determination of deterioration, stagnation, and progress; the nature of alliance; the character of equal, inferior and superior kings; forms of agreement made by

> an inferior king; neutrality after proclaiming war or after making peace; the march of combined powers; considerations about marching against an assailable enemy and a strong enemy; causes leading to the dwindling, greatness and disloyalty of the army; considerations about the combination of power; the march of combined powers; agreement of peace with or without definite terms; and peace with renegades; peace and war by adopting the double policy; the attitude of an assailable enemy; friends that deserve help; agreement for the acquisition of land; agreement undertaking a work; considerations about enemy in the rear, recruitment of lost power; measures conducive to peace with a strong and provoked enemy; the attitude of concurred king; making peace and breaking it; the conduct of a Madhyama king; a neutral king and of a circle of states.[16]

Kautilya did not try to mix ethics with politics. The end in his view should be the warfare of a particular state, whether big or small. Every state wanted to expand. For him greatest religion or morality for each was self preservation. Might was the sole criterion and right was in background in Kautilya's thinking. He dispassionately tried to solve the problems of ruler's international life.

He was not much interested in concept of non-violence as a policy for a statesman of his times. But at the same time he clarified that when the advantages derivable from peace and war are equal, one should prefer peace. In case of disadvantages, such as the loss of power and wealth, then preference should go to war.[17] Hence, most of Kautilyan theory was similar to realist assumptions.

Classical or Morgenthau's realism had been targeted from several theoretical streams and others. The major setback to it was from 1950s scientific theories of IR which do not agree with the realist view point that realism is scientific. They also criticized Morgenthau's study of human nature, which is unscientific and not testified. Neo-liberals reject it on the basis of realist theory of total rejection of role of international law and organizations. They also emphasize the role of political economy (Haas, Keohane, Nye) for the interdependence of world community. Critics of E.H. Carr's position point to the irreconcilable antinomies between realism and idealism. Carr himself did not consider state as the ultimate group unit of human society. Marxist criticized realism on the ground that realism is primarily concerned with reinforcement and reproduction of capitalist relations of production. According to Marxism, realism strengthens the institution of state which is part of superstructure for maintenance of status quo, realism is also against the logic of change which is unacceptable and dangerous for human progress.

The other attack came from the English school, whose main writers were Martin Wright and Hedly Bull (1977). They did not question the primacy of state or power politics, but developed the concept of international society as a way of introducing both historical range, and a significant role for norm-based order, into the understanding of international relations.[18]

Although, realist theory highly criticized by other streams of thought such as liberalism-neo-liberalism, neo-Marxism, post-positivist theories, yet its relevance and importance are difficult to deny.

Neo-realism

Realism emerged in the form of neo-realism after facing several challenges from various sectors. Kenneth Waltz with his *Theory of International Politics*—1979, might have rescued realism from its degeneration. A revival under the label neo-realism started in late 1970s led by this work of Kenneth Waltz' Neo-realism was the counter attack in this intellectual joust. It abandoned the conservative assumptions about human nature that underpinned classical realism, and reasserted the logic of power politics on firmer foundation of anarchic structure. It defended the centrality of state, and especially of great powers, exploring the partiality of interdependence views of international relations, and reaffirming the primacy of American power in the international system. Its success was much aided by the onset of the so-called 'Second Cold War' in 1979, which caught off balance many of the advocates of interdependence and transnationalism.[19] Kenneth Waltz, Joseph Grieco, John Mearsheimer, Kransners are prominent neo-realists.

Basic postulates of neo-realism

- States and other actors interact in an anarchic environment. This means there is no central authority to enforce rules and norms or protect the interests of the larger global community.
- The structure of system is a major determinant of an actor's behaviour. It means the states' foreign policy is largely guided by prevailing international system. Vice versa international system is also based on power-politics of states.
- States are self-interest oriented; an anarchic and competitive system pushes them to favour self-help over cooperative behaviour.
- States are rational actors, selecting strategies to maximize benefits and minimize losses.
- The most critical problem presented by anarchy is survival. When states are always struggling for power, there is anarchy at international level. In this situation, state's first preference is survival and security. This could be provided by the system of 'balance of power' or 'power management'.
- States see all other states as potential enemies and threats to their national security. This distrust and fear creates a security dilemma, and this motivates the policies of most states.[20]

Neo-realism emerged in the 1970s, partly as a response to the challenges posed by interdependency theory and partly as a corrective to traditional realism's neglect of economic forces. It was Kenneth Waltz who revived realism after a challenge posed by behaviouralism, Marxism and interdependency to realism. Robert Gilpin and Stephen Krasner also sought to reclaim a role for state in the sub-discipline of political economy, where transnational economic players threatened to undermine its primacy. Ideas such as 'regimes' and 'hegemonic stability theory' were invented to demonstrate the continuing importance of stability theory.[21] In the light of this we shall study the neo-realism from different angels of these key realist thinkers.

(a) Kenneth Waltz's Realism—Structuralism

The leading contemporary neo-realist thinker Kenneth Waltz takes some elements of classical and neo-classical realism as a starting-point. In the more traditional provinces of international relations, Waltz has attempted to bring what he sees as the scientific and methodological rigour of disciplines, such as anthropology and economics to the study of international politics. Waltz's 'neo-realism' is known as structural realism which is both a critique of traditional realism and a substantial intellectual extension of a theoretical tradition which was in danger of being outflanked by rapid changes in the contours of global politics. Waltz presents a more sophisticated theory than his predecessors in the realist tradition, to the extent that his account has often been referred to as occupying a position of intellectual hegemony in the discipline. He departs from tradition by ignoring its normative concerns and by trying to provide a scientific IR theory. Unlike Morgenthau (1985), he gives no account of human nature and he ignores the ethics of statecraft. His explanatory approach is heavily influenced by positivist model of economics.[22] The theory of neo-realism developed by Waltz dominated the discussions of international relations theory during the last quarter of 20th century, much as Morgenthau's discussions during the period between 1950 and 1975.[23]

Basic features of Waltz-New Realism

Structuralism: During the 1980s Kenneth Waltz's neo-realism has been also called structuralism. The term structural realism is preferred by those who seek to widen Waltz's analysis so that it can be combined with work in the liberal tradition than focuses on economic relations, regimes and international society, though the lives of identity here are not yet settled at the time of writing.[24] Waltz advances a structural theory of international politics. One of the defining characteristics of the structure of the international system is the distribution of capabilities, since judgments must be made about how capabilities are distributed. Realizing, he said that this theory requires the rank ordering of states according to their capabilities. Ranking the capability of states is much harder if power/capability is conceived as multidimensional. Thus, he asserts that 'the economic, military, and other capabilities of nations cannot be sectored and separately weighed.[25]

Waltz rejects unit level theories because they attempt to explain the whole (the global system) by 'examining the interactions of its parts (domestic orders). Waltz argues that to make direct link between intentions of individual actors such as the nation-states, and the results of their actions, is not acceptable. What they fail to recognize is the structural conditions which belong to international system, which impose themselves on all the units, and which therefore ultimately determine the outcomes of the interactions between states. Realists (classical) emphasize human nature and the intentions of statesman, liberals stress the importance of democracy and free trade, and Marxists highlight the class struggle between capital and labour. All are advocating unit level factor and ignoring the overriding importance of the international system which covers between the intentions of states and the results of their interactions.

Structure consists of three factors:

(i) The ordering principle of the system: The ordering principle is hierarchic at domestic level where power and authority exerted are through the compulsory jurisdiction of political and legal process. The ordering principle at international level is anarchic without any overarching authority that can regulate the behaviour of the states.

(ii) The character of the units in the system: It is similar of all states. All states (units) in the international system made functionally similar even differ vastly in their capabilities.

(iii) The distribution of the capabilities: The capacity of each state to pursue and achieve their common objectives varies according to their placement in the international system, the relative power.[26]

- National Interest: Waltz's concept of national interest is 'each state plots the course it thinks will best serve its interest'. For classical realists, the national interest is the basic guide of responsible foreign policy. It is a moral idea that must be defended and promoted by state leaders. For Waltz, however, the national interest seems to operate like an automatic signal commanding state leaders when and where to move. The difference here is: Morgenthau believes that state leaders are duty bound to conduct their foreign policies guided by national interest. Waltz's neo-realist theory hypothesis, that they will always do that more or less automatically.[27]
- Autonomy of international politics: Waltz's structural 'neo-realism' argues that by depicting an international political system as a whole, with structural and unit levels at once distinct and connected, neo-realism established the autonomy of international politics and thus makes a theory about it possible.
- State sovereignty and security are highly important: For Waltz there is anarchy in international relations. The dangers in this environment are many, not least because an effort by one state to provide for its own security is more than likely to provoke insecurity in another state, which may then respond by an arms build-up of its own and therefore become even more dangerous. This is known as the 'security dilemma'.[28] State is thus providing the security and 'state sovereignty' is also prime to Waltz theory.

- Waltz's Structural Realism after the Cold War: In his Structural Realism after the Cold War (2000), Waltz examines three developments that are seen to be transforming the post-Cold War world:

I. The expansion of democracy: The end of Cold War coincided with what many took to be a new democratic wave.... Proponents of the democratic peace thesis write as though the spread of democracy will negate the effects of anarchy. No causes of conflict and war will any longer be found at the structural level. Waltz argues again, "Democracies may live at peace with democracy but even if all states become democratic, the structure of international politics would remain anarchic. The structure of international politics is not transformed by changes internal to states, however widespread the changes may be. In the absence of an external authority, a state cannot be sure that today's friend will not be tomorrow's enemy. Indeed, democracies have at times behaved as though today's democracy is today's enemy and a present threat to them."[29]

II. The weak effects of interdependence: Waltz pointed out that interdependence hardly brings any fruit of 'perpetual peace'. That interdependence promotes war as well as peace has been said often enough. What requires emphasis is that, either way, among the forces that shape international politics, interdependence is a weak one. Interdependence within modern states is much closer than it is across states.... States, if they can afford to, shy away from becoming excessively dependent on goods and resources that may be denied to them in crisis and wars. States take measures, such as Japan's managed trade, to avoid excessive dependence on others.... Relatively independent states are in a stronger position than relative dependent ones.[30]

III. The limited role of international institutions: International institutions are instrument to fulfill the national interest. The role of international institutions diminishes if they outlined from its major concern. They play limited role for international peace, law etc. The nature and purposes of institutions change as structures vary. NATO and the WTO (Warsaw Treaty) were treaties of guarantee rather than old style military alliances. Alliances have no meaning apart from the adversary threat to which they are a response. By giving the example of NATO Waltz said, "With its old purpose dead, and the individual and collective behaviour of its members altered accordingly, how does one explain NATO's survival and expansion?" Institutions are hard to create and set in motion, but once created, institutionalists claim they may take on something of life of their own.....Waltz denying this argument of liberals "the institutionalists says, interpretation misses the point. NATO is first of all a treaty made by states. A deeply entrenched international bureaucracy can help to sustain the organization but states determine its fate".[31]

(b) John J. Mearsheimer's Security and Stability Studies, and Neo-Realism

Security studies and neo-realism, particularly in USA have suggested a more nuanced version of a realism that reflects their interests in understanding the nature of the security threats presented by the international system. John Mearsheimer an offensive realist in security studies, suggests that relative power and not absolute power is most important to states. He would suggest that leaders of countries should pursue security policies that weaken their potential enemies and increase their power relative to all others.[32] Mearsheimer builds on Waltz argument concerning the stability of bipolar systems as compared to multipolar systems. Whereas Waltz claims that bipolar systems are superior to multipolar systems because they provide peace and security. Mearshimer was worried what would happen if bi-polar system is replaced by multipolar? How would that basic system change affect the chances for peace and the dangers of war in post-Cold War Europe? 'The long peace' between 1945 and 1990 was a result of three fundamentally important conditions: The bipolar system of military power in Europe; the approximately military equality between US and Soviet union; both equipped with nuclear weapons. Mearsheimer further says, "the Cold War between the US and Soviet Union was principally responsible for transforming a historically violent region into a very peaceful place".[33] Mearsheimer's theory, building on five bed rock assumptions:

(i) Structure of the international system causes great powers to think and act offensively and to seek hegemony. Because international system is anarchic, the system comprises independent states that have no central authority above them. "Sovereignty, in other words, inheres in states because there is no higher ruling body in the international system." There is no "government over governments."

(ii) Great powers inherently posses some offensive military capability, which gives them the wherewithal to hurt and possibly destroy each other. States are potentially dangerous to each other.

(iii) States can never be certain about other states' intentions. Specifically no state can be sure that another state will not use its offensive military capabilities to attack the first state. Uncertainty about intentions is unavoidable.

(iv) Survival is the primary goal of great powers. Specifically, states seek to maintain other territorial integrity and autonomy of their domestic political order. Survival dominates their motives because, once a state is conquered, it is unlikely to be in a position to pursue other aims...states can and do pursue other goals, of course, but security is their most important objective.

(v) The fifth assumption is that great powers are rational actors. They are aware of their external environment and they think strategically about how to survive in it. They consider the preferences of other states and how their behaviour is likely to affect their own strategy for survival.[34]

(C) Robert Gilpin's Neo-realism and Political Economy

Gilpin contests the view that globalization is eroding national economies and rendering the state obsolete as an economic actor. He argues, "At the beginning of the twenty-first century, the nation state is clearly under serious attack from both above and below, and there is no doubt that there have been very important changes.... Economic globalization and transnational economic forces are eroding economic sovereignty in important ways. Nevertheless, both the extent of globalization and the consequences of economic globalization for the nation-state have been considerably exaggerated. For better or for worse, this is still a state-dominated world".

Secondly, Gilpin viewed that many of the reputed affects of globalization are the result of national policies.

Thirdly, although globalization has made macro-economic policy formation more complex and risky for states, they still retain control over their own economies. Fourthly, a broader historical perspective reveals that states have never had unfettered control of their economies.

In Gilpin's words, "The argument that the nation-state is in retreat is most applicable to the United States, Western Europe, and perhaps Japan. The end of Cold War represented the end of a century and a half of rapid economic development and political/military conflict. During this period the forces of nationalism, industrialisation, and state creation had driven the industrialized powers of Europe, US, and Japan. World War I and II and the Cold War forged modern nation-state as an economic and war making machine. This bellicose epoch appears to have ended, and the industrialized countries may be retreating to their more modest late nineteenth-century status."[35]

Neo-realism's position was somehow eroded after the end of Cold War and bi-polar system, which they favoured largely. Its state-centered theory was largely challenged by forces of globalisation and pluralists. Besides, the structural model provoked the constructivism theory invertly.

- Pluralists are discontent with the assumption of realist state behaviour. They argue that international activity is not just a matter of the behaviour of states but of other actors too. They not only neglected international actors such as MNCs or UN or IMF but show no consideration of religious movements, national movements and so on. As, they argue that Islam is a factor which should also be considered independently of the state. Similarly, the intergovernmental influence the states and are influenced by the states.
- Andrew Linklater points out, a major problem with Waltz's unit-structure relationship is that it leaves little or no room for systemic change induced by the units themselves. Waltz is convinced that states are virtually powerless to alter the system in which they find virtually trapped.
- Waltz also denies greater levels of economic interdependency amongst states pose a threat to the condition of anarchy. Despite, Rosecrance claim that the state, in the contemporary world because competition for global market shares has become more important than territorial conquest.[36]
- Constructivism (Wendt, 1992) is a rejection of positivist IR theory. Postulates—Human relations, including international relations, consist essentially of thoughts and ideas and not of material conditions or forces. Ideas, conceptions, assumptions, etc. are equally important. They are widely shared by the people. 'State sovereignty' has no material reality but exist only because people collectively believe they exist and act accordingly.
- The epistemological critiques of neo-realism by Ashley (1986) and Cox expose the conservative ideology which underwrites Waltz's theoretical approach. Neo-realism, according to Cox (1992),

reduces international relations to great power management by legitimating a political order which favors the powerful and is hostile to change.

REFERENCES

1. Scott Burchill (1995). "Realism and Neo-realism" in Scott Burchill and Andrew Linklater (ed.). *Theories of International Relations*. Hampshire and London: Macmillan. p. 79.
2. John Allphin Moore and Jerry Pubantz (2008). *The New United Nations*. Singapore: Pearsons Education. p. 3.
3. Shimko, Keith L. (2005). *International Relations-Perspectives and Controversies*. Boston and New York: Houghton Mifflin Company. p. 47.
4. James Lee and Juliet Kaarbo (2002). *Global Politics*. New York: Houghton Mifflin Company. pp. 3-4.
5. Robert L. Rothstein (2006). "On the Costs of Realism", in Richard Little and Michael Smith (eds.). *Perspectives on World Politics*. New York: Routledge. p. 335.
6. Charles W. Kegley and Eugene R. Wittkopf (1993). *World Politics Trend and Transformation.* New York: St. Martin Press. p. 29.
7. Robert Jackson and George Sorenson (2003). *Introduction to International Relations Theories and Approaches*. New York: Oxford University Press. p. 41.
8. Charles W. Kegley. *Op. cit.* p. 29.
9. Robert Jackson and George Sorenson. *Op. cit.* p. 68.
10. Henry Kissinger (1995). *Diplomacy.* London: Simon and Schuster. p. 705.
11. Scott Burchill. *Op. cit.* p. 67.
12. *Ibid.* p. 71.
13. Scott Burchill. *Op. cit.* pp. 73-74.
14. Hans J. Morgenthau (1985). *Politics Among Nations: The Struggle for Power and Politics*. New York: Knopf. pp. 4-17.
15. R. Shamasastry (1951) (Translated). *Kautilya's Arthasastra.* Mysore: Shri Raghuveer Printing Press. pp. 4-6.
16. *Ibid.*
17. T.V. Subba Rao (1981). *Non Alignment in International Law and Politics*. New Delhi: Deep and Deep Publications. p. 35.

18. Barry Buzan (1996). "The Timeless Wisdom of Realism" in Steve Smith et al. (eds.), *International Theory: Positivism and Beyond*. Cambridge: Cambridge University Press. p. 59.
19. Barry Buzan (1996). "The Timeless Wisdom of Realism", in Steve Smith et al. (eds.). *International Theory: Positivism and Beyond*. Cambridge: Cambridge University Press. p. 49.
20. Steven L. Lamy (2005). "Contemporary Mainstream Approaches: Neo-Realism and Neo-Liberalism", in John Baylis (eds.), *The Globalization of World Politics: An Introduction to International Relations*. Oxford: Oxford University Press. p. 210.
21. Scott Burchill. *Op. cit.* p. 83.
22. Robert Jackson and Georg Sorensen. *Op. cit.* p. 84.
23. David A. Baldwin (2002). "Power and International Relations" in Walter Carlsnaes et al. (eds.). *Hand Book of International Relations*. New Delhi: Sage. p. 182.
24. Barry Buzan. *Op. cit.* p. 49.
25. Kenneth Waltz (1979). *Theory of International Relations*. London: Addison-Wesley. p. 131.
26. Scott Burchill. *Op. cit.* pp. 86-87.
27. Robert Jackson. *Op. cit.* pp. 87-88.
28. Stephanie Lawson (2003). *International Relations*. Cambridge: Polity Press. p. 52.
29. Kenneth N. Waltz (2000). "Structural Realism after the Cold War", in Richard Little and Michel Smith et al. (eds., 2006). *Perspective on World Politics*. New York, London: Routledge. pp. 90-91.
30. *Ibid.* pp. 92-93.
31. *Ibid.* pp. 94-95.
32. Steven L. Lamy. *Op. cit.* pp. 210-11.
33. Robert Jackson. *Op. cit.* pp. 89-90.
34. John J. Mearsheimer (2001). "Strategies for Survival", in Richard Little, *Op. cit.* pp. 62-63.
35. Robert Gilpin (2006). "The Nation-State in the Global Economy", in Richard Little and Michael Smith. *Op cit.* pp. 45-53.
36. Robert O. Keohane (2006). "Cooperation and International Regimes", in Richard Little. *Ibid.* pp. 87-88.

5

Liberalism/Neo-liberalism and Interdependence

Liberalism is considered as the foundation of 'modernism'. It triggered renaissance movement and reforms in Europe. Usually, it was the movement of middle class against the imperial Europe. Seventeen and eighteenth centuries classical liberalism largely advocated those human rights of people which have no recognition during the medieval Europe—right to life, liberty and property. Liberalism in international relations found its place first time by the inception of twentieth century.

The term 'liberalism' to denote a political allegiance made its appearance much later in 19th century. The term was widely recognized throughout Europe in relation to a distinctive set of political ideas. Liberalist ideas resulted from the breakdown of feudalism in Europe and growth, in its place, of market capitalist society. The nineteenth century was in many ways the liberal century. As industrialization spread throughout western countries, liberal ideas triumphed.[1] Liberalism believes in individual freedom and dignity, reason, justice, toleration and diversity. It demands a *laissez-faire* state. It also rejects the *divine rights theory* of the origin of the state. Instead, it viewed that state is the outcome of social contract and it is artificial.

The Liberal tradition of international relations rooted in a very different ontology, in which humans are regarded as essentially cooperative creatures despite their confinement within states that often behave as though they were not, finds quite distinct significance in the years 1900-45 (as explained in chapter 3). While clearly the most significant inter-state attempt at international organization failed to prevent war in either Asia or Europe, Liberal theorists have nevertheless found more positive signs of internationalism.

These years are often assumed to be ones of ever greater isolationism and xenophobic nationalism in much of the rest of the world—Fascism and Nazism. Later on radical African-American activists, struggling against the intersection of race and class oppression at home, found common cause for anti-imperialists battling colonialism in Africa, the Caribbean, and Asia. Nationalists in India looked for both moral inspiration and practical guidance in anti-imperial tactics to the Irish republican tradition, especially after Britain conceded an Irish Republic in 1919.[2]

Liberals are different from realists in several important ways. Liberalism has firm belief in reason and possibility of progress. Individual is the seat of moral values and asserts that human beings should be treated as ends rather than means. Liberals emphasize ethical principles over the pursuit of power, and institutions over military capabilities.[3] There was a brief resurgence of liberal sentiments at the end of Second World War with the birth of United Nations although this beacon of hope was soon extinguished by the return of Cold war power politics. In the 1990s liberalism appeared resurgent as Western state leaders proclaimed a new world order. After 9/11 the pendulum has once again swung towards realist pole as US and its western allies sought to consolidate its power and punish those whom they define as terrorists.[4] With the result, Osama (most wanted for US) has now been killed with direct military intervention of US forces in Pakistan.

To differentiate liberalism and idealism; idealism is an approach which studies international relations/politics and is based on liberal assumptions. As there has already been mentioned that idealism became popular during the end of World War I years. It was generally based on public opinion of international community which emerged extremely against war. Liberalism, on the other hand, is a social, political and economic philosophy based on the positive view of human nature, progress and harmony of interests. This philosophy became popular in the modern era of Europe, when Europe was shading the Empires and adopting the social, educational and cultural reforms.

Liberalism is a social and political philosophy that began to flourish as Europe emerged from the medieval world which existed from the fall of the Roman Empire and the beginnings of the Renaissance in the 1300s and 1400s. The renaissance was a period of scientific, artistic, intellectual, and cultural revival that ended the stagnation of medieval times. It was a period of renewal, and liberalism provided a more optimistic social and political philosophy that challenged the major elements of conservative thought. Among the thinkers associated with the development of liberal thought were John Locke (1632-1704), Jean Jacques Rousseau (1712-78), and Immanuel Kant (1724-1804). The historical roots of liberal thought can be traced to the ancient Greeks. It is important to know the key elements of liberalism and how they differ from conservatism.[5]

The belief in progress is a core liberal assumption. But it is also a point of debate among liberals. How much progress? Scientific and technological for sure, but also social and political? What are the limits of progress? Are there any limits? Progress for whom? A small number of liberal countries or the entire world? The scope and degree of liberal optimism as regards progress has fluctuated over time. Many early liberals were inclined to be thoroughly optimistic. There was surge of utopian liberalism around the First World War. After the Second World War, however, liberal optimism became more muted. Robert Keohane, for example, cautiously notes that liberals at a minimum believe 'in at least the possibility of cumulative progress'.[6]

World War I initiated a paradigmatic revolution in the study of international relations, in which several perspectives competed for attention. While the current history approach continued to claim some disciples in the waning days of World

War I, after Russia's Bolshevik Revolution, Marxist-Leninist thought became increasingly influential, with its critique of capitalism's creation of inequality, class conflict, and imperialistic war. In the 1930s, with the rise of Adolf Hitler in Germany, national socialism (or fascism) also challenged conventional European thinking about world politics. Nazism, the German variant of national socialism, was particularly provocative. Not only did Nazism glorify the role of the state (as opposed to that of the individual) in political life, it also championed war as an instrument of national policy.[7]

Emerging as dominant, however, was a perspective known as liberalism. At the core of liberalism, is an emphasis on the impact ideas have on the behavior, equality, dignity, and liberty of the individual, and the need to protect people from excessive state regulation.[8]

World War II is not only another important event of international relations in 20th century, it also brought a challenge to liberal internationalism or idealism. This challenge was posed by Carr and Morgenthau's realism. They discarded the rational human nature and positive aspect of international politics. During 1940s realism became the dominant approach in IR. Subsequently, 1950s behavioralism challenged the objectivity and logic of realism. 1950s IR again witnessed the revamping of liberal theory. That could be called the neo-liberalism. From 1950s onwards, liberalism had been considered in many forms: Sociological liberalism; interdependence liberalism; institutional or republican liberalism.

For liberals, peace is the normal state of affairs. In Kant's words, peace can be perpetual. The laws of nature dictated harmony and co-operation between people. War is, therefore, both unnatural and irrational: It is an artificial contrivance and not a product of imperfect social relations or some peculiarity of human nature. Liberals have a belief in progress and the perfectibility of human condition. Through their faith in the power of human reason and the capacity of human beings to realize their inner potential, they remain confident that the stain of war can be removed from human experience.[9]

In the history of political thought, quite different bodies of thought are identified as 'liberal'. In popular political discourse confusion can be caused the term is applied to particular parties, movements or strands of thought within a liberal democracy. For example, many political parties have the word 'liberal' in their name; in Canada the Liberal Party is the left of political spectrum, while in Australia the Liberal Party is to the right. In Europe, liberalism is related with free market whereas in US it denotes a belief in central or federal.[10]

A common thread running through liberal thought, from Rousseau, Kant and Cobden, to Schumpeter and Doyle, is that wars were created by militaristic and undemocratic governments for their own vested interests. Wars were engineered by a 'warrior class' bent on extending their power and wealth through territorial conquest. According to Paine in *The Rights of Man*, the 'war system' was contrived to preserve the power and the employment of princes, statesmen, solders, diplomats and armaments manufactures, and to bind their tyranny ever more firmly upon the necks of the people. Wars provided governments with excuses to raise taxes, expand their bureaucratic apparatus and thus increase their control over their citizens. 'The people', on the other hand, were peace-loving by nature, and only plunged into conflict by the whims of their unrepresentative rulers.[11]

The solution of conflicts is not through war and balance of power. Liberals find it in either 'collective security system' advocated by Woodrow Wilson; or in neo-liberal 'interdependence' of Nye and Keohane.

In addition to possessing a more optimistic view of human nature, liberals are much less inclined to view social and individual conflicts as inevitable. Liberals believe that it is possible to create a social, political, and economic order that benefits everybody—an order that maximizes individual freedom and material/economic prosperity. This element of liberal thought is sometimes referred to as the 'harmony of interests'. The belief in a harmony of interests, for example, is the cornerstone of the liberal belief in the free market. In terms of justifying the free market, liberals claim that when each individual is left alone to pursue and advance his or her individual economic interests without government interference, the long-term result is growth and prosperity, which benefits everyone. Yes, Bill Gates has become a multibillionaire, but his wealth did not come at the expense of my well-being. In fact, his creations and inventions have improved my life as well. There is no conflict between his interests and mine. Much of what we see as social conflict results not from an inevitable and irreconcilable clash of interest, but the failure of people to understand their deeper mutual interests.[12]

Different forms of neo-liberalism indicated their own versions of liberalism. Republican liberalism states that democratic institutions are working more for the rights of people and less likely to wage the war against neighbors. Republican liberalism is built on the claim that liberal democracies are more peaceful and law-abiding than are other political systems. The argument is not that democracies never go to war; democracies have gone to war as often as have non-democracies. But the argument is that democracies do not fight each other. This observation was first articulated by Immanuel Kant (1992) in the late eighteenth century in reference to republican states rather than democracies.

Republican liberalism, therefore, apparently advocates democratic norms of peaceful resolution of conflicts. Peaceful and cordial relations among the democracies and economic interdependence of states.

Transnational relations are considered by sociological liberals to be increasingly important aspects of international relations. James Rosenau defines transnationalism as follows: The processes whereby international relations conducted by governments have been supplemented by relations among private individuals, groups, and societies that can and do have important consequences for the course of events') In focusing on transnational relations, sociological liberals return to an old theme in liberal thinking: The notion that relations between people are more cooperative and more supportive of peace than are relations between national governments. Richard Cobden, a leading nineteenth century liberal thinker, put the idea as follows: As little intercourse between the governments, as much connection as possible between the nations of the world. By 'nations' Cobden was referring to societies and their membership.

Karl Deutsch was a leading figure in the study of transnational relations during the 1950s. He and his associates advocated enhancing the communication and transactions between societies. Deutsch argues that a high degree of interrelations between societies leads to peaceful relations which reaches at more than mere absence of war. According to Deutsch, "larger, stronger, more politically, administratively, economically, and educationally advanced political units were found to form the cores of strength around which in most cases the integrative process developed. It leads to a security community; a group of people which has become integrated". Integration means that a 'sense of community' has been achieved: People have come to agree that their conflicts and problems can be resolved 'without resort to large-scale physical force'. Such a secured community has emerged, argues Deutsch, among the Western countries in the North Atlantic area. He lists a number of conditions that are conductive to the emergence of security communities: Increased social communication; greater mobility of persons; stronger economic ties: and a wider range of mutual human transactions.[13]

Democracies do not fight each other is "one of the strongest non-trivial or non-tautological statements that can be made about international relations". This finding then is the basis of the present optimism among many liberal scholars and policymakers concerning the prospects of long-term world peace. Their reasoning goes as follows. Because the number of democracies in the world has increased rapidly in recent years we can look forward to a more peaceful world with international relations characterized by cooperation instead of conflict. Why are democracies at peace with one another? The answer to that question has been most systematically addressed by Michael Doyle. He gives three elements behind the claim that democracy leads to peace with other democracies. The first is existence of domestic political cultures based on peaceful conflict resolution. Democracy encourages peaceful international relations because democratic governments are controlled by their citizens, who will not advocate or support wars with other democracies.[14] Liberalism also strongly believes in the functioning of international institutions. These institutions are essential for the maintenance of world peace and prosperity.

Liberal institutionalism or neo-liberal institutionalism is considered by many scholars to present the most convincing challenge to realist and neo-realist thinking. The roots of this version of neo-liberalism are found in the functional integration scholarship of the 1940s and 1950s and regional integration studies of the 1960s. These studies suggest that the way towards peace and prosperity is to have independent states pool their resources and even surrender some of their sovereignty to create integrated communities to promote economic growth or respond to regional problems. The European Union is one such institution that began as regional community for encouraging multilateral cooperation in the production of coal and steel. Proponents of integration and community-building were motivated to challenge dominant realist thinking because of the experiences of the two world wars. Rooted in liberal thinking, integration theories promoted after the Second World War were less idealistic and more pragmatic than the liberal internationalism that dominated policy debates after the First World War.[15]

The 1970s neo-liberalism is known as interdependence. 'Interdependence' is most popular and established form of neo-liberalism. 'Interdependence' challenged strongly the 'Waltz' neo-realism. Both neo-realism and interdependence neorealism believes in structural international relations.

Scholars such as Robert Keohane, Joseph Nye and Robert Axelrod developed models which shared a lot with neo-realism (Keohane 1984, 1989: Axelrod 1984; Axelrod and Keohane 1985). They accepted the two basic assumptions of international anarchy and the rational egoism of states; the aim of their analysis was to show that it was possible for rational egoists to cooperate even in an anarchical system. Drawing material from the same kind of sources as the neo-realists-in particular game theory, public choice and rational choice theory—they recognized that cooperation under anarchy was always liable to be fragile. 'Free ridder' states—who took the gains of cooperation without contributing to the costs—would always be a problem, and the 'prisoner's dilemma' game modeled very clearly the difficulty of relying on promises of cooperation made in circumstances where enforcement was impossible. However, if international regimes could be established within which information could be exchanged and commitments formalized, the possibilities for cooperation would be enhanced. Basically, interdependence model was developed for industrial democracies of west.[16]

Influenced by the emergence of trade deficits after 1970, the rapid post-war spread of multinational corporations, and the oil crisis of 1973-74, many political scientists in the United States reacted against the strong emphasis placed in the dominant realist school of international relations upon the centrality of the state and the relative autonomy of its military and political power from social and economic pressures. R.O. Keohane and J.S. Nye coined the term 'complex interdependence' to describe the new pattern of relations between mature industrial democracies in which functionally defined international regimes, comprising state agencies, specialized international organizations, and firms, managed matters as diverse as international trade, security, environmental issues, public health, and development assistance in ways which could no longer be relied upon to yield outcomes dictated by the United States as the conventionally pre-eminent power. Interdependence was also seen as an insurance against any collapse of Western security and the international economy that might follow a post-Vietnam decline in United States hegemony, since it was argued that cooperative international regimes might outlast the dominant power that had instigated them. Mere lexical coincidence has led to confusion between interdependence and neo-Marxist Latin America dependency approaches to international relations, but the two are quite unrelated.[17]

Keohane and Nye in their famous work *Power and Interdependence*, 1977, mooted the idea of interdependence. They said, In common parlance, dependence means a state of being determined or significantly affected by external forces. Interdependence, most simply defined, means mutual dependence. Interdependence in world politics refers to situations characterized by reciprocal effects among countries or among actors in different countries. These effects often result from international transactions—flows of money, goods, people and messages across international boundaries. Such transactions have increased dramatically since World War II: "Recent decades reveal a general tendency for many forms of human interconnectedness across national boundaries to be doubling every ten years." Yet this interconnectedness is not the same as interdependence. The effects of transactions of interdependence will depend on the constraints, or costs, associated with them. A country that imports all of its oil is likely to be more dependent on a continual flow of petroleum than a country importing furs, jewelry, and perfume (even of equivalent monetary value) will be on uninterrupted across to these luxury goods. Where there are reciprocal costly effects of transactions, there is interdependence. Where interactions do not have significant costly effects, there is simply interconnectedness. The distinction is vital if we are to understand the politics of interdependence.[18]

These noted scholars of IR set the idea of how interdependence can affect the world relations. Interdependence affects world politics and the behavior of states; but governmental actions also influence patterns of interdependence. By creating or accepting procedures, rules, or institutions for certain kinds of activity, governments regulate and control transnational and interstate relations. We refer to these governing arrangements as international regimes.[19]

Interdependence means mutual dependence: People and governments are affected by what happens elsewhere, by the action of their counterparts in other countries. Thus, a higher level of transnational relations between countries means a higher level of interdependence. That also reflects the process of modernization, which usually increases the level of interdependence between states. The twentieth century, especially the period since 1950, has seen the rise of a large number of highly industrialized countries. Richard Rosecrance (1986; 1995; 1999) has analyzed the effects of these developments on the policies of states. Throughout history states have sought power by means of military force and territorial expansion. But for highly industrialized countries economic development and foreign trade are more adequate and less costly means of achieving prominence and prosperity. That is because the costs of using force have increased and the benefits have declined. Why is force less beneficial for states and trade increasingly so? The principal reason, according to Rosecrance, is the changing character and basis of economic production, which is linked to modernization. In an earlier age the possession of territory and ample natural resources were the key to greatness, access to information, and financial capital are the key to success.[20]

David Mitrany in 1950s developed the model of functionalism for world peace. This functionalism should be based on technical cooperation and spillover. Later on, Ernst Haas developed a so-called neo-functionalism theory of international integration that was inspired by the intensifying cooperation between the countries of Western Europe that began in the 1950s. But he rejects the Mitrany's notion of functionalism that 'technical' matters can be separated from politics. According to Haas, integration needs political cooperation too. Integration has to do with getting self-interested political elites to intensify their cooperation. Integration is a process whereby "political actors are persuaded to shift their loyalties...towards a new center whose institutions possess or demand jurisdiction over the preexisting national states".[21]

This 'functional' process of integration depends on the national of 'spillover', when increased cooperation in one area leads to increased cooperation in other areas. Therefore, Haas justified the essentiality of political cooperation at supranational level. Consequently, interdependence model was also set forth for regional peace at the continental level.

Map V: World Physical with Soft Borders

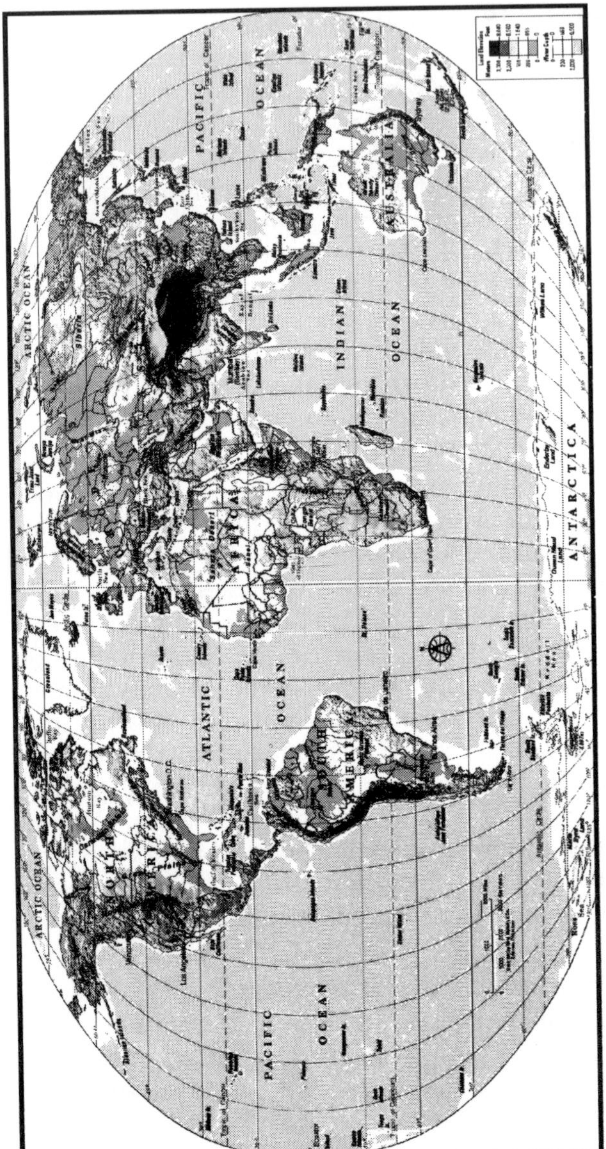

Keohane and Nye wanted the state to weave the relation based on complex interdependence. Complex interdependence has three main characteristics:

1. Multiple channels connect societies, including: informal ties between governmental elites as well as formal foreign office arrangements; informal ties among non-governmental elites (face-to-face and through telecommunication); and transnational organizations (such as multinational banks or corporations). These channels can be summarized as inter-state, trans-governmental, and transnational relations.
2. The agenda of inter-state relationships consists of multiple issues that are not arranged in clear or consistent hierarchy. This absence of hierarchy among issues means, among other things, that military security does not consistently dominate the agenda. Many issues arise from what used to be considered domestic policy, and the distinction between domestic and foreign issues becomes blurred. These issues are considered in several government departments (not just foreign offices), and at several levels. Inadequate policy coordination on these issues involves significant costs.
3. Military force is not used by governments towards other governments within the region, or on the issues, when complex interdependence prevails. It may, however, be important in these governments' relations with governments outside that region, or on other issues. Military force could, for instance, be irrelevant to resolving disagreements on economic issues among members of an alliance, yet at the same time be very important for that alliance's political and military relations with a rival bloc.

We believe, however, that our three conditions are fairly well approximated on some global issues of economic and ecological interdependence and that they come close to characterizing the entire relationship between some countries. One of our purposes here is to prove that contention.[22]

Francis Fukuyama, in his famous and controversial work *The End of History* (1992), strongly emphasised that western forms of government, political economy and political community are the ultimate destination of human civilization. He said, "liberal democracy replaces the irrational desire to be recognized as equal. A world made up of liberal democracies, that should have much less incentive for war, since all nations would reciprocally recognize one another's legitimacy. And in hundred of years those liberal democracies do not behave imperialistically toward one another, even if they are perfectly capable of going to war with states that are not democracies and do not share their fundamental values".[23]

To a significant extent, the globalization of the world economy coincided with renaissance of neo-liberal thinking in the Western world. The political triumph of the 'New Right' in Britain and the United States in particular during the late 1970s and 1980s was achieved at the expense of Keynesianism, the first coherent philosophy of state intervention in economic life. According to the Keynesian formula, the state intervened in the economy to smooth out the business cycle, provide a degree of social equity and security, and maintain full employment. Neo-liberals, who had always favored the free play of 'market forces' and a minimal role for the state in economic life, wanted to 'roll back' in the welfare state, in the process challenging the social-democratic consensus established in most Western states during the post-war period.[24]

In the last decade of the twentieth century, satisfaction with realism and neo-realism began to fall. Arguing that it was time for a new, more rigorous liberal alternative to realism, critics pointed to several shortcomings. Firstly, power politics perspectives failed to predict the peaceful end of the Cold War and international social change in general. Secondly, research suggested that the "underlying theory of war and peace flawed" because realists "oversimplified the concept of power and misunderstood the lessons of history". Thirdly, it appeared that realism's approach would "not be an adequate guide for the future of international politics", because the broadened global agenda included many questions and problems that realist theory could not cover. The problems of AIDS, environmental deterioration, global warming, economic underdevelopment, and the globalization of trade and markets were among those for which the realistic approach was seen as deficient.[25] The creation of a free liberal trading regime by the United States in the post-war period was a conscious act of state policy. The United States emerged from the Second World War with 'preponderant power' and in an unprecedented position to reconstruct the world economy so American business could trade, operate and profit without restrictions everywhere. This meant creating an open world economy conducive to the free movement of goods, capital and technology. US planners wanted to break down England's sterling bloc, create convertible currencies, and establish conditions for free trade. Crucially, raw materials had to be made available to all nations, though particularly to the advanced industrialized states, without discrimination. It was clear from official statements that the USA was ready to assume Britain's former role as the world's financial hegemon, and realized this could only be achieved by exercising considerable statepower.[26]

Even though this brand of liberalism is fairly close to a neo-realist position, most such realists remained dissatisfied with the revised and very much weakened liberal thesis. They claim that Keohane as well as several other liberal institutionalists overlook one crucial item, that of relative gains. 'Gains' are benefits that accrue to participants that cooperate. Institutional liberals claim that institutions facilitate cooperation and thus make it less likely that states will cheat on each other. That is because international institutions are transparent. They provide information to all member states and they thus foster an environment in which it is easier for states to make reliable commitments. Neo-realists reply that cheating is not the main problem in negotiation between states. The main problem is relative gains. States must worry that other states gain more from cooperation than they do. Neo-realist's claim that institutional liberals take no account of that problem; they ignore the matter of relative gains. In doing so, they fail to identify a major source of state inhibitions about international cooperation.[27]

The end of Cold War was, once, subsided by the theory of neo-realism which propounds that stability is well maintained by bipolar nuclear power structure and systemic forces are instrumental in establishing interstate relations. The unpredicted sudden demise of erastwhile USSR and communist bloc made a serious dent on dominance on realism. There was surge of classical neo-liberalism. This important event of 20th century world relations also put a question mark on relevance and objectivity of IR theory. Whatever, the elimination of 'iron curtain' and immediate spread of globalization, which is based on classical neo-liberalism, made liberalism a permanent and sound theory of IR.

The 21st century liberalism is also called market fundamentalism. Market is seen to be morally and practically superior to government and any form of political control. Besides, transnationalism and multiculturalism on cards of liberal theory. On the other hand, United States, who is the strongest advocator of neo-liberalism protected its economy during recent economic recession. US, also is still establishing its power and hegemony in world which is proved by its direct intervention earlier in Iraq and Afghanistan, and recently its intervention in Pakistan while killing Osama without even informing the latter.

REFERENCES

1. Andrew Heywood (2003). *Political Ideologies*. New York: Palgrave, Macmillan. pp. 25-26.
2. Susan L. Carruthers (2005). "International History, 1900-1945" in John Baylis and Steve Smith (eds.). *The Globalisation of World Poltics: An Introduction to International Relations*. Oxford: Oxford University Press. p. 85.
3. Charles W. Jr. Kegley and Eugene R. Wittkopf (1993). *World Politics Trend and Transformation*. New York: St. Martin Press. p. 36.

4. Tim Dunne (2011). "Liberalism" in John Baylis and Steve Smith (eds.). *Op. cit.* p. 102.
5. Keith L. Shimko (2005). *International Relations*. New York: Houghton Mifflin Company. p. 51.
6. Robert Jackson and Georg Sorensen (2003). *Introduction to International Relations*. Oxford: Oxford University Press. p. 107.
7. Charles W. Kegley and Eugene R. Wittkopf (1993). *Op. cit.* p. 27.
8. *Ibid.*
9. Scott Burchill (1996). "Liberal Internationalism" in Burchill and Andrew Linklater (eds.). *Theories of International Relations*. Hampshire and London: Macmillan. p. 31.
10. John Hoffman and Paul Graham (2010). *Introduction to Political Ideologies*. New Delhi: Pearson. p. 12.
11. Scott Burchill. *Op. cit.* p. 31.
12. Keith L Shimko. *Op. cit.* p. 52.
13. Robert Jackson and Georg Sorensen. *Op. cit.* p. 109.
14. *Ibid*. pp. 120-21.
15. Steven L. Lamy (2005). "Contemporary Mainstream Approaches: Neorealism and Neo-Liberalism", in John Baylis and Steve Smith (eds.). *Op. cit.* p. 213.
16. Chris Brown (2001). *Understanding International Relations*. New York: Palgrave. pp. 48-49.
17. Iain Mclean and Alistair Mcmillan (eds., 2003). *Oxford Concise Dictionary of Politics*. New Delhi: Oxford University Press. p. 266.
18. Robert O. Keohane and Joseph Nye (1977). *Power and Interdependence: World Politics in Transition*. Boston, MA: Little Brown and Company. pp. 8-9.
19. *Ibid.* p. 5.
20. Robert Jackson and Georg Sorensen. *Op. cit.* p. 113.
21. E.B. Hass (1958). *The Uniting of Europe: Political, Social, Economic forces 1950-1957*. Standford: Stanford University Press.
22. Robert O. Keohane and Joseph Nye. *Op. cit.* pp. 24-25.
23. Francis Fukuyama (1992). *The End of History and the Last Man*. New York: The Free Press. p. 20.

24. Scott Burchill. *Op. cit.* p. 31.
25. Charles W. Kegley and Eugene R. Wittkopf. *Op. cit.* p. 36.
26. Scott Burchill. *Op. cit.* p. 53.
27. J.M. Grieco (1993). "Anarchy and Limits of Cooperation: A Realist Critique of the Newest Liberal Institutionalism", in D. A Baldwin (ed.). *Neorealism and Neoliberalism: The Contemporary Debate*. New York: Columbia Press. p. 118.

6

Dependency Theory and World System Analysis

Dependency and World System Analysis theories are variants of Marxism. Dependency theory became an alternative to the developing countries during the late 1970s, when there was resurge of Third World in the international relations. During this time there was demand of New International Economic Order (NIEO) and rejection of Bretton Woods System which was established during the period of Second World War (1944). Dependency theory maintained that the inadequate economic development in the Third World countries (TWCs) is due to their asymmetrical dependence on the dominant affluent countries. After their political independence the poor countries are still economically being exploited by the latter. There is no interdependence (of neo-liberals), rather there is dependence of South on the North. Another important advocacy of dependency thinkers is that Third World countries need their own model of development. The western model of liberal capitalism or even of traditional Marxism, or Socialism should not be implied on poor countries. They require the decentralized and indigenous mode for their development.

The dependency theory presents a different structure to study international relations. Many theorists have developed this theory to study international relations. This theory is also called as 'Center-Periphery Model', or 'Development Theory' or 'Third World Model'. This theory's direct inclusion of

TWCs are exposed to external pressures and influences. They have to suffer if they do not make any effort to counteract these pressures. South is vulnerable to the situations in which efforts have been made to eliminate negative external influence but without any appreciable success.

World System Analysis or dependency is a historical approach to political economy with a belief in the global systemic structure and connected processes. The origin of world system theory can be traced back to the first systematic attempt to apply the ideas of Marx to the international sphere, that is, to the critique of imperialism advanced by such thinker as Hobson. According to Ray and Kaarbo, "The world economic system perspective disagrees most fundamentally with the realist state-centric assumption. Whereas realism focuses on the international system of anarchy and state competition for power, the world economic system perspective focuses on the international system of capitalism and the competition among economic classes. For this perspective, economics is the primary explanation for world politics. In this way, it is a Marxist theory. But whereas Marx concentrated on class conflict within countries, the former perspective concentrates on global class conflict. The world economic system perspective concentrates on global class conflict".[1]

Economic world system was also developed by Lenin through his theory of imperialism. Lenin's explanations of why advanced capitalist economies were impelled towards the control of backward lands was based on two main factors. One is movement of capital, the other outlined the productive process. A main thrust of capitalist development in the stage of imperialism was toward the territorial division of the world among the leading capitalist countries. This process guaranteed capital flows from the over-capitalized economies to backward countries which assured provision of raw materials in return. The consequence of imperialism with respect to dependent economies and nations was the integration of the latter into the international market. Inequality among nations and economies resulted from imperialism's development to the extent that import of raw material and export of manufactured goods were the bases of the imperialist-colonial relationship.[2]

Subject matter of IR is with a number of preconceptions and assumptions. Among the most entrenched of these is the idea that they are studying a world whose most important characteristic is division. We may harbour a desire to study international relations in order to bring states and peoples closer together, but the starting point is a potentially united world that is actually divided in political, economic and cultural terms. Although world-system theorists would not deny that such divisions exist, they would argue that the best way of understanding them is by locating them in the context of unity. The concept of a world-system suggests that the most meaningful primary unit of social constraint and social decision-making is this world-system rather than the nation-states that have been traditionally used as a unit of analysis.[3]

The simple explanation of dependency can be understood through this model

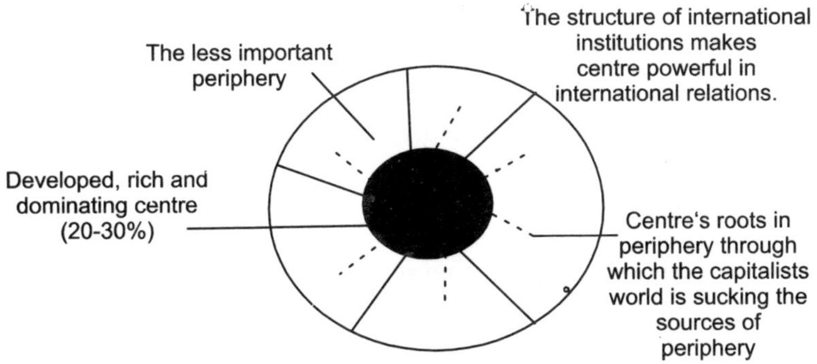

Fig. 6.1: Centre-Periphery Model

(a) Centre is the most important part of world population which dominates and had established its hegemony. Periphery is less important or neglected part of the world.

(b) 20 to 30 percent population of centre consumes 60 to 80 percent resources of the world.

(c) Vice versa 60 to 80 percent population of world only lives on the 30 percent resources of world.

(d) Periphery is dependent on centre for capital, technology and manufacturing goods.

(e) Centre is sucking the precious primary non renewable resources of periphery through capitalist class of periphery.

Although world system theory is inspired by radical dependency theories of underdevelopment, Lenin, Andre-Gunder Frank, Johan Galtung, etc. had analyzed world relations on the basis of development or core-periphery. The foremost pioneer of contemporary world-system theory is Immanual Wallerstein. Wallerstein's world system theory will be discussed later on after discussing the key features of core-periphery or dependency theory.

- The pamphlet written by Lenin *Imperialism, the Highest State of Capitalism*, published in 1917, is the most well known and influential work or base of world system analysis. Lenin accepted Marx's basic thesis that economic mode of production ultimately determines broader social and political relations: a relationship usually summarized via the famous base superstructure model. He also accepted Marx's contention that history can only be correctly understood in terms of class conflict. However, Lenin argued that the character of capitalism had changed since Marx published the first volume of *Capital* in 1867. Capitalism had entered a new stage – its highest and final stage – with the development of monopoly capitalism. Under monopoly capitalism, a two-tier structure had developed within the world economy with a dominant *core* exploiting a less-developed *periphery*. Such a structure dramatically complicates Marx's view of simple divergence of interests between the proletariat and the *bourgeoisie*.[4]
- The liberal mode of development was subject to increasing criticism during the 1960s and 1970s. That was partly in reaction to the lack of progress in many Third World Countries at the time. While growth rates in the developed world reached unprecedented

highs in the post war decades, many Third World Countries had difficulties in getting economic development underway. The most radical critique of economic liberals came from neo-Marxist underdevelopment theory which is also known under the name of 'dependency theory'. It is based on classical Marxists but is different from it (classical Marxism) in a basic respect. Unlike Marx, dependency theorists do not expect capitalist development to take root and unfold in the Third World in the same way that capitalism first took place in Western Europe and North America. And unlike Soviet Marxism, dependency theorists do not support a Soviet model with its centralized and highly authoritarian system. Instead, they argue in favor of a socialist model which is more decentralized and democratic. Dependency theory is an attack on late capitalism. It is an effort to provide the theoretical tools by which Third World Countries can defend themselves against globalizing capitalism.[5]

- Underdevelopment is not a phase of 'traditional society' experienced by all countries. Both development and underdevelopment are results of a single process of global capitalist development. Radical dependency theorists such as Andre Gunder Frank (his renown works: *Underdevelopment or Revolution* – 1969, Dependence is Dead, Long Live Dependence and the Class Struggle-1977), Samir Amin (*Unequal Development* – 1976, *Delinking: Towards a Polycentric World* – 1990). They argued that under such adverse global conditions, how can development be brought to the Third World. Through reliance on their own strength, as well as possible, outside the reach of capitalist world market exploitation.[6]
- The dependency (this theory was developed in 1960s and 1970s) theorists (Raul Prebisch, A.G. Frank, Cardozo, Santos John Galtung) not only rejected

modernization theory but also radically undermined Karl Marx's view that capitalism is able to promote development everywhere. It refers to structural inequalities in global wealth and power. Explaining low levels of development in Latin America, Asia and Africa has been enduring concern of these scholars. It addresses the exogenously imposed conditions whereby the exposure of Third World states to FDI (Foreign Direct Investment), unequal trade agreements, interest payments on debt, and the exchange of raw materials for higher-priced manufactured goods creates structurally unequal relations between the core and periphery.[7]

- Raul Prebisch's (1901-86) structural developmentalism have been the base of dependency. Prebisch experienced directly the catastrophic impact of the great depression of the 1930s on what had long been a prosperous economy and a constitutional state. Generalising from this, he reasoned that so long as industrialised states were able to react to adversed conditions with mercantilist policies, as the Europe and United States has done in 1930s, it was folly for less powerful states to plump for the grains from free trade available to them as producers of primary commodities. The terms of trade were bound to move in the long run against producers of primary products because demand for their exports was bound to grow more slowly than for the manufactures they needed to import.[8]
- Andre Gunder Frank (1967: *Capitalism and Under Development in Latin America*) concentrated upon the external mechanisms of control exerted by the centre (or metropole) upon the periphery in a state of underdevelopment for purposes of super-exploitation. Underdevelopment was not an original or inherent condition, rather it was the determined outcome of the historical relationship between dominant and subordinate states. As underdevelopment was a

product of capitalist development, it would only end when capitalist system itself collapsed. For Frank socialist revolution was the only solution.[9]

This dependency theory was developed by A.G. Frank, who is considered the founding father of this theory. He made case studies of Brazil and Chile to prove a thesis that there is a chain of exploitation linking centers and peripheries. Wealthy countries are the 'centre' (*core*) of the global capitalist system and poor countries are its 'satellite' or *periphery*. These peripheral countries are dependent on the countries in the core for exporting their products. The centre or core exploits them for cheap labour, raw material and longer markets. For dependency theorists underdevelopment in the periphery is the result of development in the center.[10]

- Johan Galtung's Structural Theory of Imperialism (1971): Galtung developed a theory of imperialism to account for inequality within and between nations and the resistance of this inequality to change. He distinguishes between *centre* and *periphery* countries and argues that those in power in the former have a community of interest with those in power in the latter. The result is a relationship which operates at the expense of the majority of the people in peripheral countries, but which is largely in the interest of the majority of the people in centre countries.

This theory takes as its point of departure two of the most glaring facts about this world: the tremendous inequality, within and between nations, in almost all aspects of human living conditions, including the power to decide over those living conditions, and the resistance of this inequality to change. The world consists of center and periphery nations; and each nation in turn, has its centers and peripheries. Hence, our concern is with the mechanism underlying this discrepancy.[11]

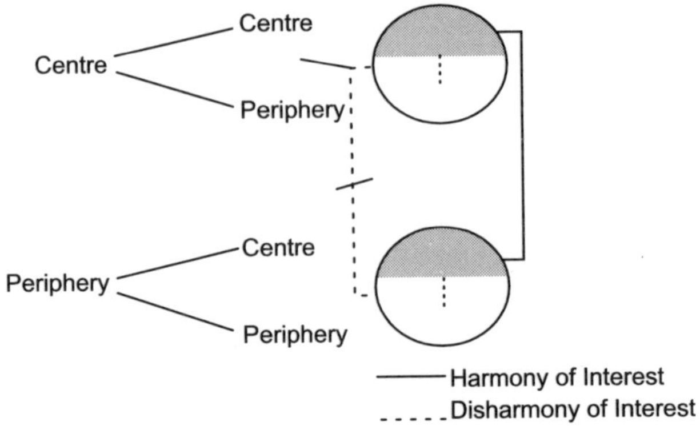

Fig. 6.2: Galtung's Model: The Structure of Imperialism.[12]

Galtung explains:

1. there is *harmony of interest* between centre in the centre nation and centre in the periphery nations.
2. there is more *disharmony of interest* within the periphery nation than within the center nations.
3. there is *disharmony of interest* between the *periphery* in the center nation and the periphery in the center nation.[13]

The LC (Living Condition) gap is not decreasing but is at best constant.

Galtung mentions five types of imperialism depending on the type of exchange between centre and periphery nations.

Table 6.1: Galtung's Five Types of Imperialism

Sr. No.	Type	Center Nations Provide	Periphery Nations Provide
1.	Economic	Processing, means of production	Raw materials, markets
2.	Political	Decisions, models	Obedience, imitators
3.	Military	Protection, means of destruction	Discipline, traditional hardware
4.	Communication	News, means of communication	Events, passengers, goods
5.	Cultural	Teaching, means of creation, autonomy	Learning, validation, dependence

- Radical dependency theory came under fire during the 1970s and went into decline. A number of countries in South East Asia, most notable the 'four Tigers' (South Korea, Taiwan, Singapore, and Hong Kong), experienced rapid economic growth combined with world market integration. This was a blow to dependency theory's prediction of stagnation and misery and seemed to support liberal modernization theory.

Secondly, critics of dependency thesis have complained of careless terminology, simplistic class analysis, lack of conceptual rigour, and excessive polemic. Dependency should be regarded more as a tool of interpretation, a critical methodology rather than a fully developed theory. It has not provided answers to Latin American problems but has provoked debate.[14]

Thirdly, dependency theory severely downplayed domestic factors in their analysis, such as the role of the state and domestic social forces. To some extent, the world systems analysis by Wallerstein set forth earlier has an answer to such critiques.

World System Analysis

The term 'world-system' is synonymous with the term 'capitalist world-economy'. Based on the German word 'Weltwiritschaft', it refers to an entry within those boundaries where there is a single overarching division of labour but which infact includes a number of separate state structures. This entity, according to world-system theorists, is a historical system whose structures operate at a different level from any existing political unit.[15]

The foremost pioneer of contemporary world-system theory is Immanuel Wallerstein. It was he who located the origins of the modern world-system in what he called 'the long sixteenth century' from around 1450 to 1670. Before this period, Western Europe was feudal, and economic production was based almost entirely on agriculture. From 1300 onwards, however, agricultural production fell rapidly as changes in the

European climate contributed to rapid increase in the incidence of epidemics among peasant population. It was not until the 1500s Europe moved towards the establishment of a capitalist world economy, in which production was oriented towards exchange in the market rather than seasonal consumption, those who produced goods earned less than their value, and the driving force of capitalism became the endless accumulation of material goods.[16]

Wallerstein builds on ideas from dependency theory about unequal exchange and underdevelopment in the periphery. But in his view some countries, such as the 'Four Tigers', may well move ahead; other countries will simply move in the opposite direction and overall, hierarchy and unequal exchange continues to characterize the capitalist world-economy. Wallerstein also protests against labeling his analysis as economistic (as understood in academics); economics and politics affect each other in a dialectical interaction.[17]

In Wallerstein's own words, "The modern world-system is not the only world-system that has existed. These were many others. It is, however, the first one that was organised and able to consolidate itself as a capitalist world-economy. Although initially formed primarily in (part of) Europe, its inner logic propelled it to seek the expansion of its outer boundaries. Over some four centuries, it proved durable and strong enough to be capable repeatedly of incorporating new areas and peoples within its division of labour until, by the late nineteenth century, its orgainsation or integrated labour processes effectively covered the entire globe, the first world-system in history to achieve this".[18]

The capitalist world-economy is a system socially structured by an integrated axial division of labour, whose guiding principle is the ceaseless accumulation of capital. The key mechanism to realise this principle has been the construction of extensive commodity chains of production that crossed multiple political boundaries.

The activities of the more profitable nodes have tended to be geographically concentrated in a few, relatively small areas of the world-economy, which we may call collectively the core zone. The less profitable nodes tend to have their units of economic activity more geographically dispersed, most of these units being located in a much larger area we may call the peripheral zone.[19]

Only the modern world-system (the capitalist economy) has evolved a political structure composed of states, each of which claims to exercise 'sovereignty' in a delimited geographical area, and which collectively are bound together in an inter-state system. Such a political structure is infact the only kind of structure that can guarantee the persistence of the partially free market which is the key requirement of a system based on the ceaseless accumulation of capital.[20]

For Wallerstein the dominant form of social organization has been what he calls 'World-systems'. Global history has marked by the rise and demise of a series of world systems. The main distinction between a world-empire and a world-economy relates to decisions about resource distribution, crudely, who gets what are made. In a world-empire a centralized political system uses its power to redistribute resources from peripheral areas to the central core area.

By contrast, in a world-economy there is no single centre of political authority, but rather we find multiple competing centers of power. Resources are not distributed by centre directly but rather through the medium of market. However, although the mechanism for resource distribution is different, the net effect of both types of system is the same, and that is the transfer of resources from the periphery to the core.[21]

- According to Wallerstein there have been three major mechanisms that have enabled world-systems to retain relative political stability. They are:
  - (i) Concentration of military strength in the hands of dominant forces.
  - (ii) Pervasiveness of an ideological commitment to the system as a whole. He means the degree to which the staff or cadres of the system feel that their own well being is wrapped up in the survival of the system as such and the competence of its leaders.

(iii) Three layered structure of world system, when and if this ceases to be the case, the world system disintegrates.[22]

- Important dimensions of Wallerstein's description of the world-economy are:
  (i) Capitalist world economy is a system socially structured by an integrated axial division of labour whose guiding principle is the ceaseless accumulation of capital.
  (ii) *Cyclical Rhythms* – The interstate structures are governed by a longer cyclical process which can be called 'hegemonic cycle' where capital accumulation is maximized and which operates via media of a partially free market.
  (iii) *Secular Trends* – There are at least seven major secular trends of capitalism. They are: 1. The process of capitalist development is a polarizing process between the beneficiaries and nonbeneficiaries for five hundred years. 2. The functioning of the capitalist system where historical differential in wages is so necessary for high profit levels. 3. The liberal development illusion. 4. The disillusionment with liberal developmentalism since the French Revolution and this disillusionment was reflected in classical antisystemic movements (Socialist or National movements). 5. Liberalism has fostered the demand for democratic restructuring and measurable welfare which resulted in the fiscal crisis. 6. Five hundred years of expanded production led to acute ecological problem. 7. The deepest pillar of the geoculture has been the faith in science. The Newtonian scientists of previous generations overplayed their hand to contribute to technological change and enhanced the world production system.
- *Crisis* – For Wallerstein when within the system crisis manifests once in the lifetime of a world system.

When all others (Cyclinical Rhythms, Secular Trends, or Contradictions work in a way that system can not continue to reproduce itself).[23]

- Wallerstein's important point of this theory is that he identifies three structural positions – core, peripheral and semi-periphary. Semi-periphery is added by him in core-periphery model. Hobden and Jones have explained Wallerstein's inter-relationship in the world economy in the following table.

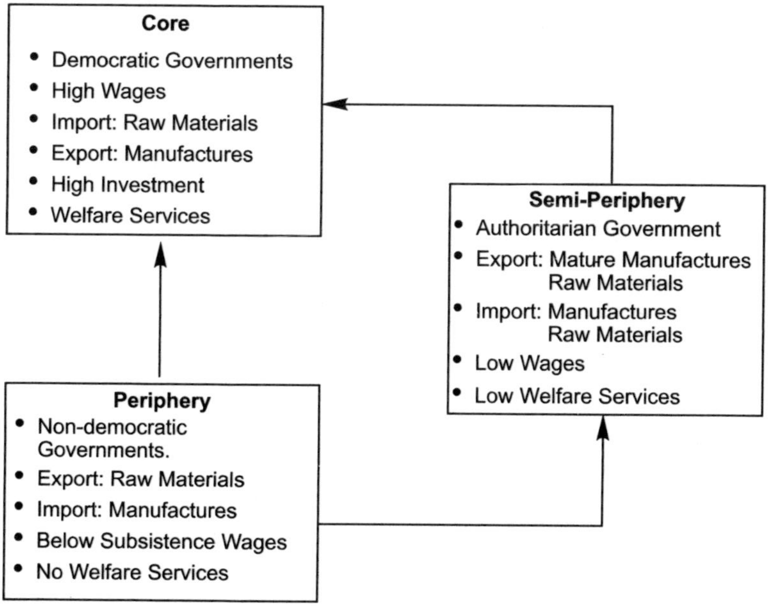

Fig. 6.3: Interrelationships in the World Economy as Described by Wallerstein.[24]

Wallerstein, however, added another economic zone (somewhat controversially) in his description of the world economy, an intermediate semi-periphery. According to him, the semi-peripheral zone has an intermediate role within the world-system displaying certain features characteristic of the core and others characteristic of the periphery. For example, although penetrated by core economic interests, the semi-periphery has its own relatively vibrant indigenously owned industrial base.[25]

Wallerstein stated that "In a world-empire, the middle stratum is in fact accorded the role of maintaining the marginally-desirable long-distance luxury trade, while the upper stratum concentrates its resources on controlling the military machinery which can collect the tribute, the crucial mode of redistributing surplus. By providing, however, for an access to a limited portion of the surplus to urbanized elements who alone, in pre-modern societies, could contribute political cohesiveness to isolated clusters of primary producer, the upper stratum effectively buys off the potential leadership of coordinated revolt. The semi-periphery is then assigned as it were a specific economic role, but the reason is less economic than political. The existence of third category means precisely that the upper stratum is not faced with the unified opposition of all the others because the middle stratum is both exploited and exploiter".[26] Semi-peripheral states are those states which combine within their boundaries a significant mix of core-like and peripheral economic activities. Semi-peripheral countries regularly run very hard to stay in place.[27]

In this way, semi-periphery, because of its hybrid nature, plays important political and economic role in the modern world system. According to world system theorists, the three zones of the world economy are linked together in an exploitative relationship in which wealth is drained away from the periphery to the centre. As a consequence, the relative positions of the zones become even more deeply entrenched; the rich get richer while the poor become poorer.[28] Periphery becomes base of exploitation by both core and semi-periphery. Therefore, exploited by core, but in turn take advantage of the periphery. Semi-periphery is a crucial buffer between core and periphery.

World systems theory refers the core to those regions that is benefitted most from change. In the period of initial expansion, this includes most of northwestern Europe (France, England and Holland, the regions were characterized by strong central governments and large mercenary armies. The latter enabled the bourgeoisie to control international commerce and extract economic surplus. The periphery, in contrast, refers to regions lacking strong central governments, dependent on coercive rather than wage labour, and whose economies depend on the export of raw materials to the core. As Latin America and East Europe were key peripheral zones in the sixteenth century.[29]

Finally, dependency or world system theorists point out that the international power structure supports the dominance of the North over the South in the international economic structures. Specifically, foreign policies of the United States are argued to work to the advantages of US business interest. All foreign aids also serves the interest of the north because aid often supports elites in dependent countries whose interest are tied more closely to the elites of richer capitalist countries than to their own countries. Foreign investment in developing countries by MNCs does much more harm than good. The economic benefits MNCs do bring tend to be concentrated in areas and among people who are already relatively well off, and so they exacerbate the already unequal distribution of wealth in developing countries. So, the present world system of political economy works to maintain the status quo.

According to Keith L. Shimko, "This vision of the world leads Marxists or neo-Marxists to a different set of concerns than those that normally animate realists and liberals. Despite their profound philosophical and theoretical differences, realists and liberals tend to focus on questions of war and peace. They may disagree about whether or not democracies are more peaceful than non democracies, but the problem of war and conflict is at the core of both liberal and realist thought. Marxist, on the other hand, are more focused on understanding the institutions and process that sustain what they see an unequal, exploitive, and unjust international order".[30]

REFERENCES

1. James Lee Ray and Juliet Kaarbo (2002). *Global Politics*. Boston, New York: Houghton Mifflin Company. p. 14.
2. Roberts J. Timmons (2007). *The Globalization and Development Reader*. US: Blackwell Publishing. p. 87.

3. Martin Griffiths and Terry O'Callaghan (2004). *Key Concepts in International Relations*. London, New York: Routledge. p. 335.
4. Stephen Hobden and Richard Wyn Jones (2005). "Marxist Theories of International Relations", in John Baylis (ed.). *The Globalization of World Politics An Introduction to International Relations*. Delhi, Oxford: Oxford University Press. p. 231.
5. Robert Jackson and Georg Sorenson (2003). *Introduction to International Relations*. Oxford, New Delhi: Oxford University Press. pp. 204-05.
6. *Ibid*. p. 205.
7. Martin Griffith. *Op. cit*. p. 72
8. Iain Mclean and Alistair McMillan (2005). *Oxford Concise Dictionary of Politics*. New York: Oxford University Press. p. 146.
9. *Ibid*.
10. Roberts J. Timmons. *Op. cit*. p. 90.
11. Johan Galtung (2006). "A Structural Theory of Imperialism", in Richard Little and Michael Smith (eds.). *Perspectives on World Politics*. London, New York: Routledge. p. 231.
12. *Ibid*. p. 235.
13. *Ibid*. p. 234.
14. Iain Mclean. *Op. cit*. p. 146.
15. Martin Griffiths. *Op. cit*. p. 335.
16. *Ibid*. p. 336.
17. Robert Jackson. *Op. cit*. p. 206.
18. Immanuel Wallerstein (1996). "The Inter-State Structure of the Modern World System", in Steve Smith et al. (eds.). *International Theory: Positivism and Beyond*. Cambridge: Cambridge University Press. p. 87.
19. *Ibid*. pp. 87-88.
20. *Ibid*. p. 89.
21. Stephen Hobden and Richard Wyn Jones (2005). "Marxist Theories of International Relations", in John Baylis and Steve Smith (eds.). *Op. cit*. p. 232.

22. Immanuel Wallerstein (1974). "The Rise and Future Demise of the World Capitalist System: Concepts for Comparative Analysis", in Richard Little. *Op. cit.* pp. 242-43.
23. Immanuel Wallerstein (1996). *Op. cit.* pp. 87-106.
24. Stephen Hobden (2005). *Op. cit.* p. 233.
25. *Ibid.* p. 232.
26. Immanual Wallerstein (1974). *Op. cit.* p. 243.
27. Immanual Wallerstein, "The Inter-State Structure of the Modern World System". *Op. cit.* p. 91.
28. Martin Griffiths. *Op. cit.* p. 337.
29. Keith L. Shimko (2005). *International Relations.* Boston, New York: Houghton Mifflin Company. pp. 55-57.
30. *Ibid.* p. 58.

7

The Alternative Approach: International/Global Political Economy

Political economy is an alternative approach to the study of international relations. IR is presently unable to deny the important role being played by international political economy (IPE) in world politics. Since its inception (1900s) the scope of the subject of international politics remained limited upto dominant issues of war and peace, national security and national interest alike. But during the period of 1970s some changes took place in international relations and these changes were due to the resurgence of developing countries at international arena and they gained ground for the establishment of a new international economic order after 1973 petroleum crisis. Consequently, International Political Economy (IPE) became relevant and new attention of IR studies.

The increasing importance of the international political economy is the result of several trends. First, transactions (trade, investment, lending) among national economies have been increasing dramatically. The number of interactions between nations has grown both in absolute terms and as a share of total economic activity. Second, there has been a rapid growth in national government responsibility for economic policies. Citizens increasingly expect their government to formulate economic and social policy objectives in addition to political objectives. Third, as these economic issues become subject to public discussion, they become more visible to individuals and groups that are potentially affected by the decisions. Because of the increased visibility of economic issues, the policy outcomes are more politicized and more controversial.[1]

Political economy generally came into existence during late fifteenth and sixteenth centuries when power was equated with wealth and wealth with power. Monarchs need to build the vast administrative set ups of their states and to finance the construction of military forces. The consolidation of the state went hand in hand with the extension of markets. But during this time the extension of the global market, the vast transactions of commerce continued to be conducted within local boundaries until the advent of the industrial revolution. The introduction of steam power revolutionized transportation both internally and internationally. Along with it, further technological advances like the introduction of refrigerated ships, the laying of submarine telegraph cables contributed to the shrinking of the world and to a deepening of the international division of labour. Subsequently, the late twentieth century brought with it recognition that the world has become a 'global village'. Hence, the study of international politics then did not considered the role of political economy in world relations whether in peace or in war. Notwithstanding, this role of political economy was either eccentric (for state protectionism) or laissez-faire (free trade or state as necessary evil).

Politics and economics affect each other. The polity is much more influenced by economic developments and the economy is dependent upon social and political developments, particularly the political policies. There is dynamic interaction between the state and market that characterizes political economy. Thus, the tensions and interactions between politics and the economy constitute the concept of political economy. Although the relative influence of politics and the market changes over time. Both are forever linked; neither exists independent of the other. Without both state and market there could be no political economy.

The approach of political economy considers that both are interdependent and cannot be studied independently. Critical to Morgenthau's viewpoint that 'politics is autonomous of economics' or social science is interdisciplinary

Political economy largely affects the process of interactions among the people and their life standards. To fulfil our basic needs we need food, clothes and shelter. Most of these provisions can be obtained in the marketplace. We cannot buy anything without money. Modern market is based on political rules. If not, it would be a 'mafia' market based on threats, bribes and force. Political rules and regulations constitute a framework within which the market functions. At the same time, economic strength is an important basis for political power. Politics and economy interact with each other in complicated and puzzling ways.

"Money makes the world go round", is an old saying. Today, more than ever, that adage is true at least in one sense: money is moving around the world at a quickening pace, as purchases at home are made increasingly of goods produced abroad. You are a participant in this process that is integrating a globalizing marketplace. When you buy a sandwich, a sweater, a car, or the gasoline to make it run, chances are exceedingly high that your purchase was produced at least in part in a foreign land. Your transaction contributed to the movement of money across borders, because the purchase you made will ultimately affect the balance of payments and the cash position of your country in international currency accounts. Congratulations! You have become an actor on the world stage and your actions have registered an international impact. As a result of your financial decisions, money will move around the world.[2]

To understand more about political economy we can explain it as: the way in which market interdependence affects international politics. The interaction of economic and political change that gives rise to intense competition among states over the global location of economic activities, especially the so-called commanding heights of modern industry, is another dimension. What is the effect of the world market on economic development and the consequent effort of states to control or at least to be in a position to influence the rules or regimes governing trade, foreign investment, and the international monetary system as well as other aspects of the international political economy. The impact of economic and political factors on each other differs from time to time. Sometimes it is interwar (1818-1939), state protectionism or at the other time liberal economy in the post-Second World War.

The institution and framework of the world economy have their roots in the planning for a new economic order which took place during the last phase of the Second World War. In 1944, policymakers gathered at Bretton Woods in the United States to consider how to resolve two very serious problems. First, they needed to ensure that the Great Depression of the 1930s would not happen again. In other words, they had to find ways to ensure a stable global monetary system and an open world trading system. Second, they needed to rebuild the war torn economies of Europe. At Bretton Woods three institutions were planned in order to promote a new world economic order. The International Monterey Fund was created to ensure a stable exchange rate regime and the provision of emergency assistance to countries facing a temporary crisis in their balance of payments regime. The International Bank for Reconstruction and Development (IBRD and later on called World Bank) was created to facilitate private investment and reconstruction in Europe. The Bank was also charged with assisting 'development' in other countries, a mandate which later became the main reason for its existence. Finally, the General Agreement on Tariffs and Trade (GATT) was signed in 1947 and became a forum of negotiations on trade liberalization.[3] The objective of these three institutions was proposed in words as of development of all member states. Practically, these institutions worked for West or developed world, specifically for reconstruction of Europe after the Second World War.

There is a latest term being used in academics called *Global Political Economy* (GPE). The terms IPE and GPE are being used interchangeably that it hardly makes any practical difference but theoretical they are differentiated. Two terms are frequently used in this context, International Political Economy, usually abbreviated to IPE, and Global Political Economy, usually abbreviated to GPE. These reveal a different emphasis, though both involve the same general issues. 'International' still involves the state even though the state might be thought to be dwindling. Indeed IPE specialists often concern themselves with the declining significance of the state in international trade and monetary affairs. 'Global' involves looking at the global political economy as a whole and stressing the global features of the system such as the division between rich and poor which cuts across state cleavages. It is often argued that we are moving from the international to the global.[4] Where issues of money transaction through technology, impact on environment, vast expansion of markets ignoring hard borders, have become important in the age of globalization. These issues are being dealt out of purview of state, and *global governance* is emerging and is successful. Globalization has led to the emergence of 'soft border' world and upto certain extent the 'borderless world'. It has increased the significance of supranational or transnational actors. These impacts of globalisation have changed the traditional features of IPE and turned IPE into GPE, which is broader in scope.

Political economy can be explained as an interdisciplinary academic discipline that explores the relationship between individuals and society and between markets and the state, using methods drawn from economics, political science and sociology. The term is derived from the Greek words *polis* [city or state] and *oikonomos* [one who manages household]. Political economy is concerned with how countries are being managed, taking into account both political and economic factors. This field, presently, encompasses several areas of inquiry, including the politics of economic relations, domestic political and economic issues, the comparative study of politics and economics.

International Political Economy (IPE) is the rapidly developing social science field of study that attempts to understand international and global problems using an eclectic interdisciplinary array of analytical tools and theoretical perspectives. IPE is a field that thrives on the process that

Joseph Schumpeter called "creative destruction". The growing prominence of IPE as a field of study is in part a result of the continuing breakdown of disciplinary boundaries between economics and politics in particular and among the social sciences generally. Increasingly, the most pressing and interesting problems are those that can best be understood from a multidisciplinary, interdisciplinary, or transdisciplinary point of view. If there is an "IPE Project" its objective is to pull down the fences that restrict intellectual inquiry in the social sciences so that important questions and problems can be examined without reference to disciplinary borders.[5]

These are the principal concerns of international political economy. This paradigm, or approach to study, is "concerned with the political determinants of international economic relations. International political economy tries to answer such questions as: How have changes in the international distribution of power among states affected the degree of openness in the international trading system? Do the domestic political economies of some states allow them to compete more effectively in international markets? Is the relative poverty of the [Global South] better explained by indigenous conditions in individual countries or by some attribute of the international economic system? When can international economic ties among states be used for political leverage?"[6]

A defining characteristic of the post World War II era has been the dramatic increase in economic integration among the liberal capitalist countries, an increasing number of developing countries, and, during the past decade, a number of former communist nations that are undertaking a transition to more open markets. This note seeks to provide an introduction to this most dynamic part of the international system, and it seeks to do so by pursuing three specific objectives. The first is to provide a descriptive overview of the key features of the global economy since World War II. To achieve this objective, the first main section of the note reviews some of the most important trading patterns, cross-border financial transactions, and foreign direct investment activities that constitute the contemporary international economy, as well as the main mechanisms and modes of political interaction between countries that structure their economic relationships. The second main objective of the note is to provide an overview of the academic field of international political economy (IPE). The IPE field, as is detailed in the second main section of the note, seeks to understand the domestic and international political and economic sources of international economic cooperation and conflict, and, as a consequence, international economic openness and closure.[7]

International Political Economy is thus a combination of the above uses of the term applied to the relationships between nation-states. IPE is mainly defined as a combination of IR and the political economy. It stresses on the interaction between the state and the market at an international level.[8]

According to Hirsch, today's field of International Political Economy (IPE) can be traced back to 1971 when Susan Strange, then at the Royal Institute of International Affairs at Chatham House, founded the International Political Economy Group (IPEG). In its early days, this company of scholars, journalists, and policy makers focused on issues like how to resuscitate the fixed exchange rate system and on the thesis of another early IPEG convener, Fred Hirsch, that comfortable middle-class people in the industrialized world would come to doubt the utility of further economic growth.[9]

Hence, IPE seeks to analyze the causes and consequences of the interaction between the state (politics) and the market (economics) on an international scale. Thomas Oatley defines IPE as the study of how economic interests and political processes interact to shape government policies.[10]

Generally, the emergence of IPE could be traced back to the 1973 world energy crisis and when oil producing countries became successful in bargaining with the West. This event awakened the developing countries towards their role and power at the international level and at organizations like UN. These energy crises led to breakdown of Bretton Woods System (1944) and there was demand for New International Economic System (NIEO) at UN level. The demand was for increasing economic share of Third World Countries (TWCs) in the IMF finance and IBRD fundings.

In the aftermath of it, IPE approach became relevant to study the international relations. Michael Veseth defines IPE as the study of a problematique, or set of related problems. The traditional IPE problematique includes analysis of the political economy of international trade, international finance, North-South relations, transnational enterprises, and hegemony. This problematique has been broadened in recent years as many scholars have sought to establish a new IPE that is less centered on international politics and the problems of the nation-state and more focused on purely economic policy issues. The issues raised by globalization which now falls clearly within the IPE problematique, seen to present the perfect foundation for a new IPE programme.[11]

There is a brief explanation of various theoretical perspectives of IPE/GPE. This theory in the academics of international relations has given different theoretical underpinning from various schools of thought.

Liberalism was emerged in West as against the economic and political hierarchy of the monarchs. Liberalism advocated free trade and that economic activity which enriches the individual and not to enhance the state's power. Liberalism criticises state's intervention in the economic activity of the individuals. Liberalism is in favour of a market-based system of resource allocation.

Liberal economic development theory makes its view point that to transform traditional society into modern society needs modernization. And modernization requires: a market economy which is free from political interference; increasing rate of economic investment; and sufficient foreign direct investment. Free trade will produce the benefits of comparative advantages. Woods explain that according to liberal theory of IPE, in free trade each country can exploit its own natural advantages, resources, and endowments and gain from specialization. The economy is oiled by freely exchangeable currencies and open markets which create a global system of prices which, like an invisible hand, ensures an efficient and equitable distribution of goods and services across the world-economy. Order in the global economy is a fairly minimal one.

The optimal role of governments and institutions is to ensure the smooth and relatively unfettered operation of markets. It is assumed that governments face a wide range of choices in the world system and likewise vis-à-vis their own societies and populations. This means that governments that fail to pursue 'good' economic policies do so because decisionmakers are either too corrupt or too ignorant of the correct economic choices they might make.[12]

Adam Smith, David Ricardo, J.S. Mill and John Maynard Keynes were the classical liberals. Adam Smith (1723-1790), considered the father of modern economics, said that the markets expand spontaneously for the satisfaction of human needs provided that governments do not interfere. To Smith, economic marketplace is the main source of progress, cooperation and prosperity. Political interference and state regulation are uneconomical, retrogressive and can lead to conflict. The law of 'comparative advantages' was developed by Ricardo which proposes the free borders and production specializations. Specialization increases efficiency and productivity.

Twentieth century (first half) liberalism is called positive liberalism, it recommended more role of the state even in the economic sphere of the individual. This was due to the rising influence of socialism. Those liberals view the 'welfare state' and state as not mere 'necessary evil' but a social agency and would improve the public utility services. But 1980s onwards made the pendulum swung back to classical laissez-faire system. It is named as economic neo-liberalism.

The reason behind this renewed liberal faith in the unfettered market is the belief that economic globalization will bring prosperity to all. During this period, the classical liberal view of political economy asserted itself forcefully through a movement that is often called neo-conservatism. The chief proponents of this tradition were Prime Minister Margaret Thatcher of Great Britain and US President Ronald Reagan. These two leaders advocated free markets at home and on the international front, and minimal state interference in all spheres of activity except security. Liberalism in the 21st century, retains all the stripes and variations of its past. Thus, there are many variations of the "liberal" perspective on political economy but the base of liberalism provided by Adam Smith and Ricardo remained integral. In the present age of globalization there is market economy or is called market fundamentalism. Market should set the rules spontaneously rather than the state interference. Economic liberalism professes that markets are consumer friendly and measure the pulse of consumer's needs. They provide competition and quality to the consumers.

American economist Milton Friedman (1993) who celebrates the fact that it is now possible to produce a product anywhere, using resources from anywhere, by a company located anywhere, to be sold anywhere. Thereafter, states can no longer interfere with production and consumption the way they used to.[13]

Classical liberalism or economic liberalism was severely challenged by Realist and Marxist theories. Here, we will also discuss these. Realists' economic version is called Mercentalism, which remained successful during the golden period of balance of power (1815-1914) and interwar period (1919-1939). Mercentalism advocates that state interest and state's jurisdiction are paramount.

Mercentalism sees competition between states as the essence of international life, with pursuit of national self-interests leading naturally to conflict and war to alter the balance of power in one's favour. Accordingly, mercantilism sees power politics determining economics and advocates government regulation of economic life to increase state wealth and security. It is an outlook influenced by the prevailing global conditions at the birth of capitalism and the system of sovereign states. Mercentalism emerged in Europe as the leading political economy philosophy after the decline of feudalism and helped to stimulate the first wave of Europe's imperialist expansion, which began in the fifteenth century. Accumulating gold and silver was seen as the route to state power and wealth, and imperialistically acquiring overseas colonies was seen as a means to that end.[14]

The mercantilist tradition stands in stark contrast to the liberal one. Mercantilists share the presumptions of realists in international relations. They do not focus on individual policy-makers and their policy choices but rather assume that the world economy is an arena of competition among states seeking to maximize relative strength and power. Simply put, the international system is like a jungle in which each state has to do what it can to survive. For this reason, the aim of every state must be to maximise its wealth and independence. States will seek to do this by ensuring their self-sufficiency in key strategic industries and commodities, and by using trade protectionism (tariffs and other limits on exports and imports), subsidies and selective investments in the domestic economy. Obviously, within this system some states have more power and capability than others. The most powerful states define the rules and limits of the system: through hegemony, alliances, and balances of power. Indeed, stability and order will only be achieved where one state can play the role of hegemon, or in other words, is willing and able to create, maintain and enforce basic rules.[15] Realism strongly supposes that nation-states are the dominant actors within the international political economy and the actual actor to study international relations. States must always seek to enhance their power by increasing the economic resources as well. Thus, the assumption of political economy understood by realism is power maximisation of the state.

There is *hegemonic stability theory* of advanced realism that advocates presence of superpower and its hegemony to establish economic and political world order. Hegemonic stability theory holds that when a single state attains a preponderance of military and economic power such that a hegemon emerges, international economic stability based on liberal principles can materialize to alleviate the fears of nationalistic-mercantilists. Unlike mercantilism, this realist worldview follows the logic of *long-cycle theory* in viewing the balancing of power among competing actors in anarchy as the key to global economic order. But hegemonic stability theory accepts the likelihood that order can best emerge at those phases in the long-term redistribution of global power when an all-powerful single hegemon uses its supremacy to enforce free-trade rules. Thus it "assumes that a liberal economic system cannot be self-sustaining but must be maintained over the long term through the actions of the dominant economy".[16]

Why is the theory of hegemonic stability important? Because if it is true, we must expect international markets to be dependent on the existence of a liberal dominant power. In the absence of such a hegemon, an open world economy will be much more difficult to sustain. There is a risk that economic relations will deteriorate into nationalistic, self-interested, protectionist competition, as it did during the world economic crisis of the 1930s, when countries pursued national policies the effect of which was 'beggar your neighbour'. The United States was already the largest economic power, but America was not willing to take on the hegemonic responsibility of creating and maintaining a liberal world economic order. That willingness emerged only after World War II which put an end to American isolationism.[17]

Robert Gilpin (2001), a renown neo-realist thinker represents the realist political-economy perspective. He well understood the increased role of economy in international politics. But he argues that there is limited nature of economic globalisation. "Despite the increasing significance of economic globalization, the integration of the world economy has been highly uneven, restricted to particular economic sectors, and not nearly as extensive as many believe. As a number of commentators have pointed out, there are many ways in which the world is less integrated today than it was in the late nineteenth century. This should remind us that although the technology leading to increased globalization may be irreversible, national policies that have been responsible for the process of economic globalization have been reversed in the past and could be reversed again in the future...." He further said that "The most important measure of the economic integration and interdependence of distinct economies is what economists call the 'law of one price'. If identical goods and services in different economies have the same or nearly equal prices, then economists consider these economies to be closely integrated with one another. However, evidence indicates that the prices of identical goods around the world differ considerably. When the law of one price is applied to the United States, it is clear that American prices differ greatly from those of other countries, especially Japan's. Price-differentials in the cost of labour around the world are particularly notable, and there are large disparities in wages. All of this clearly suggests that the world is not as integrated as many proclaim."[18]

Thus neo-realism opines that there is mutual interaction between the state and the market in present era but without state and market there would be no political economy.

The basis of all Marxist theory is economy. As well understood is Marxist critique of capitalism. The structuralist view of the Marxism is that national and international economic structures affect global political economy. According to traditional Marxism, there is class struggle between the 'oppressor and oppressed'. The oppressed are the working class. The struggle between the two arises because capitalists seek to increase their profits and this requires them to exploit ever more harshly the working class. In international relations this description of 'class relations' within a capitalist system has been applied to describe relations between the core (industrialized countries) and periphery (developing countries), and the unequal exchange which occurs between the two. Dependency theorists (who have focused mainly on Latin America) describe the ways classes and groups in the 'core' link to the 'periphery'. Underdevelopment and poverty in so many countries is explained as the result of economic, social, and political structures within countries which have been deeply influenced by their international economic relations. The global capitalist order within which these societies have emerged is, after all, a global capitalist order which reflects the interests of those who own the means of production.[19]

Lenin developed a perspective on IPE that took Marx's class struggle, based on the mode of production, and used it to explain capitalism's international effects as transmitted through the production and finance structures of rich industrial countries to the poorer developing regions of the world.

Lenin's famous summary of his views is *Imperialism: The Highest Stage of Capitalism* (1917). He argued that the process of capitalist expansion must always be unequal or uneven, between countries, industries and firms. Therefore, capitalist societies would remain unevenly developed one, with some classes prospering as others were mixed in poverty.[20]

Both the dependency and the modern world system theory described the exploitative relations between the rich or the core nations and the poor or the periphery nations. According to this viewpoint, the structure of the global political economy essentially enslaves the less developed countries of the "South" by making them dependent on the nations of the capitalist core of the "North".[21]

These three traditional theoretical perspectives present different aspects of international political economy. Liberalism supports interdependence of political economy among the state and there is least role of the state to play. Realism/ mercentalism considers state as a dominant actor to control and manage the economic activities. Marxism studies IPE while presupposing the national and international structure is instrumental.

There are new approaches of IPE, e.g., the rational choice, the feminist IPE or Green Critique of IPE. The rational choice is also called neo-utilitarianism. This borrows economic concepts to explain politics. Instead of exploring the ideas, personalities, ideologies, or historical traditions which lie behind policies and institutions, rational choice focuses on the incentive structure faced by those making decisions. It is assumed that actors' interests and preferences are known or fixed and that actors can make strategic choices as to how best to promote their interests. The terms 'rational choice' is a useful one to describe this approach since it proposes that even though a particular policy may seem stupid or wrong, it may well have been rational. 'Rational' in this sense means that for the actor or group concerned, this was the optimal choice given the specific incentives and institutional constraints and opportunities that existed at the time.[22]

Whatever happens in the social world, including in international relations, can be explained by individual choices. The rational choice critique is based on the idea that states do not think, make decisions or do things, rather, people do. There is no distinct national interest. There are only the interests of the individuals who make and influence national policies and the ways that these interests are resolved in the political marketplace. People/individuals are the appropriate levels of analysis for IPE/GPE, according to the rational choice critique. Individual actors are rational and self-interested. They want to make themselves better off.

The feminist critique of political economy studies IPE from feminist angle. They viewed that a profound analysis of poverty and injustice needs to be rooted in an understanding of unequal power relations – between and within North and South, rich and poor, ethnic groups, and women and men. It is upon the recognition and repudiation of these inequitable power relations that efforts at supporting social transformation are constructed. Overcoming the subordination that one suffers at the hands of another – the oppression of and violence against women by men, the social and economic exclusion of the poor by the wealthy, the marginalisation of indigenous peoples by dominant ethnic groups – is not only a goal important for subordinated groups themselves. It is, as critically, an essential element for the development of an authentically democratic political culture and society. This goal is pertinent to any social space, be it a public, democratically-accountable institution, a political party, an NGO or a popular organization.[23]

Generally, feminists argue that economy is in the hands of men in the gendered political economy. Men and state both are powerful and control the wealth and power respectively, world is not made up of states and markets, or bourgeoisie and the proletariats, it is made up of men and women. So the objective of feminist critique of GPE invites the gendered analysis of it and to study to which account the male dominant political economy prevails. Murphy and his associates further viewed that asymmetrical power relations between men and women must be understood in their appropriate historical and cultural contexts, and within the dynamics of continual change and reinvention that occur in all vibrant and living cultures. Within the contemporary social context in most countries in the world there exist important and dynamic elements that promote empowerment, autonomy and a transformation or gender-based roles and relations among women and men. These possibilities create the circumstances to construct new parameters for a better quality of life for everyone, and ought to be supported.[24]

Green Critique is against liberal, realist and Marxist approaches of IPE/GPE. They opine that market, state and economic structures are hard on nature. No theory considers the environment as important part of political economy to be understood. Green is an attempt to present nature as an actor to study the political economy and particularly the security. The universalism posed by globalisation, too much industrialisation, technology are harshly consuming the non-renewable natural resources but also uprooting the local communities and animal species. Any study of political economy cannot ignore the environment.

Hence, there is brief explanation of traditional theories of IPE and some new perspectives. The issues of wealth, poverty, security, market, global economic structure, gendered and environmental exploitative political economy are very important while studying the International/Global political economy.

REFERENCES

1. Karen Mingst A. (2004). *Essentials of International Relations.* New York: W.W. Norton and Company. p. 233.
2. Charles W. Kegley (2007). *World Politics Trend and Transformation.* US: Thomson Wadsworth. p. 301.
3. Ngaire Woods (2005). "International Political Economy in an Age of Globalization", in John Baylis and Steve Smith (eds.). *The Globalization of World Politics: An Introduction to International Relations.* New York: Oxford University Press. p. 326.
4. Michael Nicholson (1998). *International Relations: A Concise Introduction.* New York: Palgrave. p. 121.

5. Michael Veseth (2002). "What is International Political Economy". *http://www.ups.edutipe.*
6. Charles Kegley W. *Op. cit.* p. 301.
7. Joseph M. Grieco (October 2000). "The International Political Economy since World War II". http://www.ciaonet.org/casestudy/grjol/grjol.pdf
8. http://www.economywatch.com/political-economy/international-political-economy.html
9. Craig N. Murphy and Nelson Douglas R. "International Political Economy: A Tale of Two Heterodoxies". *http://www.tulane.edu/dnelson*
10. Thomas Oatley (2004). *International Political Economy: Interests and Institutions in the Global Economy.* Delhi: Pearson Education. p. 3.
11. http://www.ups.edu/x12490.xml
12. Ngaire Woods. *Op. cit.* p. 332.
13. Robert Jackson and Georg Sorensen (2003). *Introduction to International Relations.* US: Oxford University Press. p. 214.
14. Charles W. Kegley. *Op. cit.* p. 309.
15. Ngaire Woods (2001). "International Political Economy in an Age of Globalization". http:// www.globaleconomicgovernance.org
16. Charles W. Kegley. *Op. cit.* p. 309.
17. Robert Jackson and Georg Sorenson. *Op. cit.* p. 196.
18. Robert Gilpin (2006). "The Nation-State in the Global Economy", in Richard Little and Michael Smith (eds.). *Perspectives on World Politics.* New York: Routledge. pp. 46-47.
19. Ngaire Woods, in John Baylis and Steve Smith (2005). *Op. cit.* p. 333.
20. Balaam Bauid N. and Veseth Michael (2001). *Introduction to International Political Economy.* New Jersey: Pearson Education. pp. 76-77.
21. Cohn Theodre H. (2008). *Global Political Economy.* New York: Pearson Education. p 52.
22. Ngaire Woods, in John Baylis and Steve Smith (2005). *Op. cit.* p. 335.

23. Murphy Brain (November 2004). "Towards a Feminist Political Economy". *Inter Pares Occasional Paper Series* No. 5: 1.
24. *Ibid.*

8

Post Positivism

Since its inception before the First World War the study of international relations (IR) is growing and flourishing. The growth is not only in respect of widening of its scope but of rising debates, particularly, in terms of methodological debates. From philosophical, historical to international liberalism (Idealism), from idealism to realism and to behaviourlism, and positivism and then post-positivism. All this fall under the four major debates. The fourth major debate was between the positivism and post positivism.

Methodological controversies indicate that IR has become more of an academic discipline. Every approach whenever emerges considers itself that they have perfectly studied the international relations. Over the time weaknesses emerged in every theoretical stream. Behaviouralism and post-positivism were the methodological challenges to the existing theories of the time.

Positivism is a an academic movement characterized by an emphasis upon science and scientific method as the only source of knowledge, a sharp distinction between the realms of fact and value, and a strong hostility towards religion and traditional philosophy. Positivism believes that these are only two source of knowledge (as opposed to opinion): logical reasoning and empirical experience. A statement is meaningful only if it can be proved true or false, at least in principle, by means of the experience. The meaning of a statement is its method of verification. We know the meaning of the statement if we know the conditions under which the statement is true or false.[1] Positivism had almost dominated the academic discipline of IR from 1950s to 1990s. It has involved a commitment to unified view of science, and the adoption of methodologies of natural sciences to explain the social world.[2] Methodological issues became prominent in connection with the 'behavioral revolution' in American political science which occurred in the 1950s and 1960s. The second great debate between the behaviouralists and traditionalists is concerned with methodological issues. The behaviouralists wanted to place IR on a foundation of 'scientific' analysis. The system approach, decision making, game theory, all belong to scientific empiricism and positivism. Besides, during the Cold War the methodology associated with neo-realism prevailed in IR. This new attitude to methodology later came to be known as 'positivism' a belief that IR scholarship is an objective inquiry that is concerned with uncovering verificable facts or regularities of world politics and is based on valid scientific research techniques.[3] The behaviouralist challenge was a major setback to traditional theories particularly the classical realism of Carr and Morgenthau. 1950s and 1960s challenge of 'scientific revolution' brought back the revived realism called neo-realism, neo-liberalism. Including neo-Marxism these three theoretical 'neos' became the great positivist metanarratives. The structuralism of neo-realism (Kennth Waltz), the interdependence of neo-liberalism (Nye & Keohane) and international economic structure (dependence) or World System Analysis (Wallerstein), all tried to make their theories 'positivist'.

Thereafter, post positivism was resentment towards the inability of positivist methodology. Post positivism is a broad term that encompasses a diverse range of theoretical perspectives that have proliferated in the field since the late 1970s. It includes critical theory, constructivism, feminism and post modernism as well as the debate in normative international theory. Despite their differences, all these 'isms' can be seen as part of a post positivist era in the study of international relations. All this means is that positivism is no longer dominant in shaping the nature and limits of contemporary international relations theory, although the debate between supporters and opponents of positivism remains a controversial issue.[4] The distinction between them refers to the simple-sounding issue of whether our beliefs about the world can be tested or evaluated against any neutral or objective procedures. This is a distinction central to the branch of the philosophy of social science known as epistemology (the study of how we can claim to know, or that part of philosophy which is related with knowledge). K.J. Holsti an empirically oriented scholar, asserted in his 1985 work that international theory was in disarray. According to him the incorporation of new issues and actors challenged the hegemony of state centric analysis. Hence there is theoretical confusion.[5] Therefore postmodernism, constructivism, feminism and critical theory challenged the 'positivism', 'empiricism' as well.

Postmodernism

Postmodernism is a distinctive approach to study international relations. Postmodernists are hostile to positivists' notion that there are 'universal truths'. In mid 1980s the discipline of international relations was challenged by critical theory. Richard K. Ashley (1996), who was earlier part of critical school, later on was inspired by Pierre Bourdieu and Michel Foucault. Ashley constructed the postmodernist theory in international relations.

Postmodernist challenge to the IR discipline as a whole was spelled out in the title of James Derian's and Michael Shapiro's International/Intertextual Relations and Postmodern readings of World Politics. The explicit influences on this work are those of Foucault, Derrida, Lacan, Kristeva, Barthes. These influences are in the context of discourse analysis, deconstructionism and texuality etc.[6]

Vasquez explains that Post modernism is generally a social theory that was originated among a group of post Second World War French philosophers who rejected the philosophy of existentialism which was prevalent in France in 1940s and early 1950s. But in international relations Postmodernism entered in 1980s (and the leading post modernist thinker was Richard Ashley).[7]

Defining postmodern as incredulity towards metanarratives: this incredulity is undoubtedly a product of progress in the science. But that progress in turn presupposes it. To the obsolescence of the metanarrative apparatus of legitimatation corresponds, most notably, the crisis of metaphysical philosophy and of the university institution which in the past relied on it.[8]

In the study of international relations there is no shortage of references to the concept of 'power'. Indeed, power is normally taken to be one of the key concepts in the subject that is commonly known as 'power politics'. It has shared centre-stage with the concept of 'state' since the discipline's inception, and is viewed as the basic currency of international relations. Despite this centrality it has remained largely an underdeveloped concept. More worrying that the underdevelopment of the concept of power has been the virtual silence regarding questions of knowledge in the study of international relations until recently.[9]

Three central themes in post-modern work will be briefly discussed: the power-knowledge relationship, the performative nature of identity, and various textual strategies used by post-modern thinkers. Work on the power-knowledge relationship has been most influenced by Michel Foucault (1977; 1978; 1984; 1994). (However, this relationship is also a key concern of critical theory). Foucault was opposed to the notion dominant in rationalist theories and positivism that knowledge is immune from the workings of power. Instead, Foucault argued that power in fact produces knowledge. All power requires knowledge and all knowledge relies on and reinforces existing power relations. Thus, there is no such thing as 'truth' existing outside of power. To paraphrase Foucault, how can history has a truth if truth has a history? Truth is not something external to social setting but is instead part of them.[10]

Still, the postmodern condition is as much a stranger to disenchantment as it is to the blind positivity of delegitimation. Where, after the metanarratives, can legitimacy reside? The operativity criterion is technological; it has no relevance for judging what is true or just. Is legitimacy to be found in consensus obtaining, through discussion, as Jurgen Habermas thinks? Such consensus does violence to the heterogeneity of language games. And invention is always born of dissension. Postmodern knowledge is not simply a tool of the authorities; it refines our sensitivity to differences and reinforces our ability to tolerate the incommensurable. In contemporary society and culture – postindustrial society, postmodern culture – the question of the legitimation of knowledge is formulated in different terms. The grand narrative has lost its credibility, regardless of what mode of unification it uses, regardless of whether it is a speculative narrative or a narrative of emancipation.[11]

Der Derian opines that deconstruction is one of the only ways one can successfully analyse the international in the face of what he has heralded as a 'crisis' of modernity'; a situation in which objective reality is displaced by textuality, modes of production and supplanted by modes of information, representation gives way to simulation, imperialism takes a back seat to the Empire of Signs; the legitimacy of tradition suffers on several counts, the unifying belief in progress fragments, and conventional wisdom become one of many competing ritual of power used to discipline (international) society.[12] Postmodernists are deconstructivists who speak of theories as 'narratives' or 'metanarratives'. Narratives or metanarratives are always constructed by a theorist and they are thus always contaminated by his or her standpoint and prejudices. They can thus be deconstructed: i.e. taken apart to disclose their arbitrary elements and biased intentions. The main target of postmodernist deconstruction in IR is neo-realism. Here is a theory of Waltz which claims that only a few elements of information about sovereign states in an anarchical international system can tell us most of the big and important things we need to know about international relations. And the theory even claims to validly explain international politics 'through all the centuries we can contemplate'.[13]

Foucault commenting on Nietzsche, Genealogy, History viewed that genealogy is a form of history which historicizes those things which are thought to be beyond history, including those things or thoughts which have been buried, covered over, or excluded from view in the writing and making of history. In a sense it is concerned with writing counter-histories which expose the process of exclusion and covering which make possible the idea of history as a unified, unfolding story, with a clear beginning, middle and end. History, from a genealogical perspective, does not evidence a gradual disclosure of truth and meaning. Rather, it stages 'the endlessly repeated play of dominations'. History proceeds as a series of domination and impositions in knowledge and power, and the task of the genealogist is to unravel history to reveal the multifarious trajectories that have been fostered or closed off in the constitution of subjects, objects, fields of action and domains of knowledge. Moreover, from a genealogical perspective there is not one single, grand history, but many interwoven histories very varied in their rhythm, tempo, and power-knowledge effects.[14]

Postmodernists reject the notion of objective truth. They dispute the idea that there is or can be ever-expanding knowledge of human world. Such beliefs are intellectual illusions. Metanarrative's (such as neo-realism or neo-liberalism) claim that they have discoursed the truth about the social world. Post-modernists consider such claims as far-fetched and lacking in credibility. It is called Lyotard's incredulity towards mentanarratives.[15]

Thus, IR post modernism set the serious challenge for positivists' existentialism and the objective truth (Structuralism of neo-realism) of social world and of international relations. They claim that subjectivity is an integral part of metanaratives, therefore, there is need of deconstruction of the theory of international relations.

Constructivism

The focus of constructivism is on human awareness or consciousness and its place in world affairs. Constructivists, like critical theorists and post modernists, argue that there is no external, objective social reality as such. The social and political world is not a physical entity or material object that is outside human consciousness. The international system is not something 'out there' like the solar system.[16]

Constructivism represents yet another challenge to realism. To better understand constructivism, we need to look at its basic roots, which (as the name implies) involve "construction". Although we typically think of construction as involving physical things, like building or cars, constructivists consider how the social world is built. There are many different kinds of constructivists, but they all tend to support the idea that the physical world is much less important than the social world and that important parts of the physical world are actually built of, or "constructed" by the social world.[17]

Constructivism's origin can be traced to the 1980s when neo-realism and neo-liberal institutionalism dominated American international relations theory. Waltz aspired to make realism more rigorous, scientific, and amenable to hypothesis testing. He did so by specifying the nature of the units and their preferences, and how the structure of the international system constrains those preferences. The most important actors are states. Although Waltz was unclear whether they pursued survival, security, or power, and whether they maximized or satisfied, he is very clear that these interests suffocated any possibility that ideas, norms, or values might shape state behavior. He argued that the structure of the international system had three elements: anarchy (the absence of a supranational authority), functional non-differentation of the units (because anarchy created a self-help system, all states had to be self reliant and safeguard their security), and the distribution of power. But because the world has always been anarchy and states have always been obsessed about their survival.[18]

According to Maja Zehfuss constructivism has been something of a fashion in the 1990s and its fortunes show no sign of waning. It is hard to find young academics these days that unless they consciously work within the 'old' mainstream-do not enhance their theses with a bit of constructivist rhetoric or substance. As the realist-liberal debate grew stale and as the 'Third debate' never really took off (partly due to much incomprehension from the positivist side), it seemed as if a new, more vigorous debate could put so-called rationalists against their constructivist contenders. At least, so the positivists/rationalists must have thought, this would be a debate that could proceed on equal terms and possibly engender new research programmes. And they were not to be disappointed. Nowadays, scholars like Alexander Wendt or Peter Katzenstein perceive themselves as bridge-builders between the different approaches, and others like Emanuel Adler (1997) are claiming the 'middle ground', that is, the philosophical minefield separating the realms of positivism and postmodernism. Yet, if one thing is certain about this wave of constructivist writing, it is its inherent eclecticism (Guzzini, 2000). Constructivism is much more of an approach than a full fledged theory. Its disciples propose a variety of perspectives and pursue quite different agendas, too.[19]

Construtivists accept that there is no world government but it is not correct that there is always insecurity and states continuously rival to each other. According to constructivists, realists or liberalists are badly after the state power, national interest and institutionalism. But state and national interest are the result of social identities and they are constructed by these theoretical streams. For example, if realism advocated the survival of the state is only in balance of power then states would follow that policy. Therefore, all these beliefs, identities and social norms are constructed and these theories are in race to overpower each other. Ted Hopf has explained this situation very interestingly. The scenario is a fire in a theater where all run for the exits. But absent of knowledge of social practices of constitutive norms, structure, even in this seemingly overdetermined circumstance, is still indeterminate. Even in the theater with just one door, while all run for that exit, who goes first? Are they the strongest or the disabled, the women or the children, the aged or the infirm, or is it just a mad dash? Determining the outcome will require knowing more about the situation than about the distribution of material power or the structure of authority. One will need to know about the culture, norms, institutions, procedures, rules, and social practices that constitute the actors and the structure alike.[20]

Constructivism, a term coined by Nicholas Onuf in his important book, *The World of Our Making* (1989), met that challenge. Four background factors sponsored its meteoric rise in the 1990s. The first was the end of the cold war. Although only a handful of scholars had even contemplated the possibility that the cold war would end with a whimper and not a bang, neo-realists and neo-liberal institutionalists were especially hard-pressed to explain this outcome. Their commitment to individualism and materialism meant that they could not begin to grasp what appeared to reside at the heart of this stunning development: the revolutionary impact of ideas to transform the organization of world politics and state identities. Nor did their approaches provide insight into what might come next. The USA was enjoying a unipolar moment, but the distribution of power could not determine whether the USA would aspire to become a global hegemon or would opt to work through multilateral institutions.[21]

During the periods of uncertainty when states are unsure of how to address existing challenges they are likely to adopt those models that are perceived as successful or legitimate. In other words, they frequently adopt these models even in the absence of evidence that they are superior to existing practices. Political candidates in newly democratizing countries reorganize their party and campaign organizations in order to increase their chances on election day. Toward that end, they draw from those models of success, largely from the American context, not necessarily because they have empirical evidence that the American campaign model will increase their prospect of victory but often because it appears modern, sophisticated, and superior. Furthermore, frequently states adopt these models because of their symbolic standing. For instance, many Third World governments have adopted weapons systems that have very little military value because they convey to others that they are sophisticates and are a part of the 'club'.[22]

Take the concept of a "state". Recall that states are the central actors according to a realist perspective, and it is the pursuit of state power that drives international relations. Indeed, realists contend that all states are the same in that they are actors pursuing their objective self-interests. But what is a "state"? A realist would answer that it is a government that exercises sovereign authority over a defined territory. But, then what is a "government," and what is "sovereign authority"? Certainly the notion of "government" varies from society to society, as do conceptions of both "sovereignty" and "authority." Moreover, a constructivist might ask what these "objective interests" are, as those realists espoused. Certainly these things are not "facts" in the sense that they truly exist somewhere. Rather, they are constructed from various understandings associated with different societies and cultures. Thus, it becomes important to understand how a "state" or a society conceives of itself and it interests, rather than simply asserting that all states are the same. In a sense, constructivists are more interested in understanding the subjective than the objective and are quite hesitant to claim that certain concepts apply in the same fashion to all people.[23]

They see no inherent and inevitable reason that states must behave in any particular way. States behave as they do because they adhere to certain notions of how they should and do behave. Their behavior is determined by their identities, which are neither given nor constant. "Constructivism," notes Cynthia Weber "argues that identities and interests in international politics are not stable-they have no pre-given nature." States that behave as realists (or liberals) predict they will only so long as they accept and internalize the norms of state behavior embodied in these theories. This is not to suggest that there is no "real" world out there or that the world is and can become whatever we imagine it to be. There are realities: no world government exists, some nations do have nuclear weapons, and some nations are stronger than others. Constructivism holds, however, that the implications of these facts for the conduct of international relations depend on how people understand their significance.[24]

Constructivism thus emerged in the more fluid disciplinary context of the immediate post-Cold War period. Nonetheless, insofar as constructivism shares similar concerns to those expressed by critical theorists, a recapitulation of these differences is necessary before the debate on bridge-building across the rationalist-constructivist divide may be evaluated.

Ontologically, constructivists and rationalists differ on three points. First, constructivists are philosophical idealists rather than materialists. They argue that material structures acquire social significance only via the intersubjectively shared meaning structures through which they are mediated.[25] Constructivists do not deny the phenomenal reality of material processes such as nuclear proliferation, but they suggest that one can only understand actors' behavioural responses to said phenomena by reference to the shared meaning structures through which processes are perceived and understood. Whether nuclear proliferation will be perceived as threatening international stability.[26]

Ultimately, Constructivism's success derived from its ability to further empirical analysis in matters of central concern to neo-realism and neo-liberal institutionalism. The epistemic community literature carefully explored how expert grouping help states discover their interests and ways for producing durable cooperation. Peter Katzenstein's *The Culture of National Security* (1996) challenged standard neo-realists claims in a series of critical areas including alliance patterns, military intervention, arms, racing, great power transformation and demonstrated how identity and norms shape state interests and must be incorporated to generate superior explanations. By the end of the 1990s, Constructivism was no longer a fad or something attributed to the wild innocence of youth but instead was an increasing accepted form of analysis.[27]

Wiener in his article highlights importance of two constructivist assumptions in further developing the mosaic of constructivist theorizing. These include first, the importance of ideas as social capabilities which matter in addition to material capabilities; and secondly, the assumption of the dual quality of norms as both structuring and constituted through interaction. These two constructivist assumptions are key to the project of extending the communicative movement constructivism had initiated within international relations theory towards conversations across boundaries. Such conversations have begun for example with international lawyers. And a common yet rather contested interface between

IR and international law is the constitution of the normative structure in world politics based on discussions about incorporating the good life or, resorting to positivism.[28]

The constructivist theorists include Peter Katzenstwil (1996), Friedrich Kratochus (1989), Nicholas Onuf (1989) and Alexander Wendt (1992). Wendt's constructivism became popular over the time. According to him social structures have three elements: shared knowledge, material resources and practices. Generally, constructivism postulates the following ideas: human relations including the international relations, consists essentially of thoughts and ideas and not of material conditions or forces, intersubjective beliefs as ideas, conceptions, assumptions, etc. are the core identical elements; relations are formed and expressed by means of collective social institutions.[29]

Thus, constructivism is one of the post-positivist approach in international relations which challenge the mainstream theories and is studying mainly that how people of different social, economic, and political backgrounds sustain to manage their relations. It is an empirical approach which includes in its study the political and social world.

Critical Theory

Critical theory has been very influential school of thought in the fields of academics, ranging from aesthetics and psychology, politics to sociology and ethics. Recently its influence has begun to be felt on the discipline of international relations.[30]

Critical theory is a function of Marxism and socialism. It is, historically, a reaction to the imperialism of the advanced nations such as Britain, France or Japan throughout the 19th century. Critical theory seeks to empower those who do not benefit from those policies of imperialism, both within and outside dominant states, in the name of equality.[31]

Critical theory has its roots in a strand of thought which is often traced back to the Enlightenment and connected to the writings of Kant, Hegel and Marx. While this is an important lineage in the birth of critical theory it is not the only possible one that can be traced. There is also the imprint of classical Greek thought on autonomy and democracy to be considered, as well as the thinking of Nietzsche and Weber.[32] Its twentieth century roots, however, are usually associated with the Frankfurt school which nurtured such thinkers as Max Horkheimer, Hebert Marcuse, Theodor Adorno, Walter Benjamin and more recently, Jurgen Habermas.[33] It is due to their work that critical theory acquired a renewed potency, in which the term critical theory came to be used as the emblem of a philosophy which questions the prevailing order of social and political modernity through a method of immanent critique.[34]

Over the past ten years Marxism has inspired critical social theory and has exercised significant influence upon international theory and has emerged as a serious alternative to orthodox approaches to the field. Critical theory has enlarged the parameters of the discipline by showing how efforts to reconstruct historical materialism offer direction to International Relations in the post-positivist phase.[35]

In IR critical theory is closely linked to Marxist IPE. Two leading IR critical theorists are Robert Core (1981, 1996) and Andrew Linklater (1990, 1996). Critical theorists reject three basic postulates of positivism: an objective external reality; the subject/object distinction; and a value free social science. According to critical theorists, there is no world politics or global economics which operates in accordance with immutable social laws. The Social world is a construction of time and place. The international system is a specific construction of the most powerful states. Everything that is social, including international relations, is changeable and historical. Since world politics is constructed rather than discovered, there is no fundamental distinction between subject (the analyst) and object (the focus of analysis).[36]

Critical theorists also rejects realism and neo-liberalism. They likewise deny the reasonableness of positivism, finding that humans simply cannot find abstract "objective" truths. For critical theorists, any premise, theory, or idea has a purpose and is designed for or useful to someone or some group. That is, relationship exists between a person's knowledge and his or her actual practice or, that is, between the knower and the known. Thus, separating fact from value is difficult, or impossible. Knowledge, then, is not impartial and obtained by objective study but is, rather "constitutive" of existing values and interest.[37]

Linklater described four achievements of critical theory as a strand of social theory and as an approach to international relations. Firstly, (as arguing against positivism) knowledge does not arise from the subject's neutral engagement with an objective reality but reflects pre-existing social purposes and interests. Observers have to consider about how claims about neutrality can conceal the role knowledge plays in reproducing unsatisfactory social arrangements. Second, critical theory is opposed to the claims of empiricism about social world which assume that existing structures are immutable. The notion of immutability supports the structured inequalities of power and wealth. In principle these structures are alterable. Third, critical theory learn from weakness of Marxism. In this regard Habermas is especially significant. Habermas denies that class power is the fundamental form of social exclusion or production is the key determinant of society. Critical theory placed special emphasis on social learning which is also responsible for inclusion and exclusion. Fourthly, critical theory judges social arrangements by their capacity to embrace open dialogue with all others and their capacity to break exclusions. This theory envisages the scope to examine the possibility of post-sovereign forms of political life.[38]

Critical theorists have made some of their most important contributions through their explorations of the meaning of emancipation.

Linklater's critical international theory accepts that an adequate account of emancipatory prospects must account for the force which work against emancipation or thwart its realization. In neo-realism a case is made for explaining the recurrence and repetition of war and power politics on the basis of international anarchy. Focusing of states' struggles for power, security and control under the condition of anarchy, neo-realism concludes that the peaceful transformation of world politics is virtually impossible. Whereas neo-realism, like any traditional or problem-solving theory, fails in its incapacity to reflect on its own complicity with the international system. It fails to recognize its embeddedness in social and political life and its contribution to the prevailing order of things by accepting this order as its framework. Neo-realism, and realism in general, makes no allowance for political action guided by interests other than technical ones.

Rationalism, on the other hand, reveals that the condition of international anarchy does not preclude statecraft informed by non-technical interests. For rationalists, states do not exist in an international anarchy exclusively, they also inhabit an international society, hence Bull's cleverly paradoxical notion of 'anarchical society'. In contrast to neo-realism, rationalism argues that an exclusive focus on struggle for power, security and control among stages cannot account for the important manifestation of international order.[39] Andrew Linklater has used some of the key principles and precepts developed in Habermas's work in order to argue that emancipation in the realm of international relations should be understood in terms of the expansion of the moral boundaries of a political community. In other words, he equates emancipation with a process in which the borders of the sovereign state lose their ethical and moral significance.[40]

According to Horkheimer's well-known distinction, critical theory which may be distinguished from a traditional theory according to a specific practical purpose: "a theory is critical to the extent that it seeks human emancipation to liberate human beings from the circumstances that enslave them." Driving from Marx's thoughts, emancipation has a very central role in the writings of critical theorists. In Habermas' epistemology, critical knowledge was conceptualized as knowledge that enabled human beings to emancipate themselves from forms of domination through self-reflection. Emancipation means, according to critical approach, freeing someone from the control of another or setting free from the power of another.[41]

Horkheimer's definition that a critical theory is adequate only if it meets three criterias: it must be explanatory, practical, and normative, all at the same time. That is, it must explain what is wrong with current social reality, identify the actors to change it, and provide both clear norms for criticism and achievable practical goals for social transformation. Any truly critical theory of society, as Horkheimer further defined it in his writings as Director of the Frankfurt School's Institute for Social Research, "has as its object human beings as producers of their own historical form of life". In light of the practical goal of identifying and overcoming all the circumstances that limit human freedom, the explanatory goal could be furthered only through interdisciplinary research that includes psychological, cultural, and social dimensions, as well as institutional forms of domination. Given the emphasis among the first generation of Critical Theory on human beings as the self creating producers of their own history. A unique practical aim of social inquiry suggests itself to transform contemporary capitalism into a consensual form of social life. For Horkheimer a capitalist society could be transformed only by becoming more democratic, to make it such that "all conditions of social life that are controllable by human beings depend on real consensus" (Horkheimer, 1982) in a rational society. The normative orientation of Critical Theory, at least in its form of critical society inquiry, is therefore towards the transformation of capitalism into a "real democracy" in which such control could be exercised.[42] Democracy is an unfinished project of modernity according to the critical theorists. Firstly, critical theorists criticize the liberal democratic capitalist form of democracy, and they believe that a more democratic form, which they call "Radical Democracy", should be established.[43]

The focus on democracy as a location for cooperative, practical and transformative activity continues today in the work of Jurgen Habermas, as does the attempt to determine the nature and limits of "real democracy" in complex, pluralistic, and globalizing societies.

In contrast to classical Marxists who locate the potential for emancipation in the economic base of society, that is, the realm of production. Habermas argues that the promise of a better society lies in the realm of communication. Herbermas's central point as far as political practice is concerned, is that the route to emancipation lies through radical democracy. That is, it is through a system in which the widest possible participation is encouraged not only in word (as is the case in many western democracies) but also in deed, by actually identifying barriers to participation – be they social, economic, or cultural and overcoming them. For Habermas and his followers, participation is not to be confined within the borders of a particular sovereign state. Rights and obligations extend beyond state frontiers. This, of course, leads him directly to the concerns of international relations, and it is striking that Habermas's recent writings have begun to focus on the international realm.[44]

Habermas, for example, "opposes substantive democracy, by which he means a system where the majority can change the very nature of the government; can redefine the basic rights of the citizen; can impose its own notions of justice, property, the right of inherit, education, of right and wrong, on all of the people," critical theorists claim that democracy, by means of liberal democracy, is not open to any differences in the society, hence actually a form of domination of the majority over any kind of minorities. Radical democracy, on the other hand, demands the recognition of differences and maximum pluralism without destroying the community. Critical theorists basically aim to transform the contemporary capitalist democracy into a more consensual form of democracy which they call radical democracy.

Critical international theorists basically try to apply the ideas of critical social theorists to the international level. Deriving their thoughts from Habermas' communicative rationality, and other critical theorists, they aim to transform the current international system to a more democratic one. The relationship between individuals, non-governmental organizations and other groups must be improved by communicative rationality by bringing their ideas, problems and thoughts to the international organizations more often. Habermas believes that this will make the international political system more democratic. Critical theorists aim to build an international system which is open to any difference, such as identity, religion, ethnicity, gender, nationality, and hence more democratic. For example, the current structure of the United Nations is actually the domination of five privileged states of the Security Council over the others.

Critical theorists also suggest international and non-governmental organizations to have a place in the international system as the basic units besides states. They support maximum pluralism in the international system without destroying it.[45]

The prime feature of critical theory revolves around the concept of "unmasking." Modern science is about masking power relations. Critical theory seeks to take this type of research and show to what extent it serves the powerful and justifies their authority. In particular, this approach seeks to unmask modern, capitalist economies. It is not value-free, it is about the control of the few who own capital over the many who do not, and must serve it as a result. In international relations, the hierarchy exists from the states who control most advanced, technical capital, down to those states that are much poorer, and hence become dependent on the wealthy. International relations are unmasked as a game where the dominant powers have written the rules of trade to benefit themselves.

Critical theory sees international relations as a "zero-sum" game. That is, one person's victory as another's defeat. If one person, region or state becomes wealthy, it has done so at the expense of someone else. Those victimized by the system have a moral right to resist and rebel. Critical Theory serves those who it claims have this right. It is inseparable from socialism, equality and the war on the dominant states.[46]

Critical theory not only challenges and dismantles traditional forms of theorizing; it also problematizes and seeks to dismantle entrenched forms of social life that constrain human freedom. Critical international theory is an extension of this critique to the international domain.[47]

Critical theory can act as a first order theory about the dynamics and structure of the international system. Critical international theory is an attempt to reflect upon critical discourses of international relations and is to focus on both the similarities and differences among them by putting them into constructive criticism. And it extrapolates important insights from each, as necessary components of a more adequate theorization of international relations.

Critical theory offers an approach which distinctly raise normative issues that cooperate with the social sciences in a non-reductive way. Its domain is inquiry into the normative dimension of social activity in particular 'how actors' employ their practical knowledge and normative attitudes from complex perspectives in various sorts of contexts.

It aims to respond to the dominating theories in international relations. And it also opposes the use of knowledge to gain power by opposing positivism as the only scientific method. The purpose is to establish an alternative world which emphasizes democracy, equality, emancipation and justice.[48]

Unfortunately, when we look at the critical theory, we can't see a systematic application of these emancipatory ideas to the international political system.

Richard Wyn Jones says that there have been no systematic considerations of how critical international theory can help generate, support, or sustain emancipatory politics beyond the seminar room or conference hotel. But moving further from the thoughts about emancipation, we can claim that an international system which doesn't produce any kind of domination of one state over the others would be the international system that critical theory aims.[49]

Thus, post positivism tries to rejuvenate the theory of international relations. It highlights the methodological differences between the science and social relations. It formulates the idea that study of social relations cannot become 'pure science' and objective. Subjectivity is inherent part of study of social relations. Hence, if we agree with the post positivism, the whole base of existentialism (of neo-realism, neo-liberalism and even neo-Marxism) will be shaken. No doubt, positivists are lacking coherence, integrity and uniformity in their views, still this theory is very meaningful for giving leverage to new ideas and issues in the transforming global politics.

REFERENCES

1. Martin Griffiths and Callaghan Terry O (2004). *Key concepts in International Relations.* New York: Routledge. pp. 249-50.
2. Steve Smith (1996). "Positivism and beyond", in Steve Smith, Ken Booth and Marysia Zalewski (eds.). *International Theory: Positivism and Beyond.* Cambridge: Cambridge University. p. 11.
3. Robert Jackson and Georg Sorenson (2003). *Introduction to International Relations.* New York: Oxford University. pp. 228-29.
4. Martin Griffiths. *Op. cit.* p. 249.
5. J.Ann Tickner (1998). "International Relations: Post-Positivist and Feminist Perspectives", in Goodin Robert E. and Klingemann Hans Dieter (eds.). *A New Handbook of Political Science.* US: Oxford University. pp. 447-48.
6. Jim George (1994). *Discourses of Global Politics A Critical (Re) Introduction to International Relations.* Boulder : Lynne Rienner Publisher. p. 191.
7. Robert Jackson and Georg Sorenson. *Op. cit.* p. 250.
8. Jean Francois Lyotard (2001). "The Postmodern Conditions" in Steven Seidman and Jeffery C. Alexander (eds.). *The New Social Theory Reader.* New York: Routledge. p. 166.
9. Richard Devetak (1996). "Critical Theory", in Scott Burchill and Andrew Linklater. *Theories of International Relations.* New York : Martin Press. p. 101.
10. Steve Smith and Patricia Owens (2005). "Alternative Approches to International Theory" in John Baylis and Steve Smith (eds.). *The Globalization of World Political: An introduction to International Relations.* US: Oxford University Press. p. 285.
11. Jean Francois Lyotard. *Op. cit.* p. 167.
12. Derian. J Der (1988). "Introducing Philosphical Traditions in International Relations". *Millennium.* Vol. 17. No. 2. p. 189.
13. Robert Soreson and Georg Sorenson. *Op. cit.* pp. 251-52.
14. Richard Devetak. *Op. cit.* p. 185.

15. Robert Sorenson. *Op. cit.* pp. 250-51.
16. *Ibid.* p. 253.
17. James Lee Ray and Juliet Kaarbo (2005). *Global Politics.* New York: Boston Mifflin Company. p. 16
18. Michel Barnett (2005). "Social Constructivism", in John Baylis and Steve Smith. *Op. cit.* p. 253.
19. Maja Zehfuss (2002). *Constructivism in International Relations: The Political of Reality.* Cambridge: Cambridge University Press. http://www.inspire.org
20. Ted Hopf (1989). "The Promise of constructivism in International Relations Theory", *International Security,* Vol. 23. No. 1. p. 172.
21. Michael Barnett (2005). "Social Constructivism", in John Baylis and Steve Smith. *Op. cit.* p. 256.
22. *Ibid.* p. 265.
23. James Lee Ray and Juliet Kaarbo. *Op. cit.* p. 16.
24. Keith L. Simko (2005). *International Relations Perspectives and controversises.* New York : Houghton Muffling Company. p. 64.
25. Marta Finnermore and Kathryn Sikkink (2001). "Taking Stock: The Constructivist Research and Compartive Politics". *Annual Review of Political Science.* Vol. 4. pp. 391-416.
26. Andrew Bradley Philips (2007). "Constructivism", in Martin Griffiths (ed.). *International Theory for the Twenty First Century.* New York: Routledge. p. 75.
27. Michael Barnett. *Op. cit.* p. 257.
28. Antje Wiener (2006). "Constructivist Approaches in International Relations Theory: Puzzles and Promises". Web papers on Constitutionalism and Governance beyond the state, No. 5. www.bath.ac.uk/esml/conweb
29. Robert Jackson and Georg Sorenson. *Op cit.* p. 254.
30. Stephen Hobden and Richard WYN Jones (2005). "Marxist Theories of International Relations" in John Baylis and Steve Smith (eds.). *Op. cit.* p. 230.
31. Walter Johnson. "Critical Theory and International Relations". http:www.enow.com
32. Richard Devetak. *Op. cit.* p. 146.
33. Stephine Lawson (2004). *International Relations.* UK: Polity. p. 11.

34. Richard Devetak. *Op. cit.* p. 146.
35. Andrew Linklater (1996). "The Achievements of Critical Theories" in Steve Smith, Ken Booth and Marysia Zalewski (eds.). *Op. cit.* p. 279.
36. Robert Sorenson. *Op. cit.* p. 248.
37. John Allphin Moore and Jerry Pubantz (2008). *The New United Nations International Organization in the Twenty first Century*. New Delhi : Pearsons Publications. p. 5.
38. Andrew Linklater. *Op. cit.* p. 280.
39. Richard Devtak. *Op. cit.* p. 154.
40. Stephen Hobden and Richard WYN Jones. *Op. cit.* p. 241.
41. Michael Baaz. "Critical Theory as an International Relations Theories". http://asrudianCentre.wordpress.com
42. Critical Theory (8 March, 2005). http://plato.standfordedu/entiries
43. Michael Baaz. *Op. cit.*
44. Stephen Hobden and Richard WYN Jones. *Op. cit.* p. 241.
45. Michael Baaz. *Op. cit.*
46. Walter Johnson "Critical Theory and International Relations". http://www.enow.com
47. Richard Devetak. *Op cit.* p. 48.
48. Michael Baaz. *Op. cit.*
49. *Ibid.*

PART – III

ISSUES

9

Human Security

The concept of human security is, in principle, quite broad. It takes the individual as the nexus of its concern, the life as lived, as the true lens through which we should view the political, economic and social environment. As its most basic level, human security means freedom from fear. According to Walter Dorn "The world can never be at peace unless people have security in their daily lives."[1]

Security in its most elementary form is understood as the well-being and prosperity of the individual – the smallest building block – and then moving up the societal ladder to encompass the collective – be it tribe/clan or city or the modern nation-state, post Westphalia. The concept of human security represents a powerful but controversial attempt by sections of the academic and policy community to redefine and broaden the meaning of security. Traditionally, security meant protection of the sovereignty and territorial integrity of states from external military threats. The state was the primary actor and the dominant interpretation was that if state security was assured, individual security was of little consequence. In this matrix, the bipolar structure of IR was nurtured with technology playing a major role. The emergence of the nuclear weapons introduced new elements and soon after, security was further focused on the military nuclear axis with the two rival blocks/camps amassing a colossal number of nuclear weapons. Thus, cold war security was exclusive, military-nuclear oriented with unchallenged state primacy and conducted in bi-polar structure and perceived as a zero sum game.

In the post Cold War understanding of security, the meaning and interpretation is a complete contrast. The concept of human security challenges the state-centric notion of security by focusing on the individual as the main referent object of security. Human security is the security for the people, rather than for states or governments.[2] The power of human security concept is most clearly evident when it is contrasted with the traditional concept of national security. In the human security approach, the welfare of the human beings around the world is the object of concern rather than military and strategic interests in a particular state. The defence of human life is more important than the defence of land, and personal integrity is as important as territorial integrity.[3]

Now security is more inclusive and encompasses the political, economic, military and non-military and non-military strands with considerable emphasis on the economic performance of the nation state in an increasingly interdependent, free market, export oriented world. Simultaneously, state primacy has been diluted and the state *per se* has become less effective and relevant with the emergence of a variety of transnational forces and multinational entities and the challenge posed to state primacy by the individual and ubiquitous non-governmental organization (NGO). Thus, the PCW interpretation of security is more inclusive with a predominant economic focus even while state primacy is being diluted in a more complex global matrix where transnational and multinational forces have come to be fore in a global order.[4]

The new *mantra* in international relations is the slogan "human security". The concept of human security is being juxtaposed to the traditional concepts of national/state security. Canada has become one of the foremost advocates of human security. The term "security" means a condition in which the physical existence of something has been protected and preserved. Therefore, aiming at "national security" means attempting to protect and preserve the nation through 'military means'; and "human security" means a situation in which the life, the body and the well being of the human person have been protected through the use of physical force. Human security is not a new concept. It was discussed during 1860s at the foundation of the International Committee of the Red Cross, and during the 1940s in the UN charter, the Universal Declaration of Human Development Report (1995) of the UN Development Program used the phrase "human security" but without any implications.[5]

The idea of human security is generally thought to go back to the UNDP Report of 1994 which for the time explicitly articulated the importance of human security as a tool of policy making and implementation. The report argued that traditional definitions had been far too narrow, with the concept being largely confined to security of territory from external aggression, or as the protection of national interests in foreign policy or as global security from the threat of nuclear holocaust. According to UNDP, Human security can be said to have two main aspects. It means, first, safety from such chronic threats as hunger, diseases, repression. And second, it means protection from sudden and hurtful disruptions in the patterns of daily life, whether in homes, in jobs or in communities. Such threats can exist at all levels of national income and development. UNDPs 1994 Global Human Development Report was the first time international document which clearly and explicitly articulated human security as a concept for future vision and agenda for action.[6] The 1994 Human Development Report defined human security as people's "safety from chronic threats and protection from sudden hurtful disruptions in the patterns of daily life." Seven types of security were listed as components of human security. They are: economic security, food security, health security, environmental security, personal (physical) security, community security, and political security. The Canadian government, which has become one of the champions of the human security concept, adopted a similar definition. "Human Security means freedom from pervasive threats to people's rights, safety and lives."[7] It is closely associated with the idea, the late Mahbub ul Haq, (the consulting economists and former Pakistan finance minister and consultant of UNDP) who had earlier played a key role in the construction of the HDI (Human Development Index) and who was subsequently the moving force behind the more recent Humane Governance Index (HGI).[8] It is under his initiative, HDI and Humane Governmence Index was prepared. Simultaneously, Canada, Japan and Norway proposed human security centric governance initiatives in domestic and foreign policy options.[9]

According to Haq, human security is not about states and nations, but about individuals and people. He argues that the world is "entering in a new era of human security" in which "the entire concept of security will change dramatically" According to Haq whereas the traditional conception of security emphasizes territorial integrity and national independence as the primary values that need to be protected, human security pertains above all to the safety and well being. Human Development Report (1994) presented the concept of human security. Human development is a broader concept – a process of indenting the range of people's choice. People are safely and freely – and that they can be fairly confident that the opportunities they have today will not be lost tomorrow. With advancing globalization, new issues of global security have since emerged. When human security is under threat anywhere, it can affect people everywhere. Famines, ethnic conflicts, social disintegration, pollution and drug trafficking can no longer be confined within national borders. Some global challenges to human security arise because threats within countries rapidly spill beyond national frontiers, such as greenhouse gases and trade in drugs.

Security is one of the most fundamental human needs: an irreoutable guarantee of safety and well being, economic assurance and possibility, sociality and order, of a life lived freely without fear or hardship. That security is a universal good available to all, and a solemn pledge between citizens and their political leaders, to whom their people's security is the first duty, the over-riding goal of domestic and international policy making.[10]

At first glance, the issue seems simple. Both state security and human security should be the objectives of national policy and regional cooperation. In theory, national security creates favorable environment that is conducive to the pursuit of human security. National security enables nation states to pursue long term national development agenda without fear of being interrupted by conflict and unwanted surprises either from within or outside the country. It allows nation states to allocate their resources to productive sectors instead of military hardware acquisitions. While national development, in turn, creates opportunities that can improve the lives and conditions of the people, national security can lead to human security. Human security, in turn, provides a strong foundation for national stability.[11] The security of the people should become the upper most concern of governments. More attention needs to be paid to income and job security of the people, to environmental security and to security against crime. National security is best achieved where human security satisfactorily prevails.[12]

Human security is not concerned with weapons it is a concern with human life (physical safety and well-being) and dignity (freedom). The UNDP report suggested that the capacity of individuals to make choices, a sense of surety about the future, feelings of personal efficacy and empowerment, and community and political security are important human security values, which for the most part relate to the freedom and dignity of the individual in social and political life.

Similarly, in the Canadian approach, human security implies "an acceptable quality of life", which connotes physical safety and well-being minimally; and "a guarantee of fundamental human rights", which connotes a basic charter of political freedoms.

Broadly, if sovereignty of the state is at the heart of the traditional national security conception, human security of the individual is at the heart of human security. If national security is, at base, about territorial integrity or protection of the body politic, so human security is basically about physical integrity or protection of the individual human body from harm. If national security is also about the political freedom of a state to choose its diplomatic partners/adversaries and to regulate its external and internal affairs, so also human security is about the political freedom to lead on private life without undue interference from fellow citizens and state authorities.[13]

Security is the oldest and the most important concerns of international studies. It means that feeling of security, which at any one time may be under threat from a number of different directions. Clearly, one such is external military threat, but is also the case that depletion of the ozone layer, mass unemployment, large-scale drug trafficking, terrorism, crime and the arrival on its borders of large numbers of refugees. Moreover, the security of individuals is also bound up with these threats in so far as individuals are citizens of state. More importantly, in circumstances where the security of the individual may actually be threatened by the state itself. Denial of human rights, ill treatment and persecution for reasons of gender or sexual orientation, the deprivations of famine and poverty, these are all factors which threaten the security of individuals.

There are two key versions of human security – the institutional approach and the emancipatory approach – while one sees the creation of liberal institutions to protect human security as paramount, the other aims at the empowerment of individuals and the removal of unnecessary constraints over their lives. Indeed, human security is designed and constructed with the notion of others in mind, and its provision is dependent upon an external act of definition as well as the capacity of human security actors to act. The institutionalist approach is derived from liberal thinking in IR and in policy more recently, and in particular is associated with peace building consensus on the 'liberal peace' though this may now be more accurately called a neo-liberal place. This certainly aspires the human security in its broader forms, but in fact focuses narrowly in terms of basic security plus the construction of effective institutions of governance through which human security can be imported into post conflict development settings. This top-down perspective takes human security to be dependent upon security and strong states and international intervention driven by hegemonic states that establish the necessary institutions in order to provide for very basic forms of human security mainly physical security.

The second approach derives from the critical impulse in IR, and offers a focus on emancipation as the aim of human security. This bottom-up approach means that individuals are empowered to negotiate and develop a form of human security that is fitted to their needs, political, economic and social, but also provides them the necessary tools to do so. This, by necessity, focuses on a broad notion of human security and on its external providers, but is aimed at local agency as its ultimate expression. Human security is therefore focused upon emancipation from oppression, domination, and hegemony, as well as from want.

Because human security is constructed within the context of democratization, the rule of law, human rights, free trade, globalized markets, and neoliberal economic development, it is most strongly characterized by an institutional approach. The actors generally associated with human security are foreign state donors, donor funded non-governmental organizations (NGOs), international organizations (IGs), international agencies, international financial institutions (IFIs), and regional organizations, all of them present human security as a universal set of very basic security needs.[14]

The real wealth of a nation is its people and the purpose of development is to create an enabling environment for people to enjoy long, wealthy and creative lives. This simple but powerful truth is too forgotten in the pursuit of material and financial wealth.[15]

In the globalized world, the very concept of security was changing as governments concerned themselves less with the military balance and territorial disputes, and more with such issues as trade, the environment, terrorism and narcotics. There are the challenges which are both national and transnational. The communications revolution and growing economic interdependence appeared to challenge national sovereignty, leaving states at the mercy of global trends. The safety and security of civilians, and their welfare, has traditionally been the responsibility of nation-states, it has become clear that, in a globalized world, these states no longer possess all of the means to deliver.

Contemporary globalization that is being shaped by technological changes, involving corporations as major players, is uneven. It involves the reconfiguration of states and goes together with regionalization. But globalisation before and after 9/11 and the war on terrorism is marked by two major differences from which other differences follows. First, the United States now shows aggressive unilateralism that marks a shift from a mixed international system of unimultipolarity to unipolarity. Second, before 9/11 matters of security were background issues in globalization, including conflict management in the global margins or geopolitics that rarely figured on the front pages, now American homeland defence and an offensive war mode define the overall terrain. From globalization centred primarily on economic dynamics (international trade, finance, development), globalisation now centers on security and geopolitics, and the whole world has become a potential background.[16]

In the globalizing world of shrinking time, shrinking space and disappearing borders, people are confronting new threats to human security – sudden and hurtful disruption in the pattern of daily life. Globalization has given new characteristics to conflict. Feeding these conflicts is the global traffic in weapons, involving new actors and blurring political and business interests. In the power vacuum of the post cold war era, military companies and mercenary armies began offering training to governments and corporations. Accountable only those who pay them, these hired military securities pose a severe threat to human security.[17] Canada's human security agenda is ultimately aimed at developing new concepts, adapting diplomatic practice and updating the institution on which the international system is based, with a view to enhancing the security of all people.[18]

The charter of the United Nations embodies the view that security cannot be achieved by a single state in isolation. The phrase "international place and security" implies that the security of one state depends on the security of other states. A human security perspective builds on this logic by nothing that the security of people in one part of the world depends on the security of people elsewhere. A secure and stable world order is built both from the top-down, and from the bottom-up. The security of states placed and security, are ultimately constructed on the foundation of people who are secure.[19]

UN specialized agencies play a crucial role in promoting human security. For example, the UN Development Programme and the World Health Organization (WHO) have been at the forefront of fighting poverty and diseases respectively. Other UN agencies such as the UN High Commissioner for Refugees (UNHCR), the UN Children's Fund (UNICEF), and the UN Development Fund for Women (UNIFEM), have played a central role in getting particular issues, such as refugees and the right of children and women, on the agenda for discussion, and in providing a platform for advocacy and action.

The concept of human security represents an ongoing effort to put the individual at the centre of national and global security concerns while expanding the range of challenges that can threaten individual safety and well being, to encompass armed conflict as well as social, economic and ecological forces. To be sure, human security has a long way to go before being universally accepted as a conceptual framework or as a policy tool for national governments and the international community. Nonetheless, there can be little doubt that threats to human security, whether understood as freedom from fear or freedom from want, are real-world challenges which cannot be wished away or dismissed because of a lack of agreement over the concept and meaning of human security.[20]

The advocates of human security find the concept to be an important step forward in highlighting the dangers to human safety and survival posed by poverty, disease, environmental stress, human rights abuses, etc. The aim of the human security agenda is to construct a global society in which the safety and well being of the individual is an international priority and a motivating force for international action : a society in which international humanitarian standards and the rule of law are advanced, woven into a coherent web, protecting the individual, where those who violate these standards are held fully accountable: and finally, a society in which our global, regional and bilateral institutions, present and future, are built and equipped to promote and enforce these standards. National security is best achieved where human security satisfactorily prevails. There is little use in accumulating weapons and military power. While people suffer from want deprivation.[21]

In conclusion we can say that human security can be achieved in that environment where all the members of family (specially women) are enjoying the equal rights of opportunities where they can develop their best selves. Clean and green environment, gender equality, cultural freedom and enjoyment, fulfillment of basic needs, freedom from hegemony of anyone else, state or any other state, any other community-all are integral part of human security.

REFERENCES

1. Walter Dorn (2011). "Human Security: An Overview". http://www.walterdorn.org/pub/23
2. C. Uday Bhaskar (1997). "Post Cold War Security". *Strategic Analysis*, Vol. XXI. No. 6. p. 196.
3. Walter Dorn. *Op. cit.*
4. C. Uday Bhaskar. *Op. cit.* p. 196
5. M.V. Naidu (1996). *Dimensions of Peace.* Oakuile, Ontario: MIT Press. p. 176.
6. Sudha Menon. "Human Security: Concept and Practice", http://mpra.ub.uni-munechen.de.pdf
7. Kanti Bajpai (2003). "The Idea of Human Security", *International Studies*, Vol. 40. p. 195.
8. Walter Dorn. *Op. cit.*
9. Sudha Menon. *Op. cit.*
10. Kanti Bajpai. *Op. cit.* p. 218.
11. M.C. Abad Jr. (2000). "The Challenge of Balancing State Security with Human Security". *The Indonesian Quarterly*, Vol. XXVIII, No. 4. pp. 403-04.

12. Bartran Bastimpilla (1998). "Role of Human Security in Regional Security and Peace in South Asia". *Regional Studies*, Vol. 16, No. 4. p. 66.

13. Kanti Bajpai. *Op. cit.* pp. 208-09.

14. John Keane (2003). *Global Civil Society*. Cambridge: Cambridge University Press. p. 2.

15. UNDP, Redefining Security (1994). http://hdr.undp.org/reports/global/1994/en/pdf

16. Jyrki Kakoven, Sanjay Chaturvedi (2005). *Globalization: Spaces, Identities and Securities*. New Delhi: South Asian Publishers.

17. HRD (1999). "Globalization with Human Face". p. 5, http//undp.org/en/reports/global/hdr1999

18. David Preston and Don Hubert (2000). "Towards Freedom From Fear: An Agenda for Human Security". *BISS Journal*, Vol. 21, No. 3. p. 351.

19. *Ibid.* p. 359.

20. Amitav Acharya (2011). "Human Security", in John Baylis, Steve Smith and Patricia Owens (eds.). *The Globalization of World Politics: An Introduction to International Relations*. Oxford: Oxford University Press. p. 492.

21. Bertram Bastiampillai (1998). "Role of Human security in Regional Security in Regional Security and Peace in South Asia". *Regional Studies*, Vol. 16. No. 4. p. 66.

10

Gender Sensitization of World Politics

The use of gender in academics has acquired great importance in social science. This issue is getting more and more importance in political science as well as in international relations. Generally, global politics deals with this issue more efficiently than IR. We live in a world which is organized around the idea that women and men have different capabilities, and different needs and desires. The first thing to deal with the distinction sociologists have made since the 1970s between sex and gender. However, it is generally agreed that gender differences are to be understood as a central feature of patriarchy, a social system in which men have become dominant in relation to women.

Gender issues have received increasing attention in many areas of the social sciences in recent decades. The starting point for introducing gender to international relations is often the debate about basic inequalities between men and women and the consequences of such inequalities for world politics. As compared to men, women are a disadvantaged group in the world. It seems that woman has been missing, as if, in the world history, society, meetings, conferences or organizations in a masculanised world.[1]

Women are rather the first to experience subordination and domination than the slaves. From the primitive times discrimination against women in society and in international relations is confirmed.

Gender-based prejudice is prevalent throughout much of the world, despite legal and other measures to overcome inequalities. The World Bank suggests that to improve this matter, 'extra efforts' must be made 'to raise awareness about culturally based attitudes' towards woman; this is because 'values, norms, and social institutions' that traditionally privilege men can also serve to reinforce persistent inequalities between males and females that in turn can become the basis of severe deprivation and conflict. Feminist agendas focus upon the lesser political position of woman compared to men. According to Gelb and Palley (1996), feminism "is a movement seeking to operationalize self-determination for woman in political, economic and social roles". Feminist concerns are increasingly reflected in political analysis, leading a growing number of political theorists explicitly to consider the issue equality assessing comparatively the nature of individual systems.[2]

Gender is misunderstood and often used as a code word for women. Hence, it draws the attention towards women. The word 'gender' comes from the English word *gender* and French word *Latin la genus*, both words mean 'kind', 'type', or sort.[3] Gender can be defined as 'masculine', 'feminine'. The use of gender word for women does draw the attention to ways in which dominant groups can normalize or naturalize their own identities. Of course men have gender too—for example 'just white people are also having race'.[4]

The terms 'gender' and 'sex' are confused. Sex is used for biological differences. Gender is used in terms of social behaviour. Gender based social behaviour is constructed in the society where women is discriminated. Hence gender is social institutionalization of sexual inequalities and being assigned to them their relative social roles. These roles are marginalized in our society such as: home cooking, child rearing, elders care. These roles deny power to women because there is no financial control in women's hands. Therefore they are the 'second sex'.

Introducing gender to IR is often the debate about basic inequalities between men and women and the consequences of such inequalities for world politics, compared to men, women as a disadvantaged group in the world. Women own about one percent of the world's property and make up less than five percent of the heads of state and cabinet ministers. Women put in about 60 percent of all working hours, but they take home 10 percent of all income. 60% of all illiterates are women. They are 80% of all refugees. The argument is that we presently live in a gendered world in which values are associated with 'masculinity' (e.g. rationality, activity, strength) are assigned higher value and status than values associated with 'femininity' (e.g. emotionality, passivity, weakness). This amounts to a gender hierarchy; a system of power in which men are privileged over women.

Fig. 10.1: Women Woes

(Figure 10.1 shows that women have many hands to do household work, child rearing, elders caring, etc., still their work is no work. This over burdened work is unpaid. Even those who are doing paid jobs along with their household responsibilities are not having control over their earnings).

The another question is "what are the consequences of gender issues for the core problems in IR?" Feminist IR scholars argue that war and peace, conflict and cooperation are gendered activities. On the one hand, the military and indeed most activities connected with war and conflict and the conduct of foreign policy are conducted by men and take place in a universe dominated by male values. Foreign policy and military policy is largely a male preserve. On the other hand, women are victims of war as wives of army men, as refugees, as prostitutes working in army bases, etc., but they are not involved in policy issues concerned with war and conflict. Therefore, gender inequality is in itself a source of conflict.

There is no doubt that the society, as it has existed until now, has made different hapless and helpless sections of the society its victims and women are not an exception. This happens not only at the local levels but throughout mankind.

If woman are the central victims of the international system as it is currently organized, there is little sense in defending that system on the basis of arguments that it provides protection to those who cannot defend themselves. Such arguments are implicitly gendered. As Cockburn states, "when men are sent to war to protect hearth and home, one of the things they will be told they die for is to keep their womenfolk safe from defilement by enemy men". The language of war, which separates the 'front' from the 'home front' has relied on the protection of the latter for its justification, and has thereby been constitutive of war. The gendered construction of war separates men and woman into 'just warriors' who protect and 'beautiful soul's who are protected.[5] The reality is very different.

The hypocritical attitude of men towards their own women and the other women makes the task rather difficult. Then, at times in the name of honour of the family or the credibility of the women, women are told to remain silent.

Due to their social conditioning, the victims of sexual violence are often hesitant to talk about it, which allows such abuse to go on undetected for years. They are further discouraged or intimidated by the fact that society normally believes that woman who undergo sexual violence are also responsible for provoking the perpetrators. Yasmeen Hassan in her study of domestic violence concludes about woman that: 'She can meet this burden only by making herself as invisible and unattractive as possible.'[6]

Gender, religion, language, ethnicity and age are recognized as highly relevant – and this is comparable with the range of factors on which feminists focuses.

The women who have perceived the lot of women community have come to realise that the attitude and behaviour of the society all around has to be changed. But has proved to be a Himalayan task and inertia prevails everywhere.

Feminists are providing important critiques of the state and state system that call into question the cognitive and philosophic underpinnings of international relations. Is war the problem and the state the solution? Or is the state is currently constructed – reproducing certain conception of masculinity – the problem and violence and domination consequences of that construction of the state?[7] The society has all along looked at homo sapiens from two angles – male and female. But they forget they are both human beings after all.

Generally, the feminist movement starting from the French Revolution (Mary Wollstonecraft wrote *Vindication of the Rights of Women* in 1792) had reached to the third wave of feminism, but in IR feminism gained ground only in the late 1980s. Cinthia Enloe (*Bananas, Beaches, and Bases: Making Feminist Senses of International Relations,* 1990); Jean Bethke Elhstain (*Women and War*, 1987), Ann Tickner and Christine Sylvester are most prominent IR radical feminists, who tried to make IR gender sensitive.

Women's experiences and ideas about world politics were rarely admitted. In an early feminist intervention in the discipline, Cynthia Enloe asked a question in 1989: 'Where are the women?' – to identify places where women are not, because they are women.[8] It means that women are invisible in the international relations, foreign policy, international organizations affairs, as they have least or no participation in international politics.

Men were constituted as just christian warriors, fighters, and defenders of righteous causes. Women, unevenly and variously depending upon social location, got solidified into a culturally sanctioned vision of virtuous, nonviolent womanhood that I call the 'beautiful soul,' drawing upon Hegel's Phenomenology. [9]

Thus, the following are the key concept related to global gender issues:

Sex: biological difference, born male or female; the sex act; sexual difference.

Gender: what it means to be male or female at a particular place or time; the social construction of sexual differences.

Gender Relations: power relations: the relational construction of masculinity and femininity, in which the masculine is usefully privileged; and which are contested, and changing.

Feminism: a political project to understand so as to change women's inequality, exploitation, or oppression. For some, aiming to move beyond gender, so that it no longer matters; for others, to validate women's interests, experiences, and choices; for others, to work for more equal and inclusive social relations overall.

Gendered Division of Labour (GDL): the notion of women's work, which everywhere includes women's primary responsibility for childcare and housework, and which designates many public and paid forms of work as 'women's' or 'men's' too.

Feminization of Labour: recognizing the increasing global demand for women as 'cheap labour', on the global assembly line and in the provision of paid as well as unpaid reproductive labour and care.

Feminist Theoretical Perspective

Realism's preoccupation with conflict, domination, and war reflects a more masculine way of thinking about human and state relations. Thus far from accepting a dog eats dog conception of autonomous states vying for supremacy as if it were a "real property of the international system, feminist argue that this is merely a masculine construction of global politics."[10] Feminist have been particularly critical of realism because they see it as a theory of international relations, *of*, *by*, and *for* men. Realism sees the world through a masculine lens but pretends to provide an 'objective' portrait of how the world works. Realism treats a world shaped by men and permeated to its core by masculine gender assumptions as a genderless and universal reality.[11]

It seems that a feminist analysis will have to re-analysed key concepts such as power, sovereignty, and reciprocity. It will ask whether male constructions of these concepts have affected how we think about international relations, and how our thinking might be changed by reflecting on the concepts.

Consider, for example, the concept of power. Morgenthau defines power rather crudely as "man's control over the minds and actions of other men". Kenneth N. Waltz views power not as a relationship but as "the old and simple notion that an agent is powerful to the extent that he affects others more than they affect him".[12]

Another feminist critique of realism concerns how realists define and emphasize power in IR discussions. Feminists would ask: who defines power, who has it, and how it is used? If power is defined by a patriarchal and realist society, which seeks global balances of power, then power is equated with military and economic strength. But how would this change if the discussion included women's viewpoints? Would the indicators of power be measured differently? Would power be seen as leadership and peace agreements, or might it be measured in terms of the ability to achieve transnational cooperation?[13]

Liberal feminism advocates equal rights for men and women. They point out that basic liberal rights of life, liberty and property have not been extended in equal measure to women. Mary Wollstonecraft wrote *Vindication of Rights of Women* in 1792, arguing that women should have the same access as men to economic opportunities and to education. Contemporary liberal feminists want women to be more active in world politics to eliminate unequal access to power and influence and achieve equal rights for men and women. Koehane advocated such a theory of IR that could examine from 'below' i.e. from the standpoint of those that have been excluded from the power.

Liberal feminism also rejects biological determinism, but rather than focusing on the similarities between man and women and the entitlement for women to the same rights and responsibilities that men enjoy. From this point of view, women can contribute in the same ways as do men with equal capability (e.g. as women leaders, soldiers, and suicide bombers) although political, economic and social structures, in addition to gender stereotypes, often block their entry into such positions.[14]

Liberal feminism has equal rights for men and women as major concern. The core concern of liberalism is the freedom and happiness of individual human beings. Liberal feminists point out that basic liberal rights of life, liberty and property have not been extended in equal measure to women. The contemporary liberal feminists want to make women more prominent in world politics, to eliminate unequal access to power and influence if men and women, and thus to achieve equal rights for men and women.[15]

Marxist feminism, as Barrett and Tong viewed, ascribes inferior position of women to the economic, social and political structures of the capitalist system. Friedrich Engels in the *Origin of Family, Private Property and State* (1884) argued that capitalism established a division between 'productive' work in the factory and 'invisible' work in the private sphere at home. Women taking care of the unpaid and invisible work. This reduced women to second class citizen. Road to equal treatment of women is an overthrow of the capitalist system. Mitchell describes that socialist feminist attempt to combine the insights of Marxists feminism with an analysis of patriarchy, i.e. a male centred and male dominated household. The oppression of women is seen to follow inevitable from the dual systems of capitalism and patriarchy. "Capitalism is the oppressive mode of production and patriarchy is the oppressive mode of reproduction."[16]

Radical feminist see women's subordination as universal, though taking different forms at different times. Some argue women are a sex-class, systematically and everywhere subject to men's sex-right, or their claims for access to their bodies, children and labour. Violence against women is seen as key to keeping women resourceless and 'in their place'. They also draw attention to sexuality as politics. Cultural feminists include those who see women as different from men, more nurturing and peaceable forces. They do not reject 'women's values', as liberal feminists do, but they argue that these values are just that world politics, and ecology, now need. Some cultural feminists are accused of essentialism, of representing these values as naturally women's and so reinforcing the gendered stereotypes that underpin women's oppression.[17]

Critical Theory: Three particular strands of what may, broadly speaking, be defined as 'critical theory' in International Relations (IR) can be identified. First, influenced by Habermas and earlier members of the Frankfurt School, Robert Cox, Andrew Linklater and other IR theorists have sought to shift the emphasis within the academic study of IR from 'positivist' and 'empiricist' perspectives that try to employ scientific methodologies (such as rational choice theory) to conceiving of theory in 'transformative' and 'emancipatory' terms. Secondly, Marxists and neo-Marxists have focused on global capitalism as the principle international structure, rather than the international anarchy favoured by realists, and on the oppressive and exploitative consequences to which they see this as giving rise. Finally, feminists, proceeding from the absences of any references to gender in most IR literature, have argued that power structures and 'discursive practice' have produced unequal and hierarchical relationship that particularly affect woman. For critical theorists, any security agenda worth its name must be primarily concerned with the quest for human emancipation. Critical theory, like feminism, therefore has a very strong normative thrust. And it is by no means simply to understand the world, but very much concerned with changing it. Another point to note is that the focus on emancipation renders critical theory a progressive modernist political project with roots in Enlightenment philosophy.[18]

There are clearly links between all the three critical perspectives as well as differences between them and indeed within each approach and are more generally applicable than the other three theories, which specially relate to international organization. However, to the degree that IGOs, quite literally in certain respects, 'institutionalize' established modes of thinking and the power structures, in these respects, they may also incorporate and legitimize existing power relations together with the inequalities and oppressions these may embody. For example, the World Bank and IMF have internalized the dominant neo-liberal economic ideas in promoting structural adjustment and other programmes that may have a severe effect on various disadvantaged groups. Kelly-Kate S. Pease has usefully distinguished different theoretical interpretations, including Marxism and feminism, of a range of IGO related issues.[19]

Emancipatory Theory: An emancipatory theory is one that recognizes that one of the goals of theory is a commitment to overthrowing an existing social order and thereby generating positive change for (particularly oppressed) groups of people. Within IR emancipatory approaches are associated with Marxists (including the work of the Neo-Gramscians) and feminism. Emancipatory theories are therefore normative theories; however, not all normative theories are emancipatory theories because they lack a commitment to radical social change.[20]

The emancipatory theories have come handy when it comes to making concerted efforts to allay the fears and worries of women. These theories have heartened the women to raise their voice and make a dent upon the agendas, decisions and policies worldwide.

Of course, we see some legislation proposing to empower the fair sex but mostly it boils down the lip-service and is a cultural setting in which the laws are supposed to be enforced, the social customs, male-dominated societies do not let them work.

Much of the feminist perspective in international politics is consistent with the constructivist perspective. Feminist constructivism examines the hidden assumptions about gender in the understating and practice of global politics. Indeed, feminist construction rejects the idea that there is a universal truth, instead arguing that gender and the way gender is defined colours different understandings of world politics. Feminists argue, for example, that international relations theorizing is largely based on masculine assumptions and reasoning. Specially, the principles of realism and its vocabulary are rather masculine in perspective. Realism's preoccupation with conflict, domination, and war, for example, reflects a more masculine way of thinking about human and state relations.[21]

We have different feminist theories of international relations. A broad kind of consensus has not been possible and we see lack of agreement among feminists on some significant issues. There is no single feminist theory of international relations. A core of concerns and beliefs may unite a variety of feminist perspectives, but there is also a range of significant issues on which feminists disagree. Rather than cataloging all the different variants of feminist thought, it is more useful to focus on the assumptions, issues, and concerns that unify most feminist analyses. Feminists of all stripes appear in agreement in their conviction that traditional approaches and research gave systemically excluded woman and issues concerned to them. For example, the literature on war in international relations could fill a large liberty. There are endless studies on whether war is more likely when only two major powers or three or more powers are present. The number of studies on how war affects the lives of woman could fit on a very small shelf.

Thus, the philosophers, statesmen, social reformers have made efforts and written in favour of giving the women an equal status, opportunity and property, they have not.

The first terrain of finding takes us to expectations people generally bring to certain types of bodies, particularly those of "woman." This is the turf of feminism: feminists theorists have continuously sought to apprehend the links between bodies, sex, gender, and power.[22] Different groups, organisations and movements have looked at their problems and the solutions, in different ways depending upon them own social, cultural and socio-economic and political and academic background.

Gender Politics and the Subordinate Status of Woman

In population conferences during the twentieth century's final decade, the critical role of women was recognized as a human rights concern, and a global consensus emerged about the need to improve the status of woman if human development was to progress. These conferences are signposts that increasingly depict women's control of their own bodies and reproductive fate as a basic human right, recognizable under international law. The conferences have educated the world to the incontrovertible evidence that woman's status in society, and especially their education, has an important influence on human development, and that woman's treatment is a global rights issue that affects everyone.[23]

As measured by the UN's Gender Empowerment Measure (GEM), woman throughout the world continue to be disadvantaged relative to men across a broad spectrum of educational statistics, such as literacy rates, school and college enrolments, and targeted educational resources. Woman, for example, enjoy less access to advanced study and training in professional fields, such as science, engineering, law, and business. In addition, within occupational groups, they are almost always in less-prestigious jobs, they face formidable barriers to political involvement, and everywhere they receive less pay than men.[24]

A great hope was pinned upon the UN system. UN Charters had sought to work for the equality of all, irrespective of sex, but the problem is that the writers, philosophers, politicians, academicians, decision-makers in the higher level happens to be males mostly while only the wearer knows where the shoe pinches.

The UN charter, in its preamble, declared their faith "in the fundamental human rights, in the dignity and worth of human person in the equal rights of men and women and of nations large and small". The UN charter also enuisages that one of the purposes is to achieve international cooperation in promoting and encouraging respect for human rights and international freedom for all people without distinction as to race, sex, language or religion. The provision of the charter regarding equal right of woman have been further refined and developed by adopting international laws and treaties on woman's rights. The UN has set a common standard for measuring how societies advance equally between men and women.[25]

A large number of treaties, conventions and conferences have materialised but UN having no coercive power to make legal sanctions possible, these have been confined mostly to the paper, e.g. UN Conference on Human Rights, Tehran (1969); International Women's Year Conference, Mexico City (1975); Convention on the Elimination of All Forms of Discrimination against Women, New York (1979); World Population Conference, Mexico (1984); UN World Conference on Human Rights, Vienna (1993); UN Fourth World Conference on Women, Beijing (1995); UN Conference on Human Rights Obligations and Multinational Corporations, Geneva (2004); UN Conference on Sexual and Reproductive Rights, New York (2004); UN Conference on Children (2005), etc.

A lot of money, efforts, time, energy, political will and the intention is needed if we have to see to it that the day comes when women would sit at the same pedestal as man and work shoulder to shoulder with man to accelerate human development and push the civilisation uphill.

For example, the first World conference for Woman in 1975 led to the creation of the UN Development Fund for Woman (UNIFEM) to support projects run by woman in developing countries. The International Research and Training Institute for the Advancement of Woman (INSTRAW) was formed in 1982, following the second women's conference. Out of the first conference also came the UN decade for

Woman (1975-1985) and a charge to ECOSOC and the specialized agencies to gather data on the status of Woman. The Platform for Action approved by the 1995 Fourth World-Conference on Woman in Beijing called for the "empowerment of all woman" through ensuring "woman's equal access to economic resources including land, credit, science and technology, vocational training, information, communication, and markets (UN 1995)."[26]

Inefficiency and corruption seem to have become the order of the day in all walks of life. The same malady ails the organisation, people and government officials when it comes to doing something for the upliftment of the women and meeting out justice to them. Inefficiency in investigation, corruption and undue influence and sometimes corruption within law enforcement hierarchy surface as other contributing factors that have created a criminal justice system that is weighted against woman victims of violence. The substantive and procedural criminal laws, as well as the culture of law enforcement of a woman's basic right to life and personal security are often trivialized in the administration of criminal justice.[27] It is unfortunate that we all the times, everywhere look at the world as male half and female half. It is enormous. The unit of analysis has to be individual not sex.

International security has always been a major concern – now, in the age of nuclear weapons and the sophistication where everyone feels insecure.

Gendering International Security

Feminist perspective on security have raised different issues, engaged in different debates and used different methodologies from traditional international security studies. Feminists have questioned the foundational stories of IR on which explanations about the 'security dilemma' have analyzed the 'masculinity' of strategic discourse and its consequences for strategic policy. Examining the effects of war on women, they have challenged the claim that women are a 'protected category'. They have also entered into the long-standing debate as to whether women are more peaceful than men; recently, an emerged empirical literature is linking this debate to the issue of the democratic peace.[28] The trafficking of women and children is a stigma on the bad face of our society.

An estimated 1.2 million women and girls enter global commercial sex marked every year (UNDP, 2000) through human trafficking, of whom 35 percent are estimated to be under 18. Ranked as the third most serious illegal trades after drugs and weapons, it is considered a modern form of slavery. Human trafficking is the illegal moving and selling of human beings across countries and continents in exchange for financial or other compensation. Trafficking often involves coercion, deception, and even abduction.[29]

Women can hope to see themselves in a better position only if they too get the opportunities to attain, maintain and translate their power into action. But all is not well in the field too. The UN Charter recognizes that everyone has the right to take part in the government of his country directly or, indirectly through freely chosen representatives. The UN has consistently advocated that addressing the issue of equal rights for women is a means to solving a number of socio-economic problems, including uncontrolled population growth and non-sustainable development. It is now widely accepted that investing in women leads to higher economic growth, better and higher education for entire nations.[30] What appeals is the observation by the international feminist lobby that the colonial racial order was also gendered. Is the neo-colonization suffering from the same malady? This can be a useful, interesting and fruitful exercise, if future researchers apply their minds to this problem. Colonialism was emasculating. A transnational perspective (of the feminist nature) is emerging that contains the intersection of race and gender. This would offer a richer analysis than a perspective that examines race alone.

Feminists supportive of women's international rights have often embraced the "first generation" of human rights with caution. As the political rights of the UN declaration, these remain most closely associated with liberal assumptions about individuals and seem insensitive to the economic and family-centre forms of oppression that historically have hindered women's choices. The UN declaration has changed over time, adding rights and promoting institutions that now attempt to overcome social and economic disadvantages based on gender. While resistance to acknowledge, economic rights has not always been encouraging, many now say that the current commitment to women's rights looks more proposing. As a result, today's practical advances should eliminate earlier theoretical quibbles and contentious charges that rights operate with a "masculine," Western bias, and need not prove terribly damaging.[31]

Gendering Globalization: Applying a 'gender lens' to globalization, to reveal that women are differently positioned in relation to globalization processes and differently impacted upon by them; and that women become global players in response to these gendered effects.[32]

New configuration of feminist practice through the discourse of human rights, the increased representation of women in parliaments and cabinets around the world and by increased theoretical interest in conceptualising the complexities of the issue of representation and the state[33] are significant trends due to globalization. Feminist political activists have been important players in the construction of newly globalized world. New kinds of alliances, political forms, political strategies and substantive fields have been involved in the context of changing gendered global power relations. Feminists are increasingly using transnational networks to pressure national parliaments.[34] It is now realised that alongwith other social dimensions, gender too should be incorporated into foreign policy.

Gender is a social dimension which can bear on foreign policy, but even more indirectly. The concern with gender which has burgeoned in IR studies over the past fifteen years has primarily been a normative and philosophical one. There are important cases to be made about the differential sufferings of women in development, and about their neglected part in war. The view that orthodox thinking about international relations has been too suffused with masculnist value also has a great deal to be said for it.[35]

We should admit that if men are more aggressive, women have more patience; if men are competitive, women are co operative; if men are violent, women are peaceful; if men are rational, women are loving; and if women are nurturing, men are emotionally distant. To be men means not to be a woman. The distinct attributes of women are to be appreciated for peaceful, non-violent and healthy world politics behaviour.

REFERENCES

1. Mary Holmes (2007). *What is Gender? Sociological Approaches*. New Delhi: Sage Publications. p. 2.
2. Jeffrey Haynes (2005). *Comparative Politics in a Globalizing World*. Cambridge: Polity. p. 287.
3. Robert Jackson and Georg Sorenson (2008). *Introduction to International Relations*. New Delhi: Oxford University Press. p. 272.
4. "Gender Identity". *Encyclopedia Britannica*. http://en.wiki.org/feminism
5. J.B. Elhstain (1987). *Women and War*. New York: Basic. p. 7
6. Hina Jilani and Eman M. Ahmad (2004). "Violence against Women: The Legal System and Institutional Responses in Pakistan", in Savitri Goonesekere (ed.). *Violence, Law and Women's Rights in South Asia*. New Delhi, London: Sage. p. 164.
7. Jean Bethke Elhtain (2006). "Reflections on War and Political Discourse: realism, just war, and feminism in a Nuclear Age", in Richard Little and Michael Smith (eds.). *Perspectives on World Politics*. London, New York: Routledge. p. 371.
8. Jan Jindey Pitman (2005). "Gender", in John Baylis and Steve Smith (eds.). *The Globalization of World Politics: An Introduction to International Relations*. New Delhi: Oxford University Press. p. 670.
9. Jean Bethke Elhtain (2006). *Op. cit.* p. 371.
10. James Lee Ray and Juliet Kaarbo (2002). *Global Politics*. Boston, New York: Houghton Mifflin Company. pp. 18-19.
11. Keith L. Shimko (2005). *International Relations Perspectives and Controversies*. Boston, New York: Houghton Miffin Company. p. 62.

12. Robert O' Keohane (1989). "International Relations Theory: Contributions of a Feminist Standpoint". *Millennium: Journal of International Studies*, Vol. 18, No. 2. p. 246.
13. Ruiz Tricia. "Feminist Theory and International Relations: The Feminist Challenge to Realism and Liberalism". http//www.csustan.edu/honors/documents/journalspdf
14. James Lee Ray and Juliet Kaarbo. *Op. cit.* p. 21.
15. Robert Jackson and Georg Sorenson (2003). *Op. cit.* p. 278.
16. *Ibid.* p. 279.
17. Jan Jindey Pitman (2005). *Op. cit.* p. 673.
18. Stephanie Lawson (2004). *International Relations.* Cambridge: Polity Press. p. 88.
19. David Armstrong, Lorna Lloya and John Redmond (2004). *International Organisation in World Politics.* New Hemisphere: Palgrave, Macmillan. p. 13.
20. Peter Sutch and Juanita Elias (2007). *Basics International Relations.* London, New York: Routledge. p. 181.
21. James Lee Ray and Juliet Kaarbo. *Op. cit.* p. 18.
22. Jean Bethke Elhtain (2006). *Op. cit.* pp. 371-72.
23. Jan Jindey Pitman (2005). *Op. cit.* p. 685.
24. Charles W. Kegley (2007). *World Politics Trend and Transformation.* Belmont (USA): Thomson Wadsworth. p. 239.
25. Nisar-ul-Haq (January-March 2005). "The United Nations and Elimination of Discrimination against Women". *The Indian Journal of Political Science.* Vol. LXVI. No. 1. p. 103.
26. Margaret P. Karns and Karen A. Mingst (2005). *International Organisations: The Politics and Processes of Global Governance.* New Delhi etc.: Viva Books. p. 86.
27. Savitri Goonesekere. *Op. cit.* p. 56.
28. J. Ann Tickner (2002). "Feminist Perspectives on International Relations", in Walter Carlsnaes et al. (eds.). *Handbook of International Relations.* London, New Delhi: Sage. p. 283.
29. Jini L. Roby (March 2005). "Women and Children in the Global Sex Trade". *International Social Work.* Vol. 48. No. 2. p. 136.
30. Nisar-ul-Haq. *Op. cit.* p. 105.

31. Ellen M. Freebery (2004). "Translating a Liberal Feminism Revisiting Susan Okin on Freedom, Culture and Women's Rights", in Mahmood Monshipouri et al. (eds.). *Constructing Human Rights in the Age of Globalisation*. New Delhi: Prentice Hall. p. 89.
32. Jan Jindy, Pettman. "Gender Issues", in John Baylis. *Op. cit.* p. 685.
33. Sylvia Walby (2002). "Feminism in Global Politics". *Economy and Society*. www.informaworld.com. p. 534.
34. Ann Philips (1995). *The Politics of Presence: The Political Representation of Gender, Ethnicity and Race*. New York: Oxford University Press. p. 5.
35. Christopher Hill (2003). *The Changing Politics of Foreign Policy*. New Hampshire: Palgrave, Macmillan. p. 243.

11

Environment: Contrasting Conceptions and Global Responsibility

The concept of security has traditionally been related more to states than to people. Since the seventeenth century, when the current system of states began to emerge, international security has been understood and practiced with reference to the needs and interests of states. Although, in its early origins, the state was conceived as an instrument for producing security for its citizens, it became the subject of security with the establishment and retrenchment of the state-system. Notwithstanding the alternative conceptions of security that have always existed, this stale-based and external-directed conception of security has prevailed and shaped the practices of governments. Critical voices calling for the importance of protecting human beings or the global environment aside, twentieth-century thinking and practices concerning security were characterized by this way of thinking. The emphasis the United Nations has put on sovereignty and the inviolability of territorial boundaries can be viewed as an indication of the institutionalization of this approach.

Even though state-based conceptions of security have taken precedence, alternative ways of thinking that give priority to individual and societal dimensions of security have also been proposed. Security was not to be thought only from military point of view. So multisectoral approach was suggested to the study of security. Five sectors are identified: the military sector, the environmental sector, the economic sector, the societal sector and the political sector. Each of these may be securitized, yet they are likely to display distinctive patterns of interaction in this process.[1]

It has been argued that the conceptualization of security underlying traditional security studies:

- Tends to reify the prevailing status quo because of its scientific objectivist epistemology (and, indeed, is a paradigmatic example of Horkshimer's traditional theory).
- Is as historical and deeply resistant to notions of contingency and change because of its state-centric ontology.
- Is blind to the way in which notions of security are dependent on deeper assumptions concerning the nature of politics.
- Focuses exclusively on a narrowly understanding of security.[2]

Time and again, thus, the world was reminded of its narrow understanding of the concept of security. A holistic approach was needed if the nest was to be kept clean and intact.

Thus, now environmental security is high on the agenda in many places, partly because of the high density and small size of units in Europe making many environmental issues border-crossing: e.g., the Danube dam, nuclear power plants in the former east, air pollution mostly blowing eastwards, and upstream pollution (such as that of Swiss medical giants) threatening downstream areas along the Rhine. These issues does not so far tie much into the two master discourses, although the EU has made some attempts to merge integration and environmentalism.[3] Proper international legislation, its execution and enforcement was obligatory.

The conditions and influences of the area in which an organism lives is called its environment. The relationship between living organisms and their environment forms part of the subject of ecology. "Concern that large parts of the physical environment are suffering from misuse and over-exploitation is central to conservation."[4]

By the twentieth century, environmental issues had been on the international agenda for a whole generation of political leaders, government officials, scientists and concerned citizens.[5] Environmental problems threaten the globe. Some ecological problems threaten the globe. Some ecological problem, such as global warming, actually carry claims to globality in the very name by which they are known, while other problems such as acid rain, lend themselves to depiction in terms of threats to the well being of the planet. No humans and virtually no plants or animals are exempted from these problems.[6]

Fig. 11.1: Human Activity and Ocean Imbalances

Global environmental change has the potential to have serious impacts on human food security, economic security and health security. As with many other issues – managing the global economy, human rights, combating diseases, such as HIV/AIDS, and controlling terrorism and the proliferation and global spread of weapons of mass destruction – the global environment represents a series of problems that are so complex

Map VI: Environmental Degradation

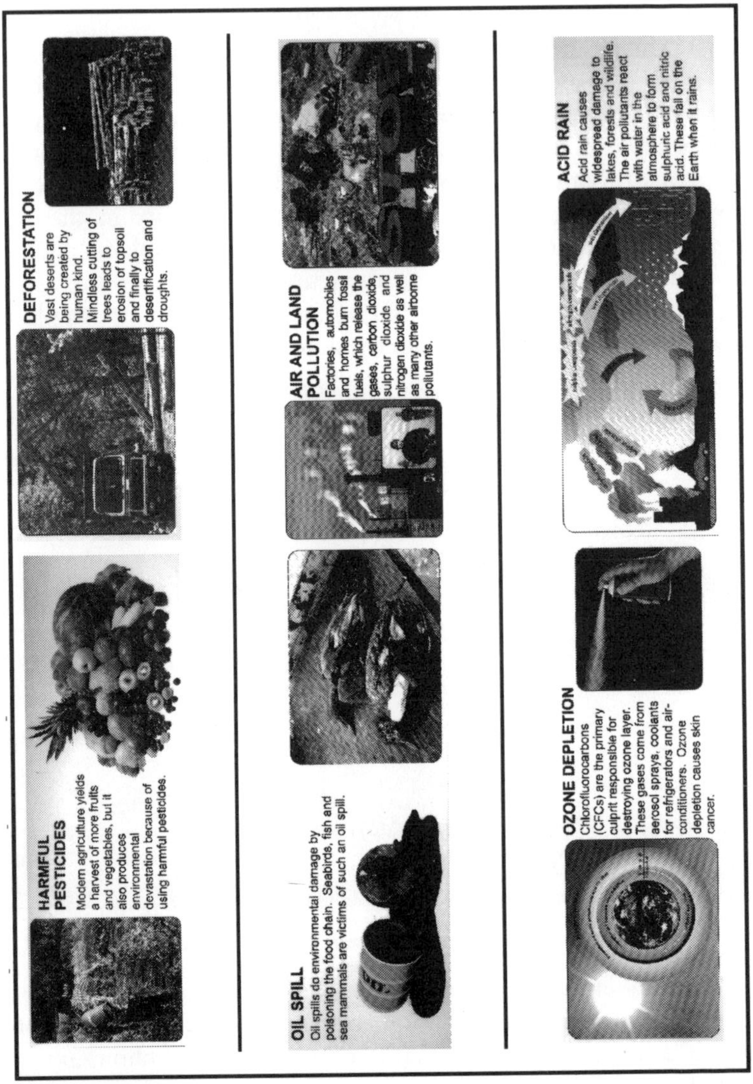

and widespread that unilateral measures or measures overtaken by countries acting on their own initiatives are not enough to prevent them. With the advent of modern technologies in the twentieth century, scientists increased their capacity to measure and predict the extent of human impact on the atmosphere, the burning of fossil fuel, the omission of ozone depletion substances, or long range air pollution, etc. Ozone layer depletion and climate change are invisible to the naked eyes, but their impacts are very real, and in a sense, represent the tragedy of commons.[7]

The environmental effects of development were apparent soon. Unlike "environmentalist" issues, in affluent parts of the first world, the notion of access to the "environment", in non-elite sections of the developing world, is inextricable from demands for economic and social justice. Excessive pollution can kill – it violates individuals' right to life. Less immediate, but just as severe, has been the destruction of life wrought by development projects in areas where residents have had little outside contact. Diseases to which locals have had little immunity are brought in by project workers; the sudden impact of human flows brought by the project's roads and infrastructure is devastating to human lives and environments. Less direct still, but again just as severe are the effects of patenting on the prices of drugs and pharmaceuticals. Multinational control of patented drugs tends to price medicines outside, the affordable range for working and middle-class people in the developing world, often excluding them from life-saving medications and resulting in their untimely and avoidable death.

The major theoretical perspective for understanding global politics can shed light on international environmental cooperation, even though it is a fairly new area in world politics. In looking at the prospects for environmental cooperation, realism, for example, would expect cooperation to be very difficult, given states' self-interested motivations to guard their power and autonomy. Furthermore, environmental issues are the stuff of "low politics" and do not demand the attention of states compared to "high politics", such as national defense. When cooperation does occur, realism would expect international agreements to reflect the interests of the most powerful states strongly. On the issue of climate change, for example, realists would point out the influence of the

United States. In the negotiations on the Framework Convention on Climate Change, "the United States opposed the others (particularly a number of European countries) that wanted a timetable for greenhouse gas emission reductions. Largely because of the U.S. position, the members of the international community could only agree to the provision that industrialized countries would try to ensure that their greenhouse gas emissions in the year 2000 were no higher than they were in 1990."[8] A European Community Scheme was introduced in 1985 to protest area of ecological and landscape importance from drainage and loss caused by agriculture largely. Realism is providing an account of the historically remarkable degree of international environmental cooperation. The interstate conflict is resulting from the impact of environment degradation on the balance of power or there is failure to agree on the management of a particularly important environmental problem. Such a perspective runs the risk of missing the most important dimensions of environmental security. The risk of environmental degradation is undermining the social fabric of weak states and provoking internal social disruption and violence.[9]

Liberals remain inclined to believe the reality of ecological interdependence. Problems can be solved only by new and more far reaching mechanism of cooperation. Moreover the liberal advocate increased scientific understanding of environmental problems that will work to reduce state interests and to facilitate international cooperation.[10] Thus liberals or neo-liberals find the solution in the advanced eco friendly technology instead of change in consumption or production patterns.

Thus, modernists consider environment as not a very big problem. Progress in knowledge and technology will enable us to protect the environment. According to them more people and increased income produce problems in the short run. These problems present opportunity, and prompt the search for solutions. In a free society, solutions are eventually found, though many people fall along the way at cost to themselves. In the long run the new developments leave us better off than if the problems had not arisen.[11]

The Marxists blame capitalism (as mode of production), is instrumental in the environmental degradation. The humanist eco-Marxists reject that Marxist view of technology which envisages the idea that some level of production may have to be foregone for the sake of environment. Merely overthrowing the capitalist class is insufficient according to this eco-Marxist. The proletariat government must also limit its destruction of the environment. This group advocates that technology and development which is for the sake of mastering the nature.

In the 1970s, feminists drew parallels between male control over nature and men's control over women as connected. Masculine's science and industrialization assault on the ecological health of the planet. According to Carolyn Merchant, the roots of the world's environmental dilemma to the world view was developed by the founding fathers of modern science that conceptualised reality as a machine rather than as a living organism. This conceptualisation had resulted in the death of nature as a living being and acceleration of the exploitation of human and natural resources in the name of culture and progress.[12]

There is now a well-developed literature on Green Political Theory (GPT) which provides a useful base for Green Ideas about IR. Three major works suggest slightly different ideas about the defining characteristics of Green Politics. Eckersley suggests that the defining characteristic is egocentrism – the rejection of an anthropocentric world-view, which places moral value only on humans in favour of one which places independent value also on ecosystems and all living beings. Goodin also places ethics at the centre of the Green position, suggesting that a 'Green theory of view' is at the core of Green political theory. His formulation is that for a Green theory of value, the source of value in things is the fact that they have a history of having been created by natural process rather than by artificial human ones.[13]

Eckersley (1992, Environmentalism and Political Theory: Towards an Ecocentric Approach), an ecoradical, opines that only ecocentric Green Political theory is capable of providing the kind of comprehensive framework we need to use in a lasting resolution to the ecological crisis. An ecocentric polity would be one in which there is a democratic state legistature; a great dispersal of political and economic power both within and between communities; a far more extensive range of marco-controls on market activity; and the flowering of an ecocentric emancipatory culture. Therefore, environment is a very serious problem. Dramatic change of lifestyle plus population control to promote sustainable development is necessary.

Dobson has two defining characteristics of Green Politics. One is the rejection of anthropocentrism, as outlined by Eckersley. The other, however, is the 'limits to growth' argument about the nature of the environmental crisis. Greens suggest that it is the exponential economic growth experienced during the last two centuries which is at the root cause of the current environmental crisis. Thus it is not the belief in an environmental crisis which is defining, but the particular (and unique) understanding which Greens have of the nature of that crisis which makes them distinctive.[14]

One distinguished personality Mahatma Gandhi should be considered as an eco-radical environmentalist. Although he had not directly touched the environment issue but his views were highly environment friendly. He was against urbanization and had firm faith in nature and decentralised self sustained village economy. He was badly against western model of development which was based on industrialization, machine and technology. He said, "Machine is like a snake hole which may contain from one to hundred snakes. Where there is machinery there are large cities... Honest physicians will tell you that where means of artificial locomotion have increased the health of the people suffered".[15] He further said, "The west had a surfeit of industrialism and exploitation.... The fact is that this industrial civilization is a disease because it is all evil".[16] According to him, "Industrialism is, I am afraid, going to be a curse for mankind.... The future of Industrialism is dark".[17] Gandhi was extremely against western model and wished, "Our concern is therefore is to destroy industrialism at any cost".[18] Thus Gandhian thought envisaged a world which is based on equality, manual labour, simplicity and without the evil industrialism.

The United Nations projects that world population will increase from 5.7 billion in 1992 to 12.5 billion in the middle of the next century. In the last half century, the world's population has doubled and its economy has increased fivefold. In a world of global markets, shortages of food and water cease to be a matter of purely local or national concern, and the destruction of environmental capital, through overuse or, by contamination of waste products, reduces the world's long-term carrying capacity for everyone.[19]

Environmental rights in this sense are different in kind from biocentric 'rights of nature', or from legislation protecting the right of 'the environment' to be protected from human harm. In each, of, the cases mentioned above, the human right to life cannot be defended without intervening if the process by which privatization and degradation of a resource occur at the hands of an institution that has no local accountability.[20] All human beings have a fundamental right to freedom, equality and adequate environment. Conditions of life in an environment of quality that permits a life of dignity and well being and bears a solemn responsibility to protect and improve the environment for present and future generations. A new development approach became the need of the hour.

World Commission on Environment and Development (WCED) is headed by the then Prime Minister Gro Harlem Brundtland of Norway and is composed of eminent persons. Its task was to formulate a new development approach around the concept of sustainable development. The 1987 Brundtland Commission Report (World Commission 1987 – Our Common Future) called for development for the present without compromising the needs of future generations.[21]

The oceans were the first areas to be recognized as global commons. Seaborne commerce, warfare and fishing have engendered a long history of international conflict and attempts at rule making. Traditionally, national jurisdiction extended to three-miles limit, and beyond that the oceans were open to free use. The rights and rules and the prevailing technology is well illustrated.

The oceans had suffered due to oil spills, over-fishing, dumping of garbage. The pearls of Bosra, thus, were no more available, the shells which had previously yielded pearls of the highest quality lay empty. The world agreed to sign treaties.

Indeed, this could take the form of a global charter of social rights, an authoritative interpretation of the Covenants aimed at translating the general and abstract principles of social rights into specific and attainable social standards worldwide.[22] It was thought that the entire tree was responsible even if a single leaf turned yellow.

The encouragement that globalization lends to normative reflection comes from a perception that it further breaks down those very intellectual barriers that have traditionally held it at bay. While IR theory has, of course, been prepared to countenance the idea of 'duties beyond borders', it was always coy about doing so and realized that this entailed, in the very act, a step across a still significant moral boundary. To the extent that globalization enjoins us to be less preoccupied with territories and borders, it creates a more hospitable intellectual atmosphere within which to advance the normative project. Unhappily, it does so by simplification.[23]

The cold war has hindered a number of joint actions. Thus, they could not shake hands. But a normative longing witnessed cooperation even during conflict.

Until the late 1980s, the Soviet Union and the United States acknowledged few shared interests. Nevertheless, even during the 'new cold war' of the Reagan-Brezhnev era the superpowers possessed sufficient common interest to make the states-system work. For example, they demonstrated a common interest in the solution of many relatively non-political problems, in fields such as transport and communications (including space exploration), and disease and pollution control (with particular attention, following the Chernobyl meltdown, to nuclear power stations). But, vastly more important, the superpowers shared an interest in the avoidable of nuclear war.[24]

Biodiversity has become a hot global issue, and the magnitude of the danger has spread geographically because human activity has disrupted or destroyed many biologically rich areas. Scientists describe the current era as the greatest period of mass extinction since the disappearance of the dinosaurs. Thousands of plant and animal species already have disappeared because of the degradation of their environments.[25]

The major problems like security, stability, peace, environment and development were all interconnected. Stable peace is a relationship between two in which neither side considers employing force, or even making a threat of force, in any dispute, even serious disputes, between them. Deterrence and compellence backed by threats of force are simply excluded as instruments of policy. Two states that enjoy stable peace may continue to have serious disputes, but they share a firm understanding that such disputes must be dealt with by nonmilitary means. For example, in the Suez crisis of 1956, President Eisenhower made strong, credible threats of economic sanctions to purpose the British to withdraw their forces from the Suez Canal area.[26]

Why do only of the many human impacts on the global environment capture international political and policy attention? Who do some that receive policy attention later 'vanish without a trace' while others are actively addressed? And, what determines how issues are discussed, whether in economic, moral, equity, or other framings?[27]

The carrying capacity of the Mother Earth was limited but the Homo-sapiens-centred thought and behaviour overlooked the fact that all life is one and man had flourished at the cost of other animals and plant species. Malthus predicted that it would lead to the vengeance of the nature.

More than twice as many people inhabit the earth today as when the post-war era began, indeed, more people have been added to the world's population in the past five decades than in all the previous millennia of human existence.... Developing countries already have 78 percent of the people in the world; as much as 94 percent of the current increase is also taking place in these countries. Evidence has accumulated of widespread ecological degradation resulting from human activity: soils losing fertility or being eroded, overgrazed grasslands, desertification, dwindling fisheries, disappearing species, shrinking forests, polluted air and water. These have been joined by the newer problems of climate change and zone depletion (The Commission on Global Governance, 1995).[28]

The Policies of the International Environment Regimes

One of the first principles of traditional international law is that state sovereignty involves control over natural resources and local economic activity. Some such principle is implied by the nature of modern state unlike, for example, some medieval institutions, contemporary political forms have been territorial since at least the seventeenth century, and territoriality involves a claim of ownership over natural resources. Moreover, the nature of capitalist economies as they have developed over the same time period has been such that it was inevitable that in the advanced industrial countries 'ownership' would not be interpreted as 'stewardship' but as 'dominion'. Natural resources were there to be exploited for gain by landowners, the state, and perhaps, at least in modern welfare capitalist societies, the people. However, even in the latter case, 'the people' means 'citizens of the state in question' and not people generally: until comparatively recently, the idea that a state might be held accountable for economic activities conducted on its territory would have seemed incompatible with the first principles of the system.[29]

One is tempted to spell it out in clear words that the inherent breeding instinct of the female of the species has manifested itself in the form of a positive input because the heart of the feminists goes out to peace, sustainable development and protection of the species.

Our activities are more closely linked than ever before, from what we produce, consume, or watch on television to diseases like AIDS or environmental problems like global warming that affects health and well-being. Values and ideas such as equity, human rights and social justice are gradually spreading through international agencies, the internet and people to people contact. Moreover, the 'unprecedented intensity' of global linkages have blurred distinctions 'between international and domestic, external and internal affairs'. US agricultural subsidies and trade adversely affect the lives of thousands of small farmers in Mexico and steel tariffs may harm Brazilian workers.[30]

The developed world with the so-called scientific approach has sought to tame nature but let us learn how to live in harmony with nature otherwise more titanic wrecks, nuclear disasters, tsunamis, earthquakes, landslides and famines. "The environment security was the primary example in academic rethinking of security, and was picked up by the policy side".[31]

Environment issues emerged in the late twentieth century as a major focus of international concern and activity. They relate to globalization themes in several ways. Many environment problems are intrinsically international or global, stimulating international political activities in response. Others, through local, are experienced across the world. Virtually all environmental issues are intimately linked to the dynamics of globalized political economic process. Much international political activity related to the environment has focused on the development and environment and implementation of these regimes, involving a wide range of actors and process. Since the late 1980s and particularly since the UNCED summit in 1992, many international political processes have engaged with the linked issues of development and environment, and the contested notion of sustainable development. By the end of the 1990s, the relationship between the WTO regimes to promote and govern a globalized market economy and international environmental regimes was high on the political agenda, influencing the design of the rules of environment regimes as well as providing a focus for political mobilization and dispute. Although established perspectives within international relations theory provide important insights into the character and outcomes of such activities, international environmental issue nevertheless pose significant new challenges for students of international relations.[32] Let us take a pledge as students, scholars and statesman to undo the harm done by politicians, the so-called warriors whose behaviour is like that of cheetahs and parrots who destroy more and bite more than what they can chew. The lion is a gentleman and is contented with only that much that is required to keep its body and soul together. One is reminded of small-sized book by Dr. Merodith, *The Choice is Yours*.

Some scholars predict that political parties are in inexorable decline as representative bodies and effective political actors and will largely be replaced by NGOs. Others contend that if political parties manage to incorporate support from new organizations and social movements and adapt their agendas to face new issues, they will retain their niche against the inroads of NGOs. For Tarrow, in either case, the outcome will be affected by "the institutional context in which both parties and NGOs operate and by the issues by they deal with". The case of organizing opinion in representative systems and finding legitimate channels for its expression induces many movements to turn to elections. Over time, "a movement turns into a party or enters a party in order to influence its policies.... At its most successful, the electoral strategy produced Green parties in parts of northern Europe, parties that rapidly become part of the parliamentary game of politics."[33] However, despite some often limited successes, green parties have rarely done well in domestic elections in Europe, often because electrical systems were a disadvantage to them, while many voters still see politics as chiefly about setting traditional questions that focus on economic distributive issues.[34] Mahatma Gandhi, who was showered by praise by Einstein (whose letter to Roosevelt, though led to nuclear attack by US on Japan) may have the answer.

It is true that the environmental problems are more challenging today than ever before. Its also a reality that we have to fight against the menace. In search of different approaches to tackle environmental challenges, we are naturally attracted towards the Gandhian approach. Nowaday Gandhian ideas, approaches and alternatives to social transformation and development are a debate of global concern. The voluminous writings of Mahatma Gandhi are replete with references to his concern for protection and preservation of environment. However, only a few writers recognize Gandhi as an early environmentalist. But it would be quite appropriate to call Mahatma Gandhi as one of the champions of environment protection. The life and work of Gandhi have had a considerable influence on the contemporary environmental movements in India. The movement truly began with the 'Chipko Andolan' in April 1973. From the 'Chipko Andolan' to 'Narmada Bachao Andolan', environment activists have relied heavily on Gandhian techniques of non-violent protest, and have drawn abundantly on Gandhi's polemic against heavy industrialization.[35]

Some key global treaties establishing environmental treaty regimes:

- 1972 Convention for the Protection of the World Cultural and Natural Heritage.
- 1973 Convention on International Trade in Endangered Species of Wild Fauna and Flora.
- 1979 Convention on the Conservation of Migratory Species of Wild Animals.
- 1979 Convention on Long Range Transboundary Air Pollution.
- 1982 Third United Nations Convention on the Law of the Sea, Part XII.
- 1985 Convention for the Protection of the Ozone Layer.
- 1986 Convention on Early Notification of a Nuclear Accident.
- 1989 Convention on the Control of Transboundary Movements of Hazardous Wastes and their Disposal.
- 1992 Framework Convention on Climate Change.
- 1992 Convention on the Protection and Use of Transboundary Watercourses and Lakes.
- 1992 Convention on Biological Diversity.
- 1997 Kyoto Protocol.
- 2001 Stockholm Convention on Persistent Organic Pollutants.
- 2009 Copenhagan failed Conference.

Something concrete in tangible terms was required. Thus, action was needed and talking only was not sufficient.The Kyoto Treaty has been a big landmark but the contrasting conceptions, narrow-thinking, a neck to neck race (as if against time) of the so-called rapid development seemed to come in the way.

On climate change, IPCC was created by the United Nations Environment Programme (UNEP) and the World Meteorological Organization (WMO) to assess the scientific knowledge on global warming. The IPCC concluded in 1990 that there was broad international consensus that climate change was human-induced. That report led way to an international convention for climate change, the United Nations Framework Convention on Climate change (UNFCCC), signed by over 150 countries at the Rio Earth Summit in 1992.[36]

Kyoto Treaty

One of the most controversial policy issues in recent years has been the Kyoto Treaty on global warming. Signed in 1997, the treaty was designed to reduce the emission of the greenhouse gases that cause global warming.

In 1997, at the Conference of Parties III (COP_3), Kyoto, Japan, the Kyoto conference on climate change took place. There, developed counties agreed to specific targets for cutting their emissions of greenhouse gases. A general framework was defined for this, with specifics to be detailed over the next few years. This became known as the Kyoto protocol. The US proposed to just stabilize emission and not to cut them at all, while the European Union called for a 15% cut. In the end, there was a trade off, and industrialized counties were committed to an overall reduction of emissions of greenhouse gases to 5.2% below 1990 levels for the period 2008-2012. (The Intergovernmental Panel on climate change said in its 1990 report that a 60% reduction in emissions was needed...) as with the following COP meetings, there was enormous media propaganda by affected big businesses and by counties such as the US who were openly hostile to the treaty.

Infact, one of the first things George Bush did when he came to power was to oppose the Kyoto Protocol. In 2001, however, President George W. Bush announced that he would not submit the treaty for senate ratification. This policy reversal by the United States unleashed a chorus of criticisms abroad, especially in Europe. The Kyoto process and treaty highlighted many of the issues and uncertainties of scientific models and predictions, ideological disagreements about solutions. The obstacles to dealing with these problems in a world of sovereign states became clear. Two statements: the first is by then Vice President Albert Gore expressing support for the Kyoto process shortly before the agreement was signed. The second is the text of President George W. Bush's statement announcing his decision not to seek senate ratification of the agreement. What lessons can we learn from the obstacles to solving commons problems on a global scale?[37] The US objection to Kyoto Protocol was that developing countries like India and China are not party of it. On the other side, India and China which had not been responsible for the historical emissions to the atmosphere, were not required to reduce emissions. Although the treaty is useless on the US side but the European Union ratified it on May 31, 2002. Russia also unilaterally accepted it.

Moreover, the Copenhagen Conference revealed again the US behaviour towards Kyoto Protocol. To keep the process online, conference in Copenhagan was held in December 2009. The parties of the UNFCCC (United Nations Framework Convention on Climate Change) meet for the last time on government level need to be renewed. Therefore the Climate Conference in Copenhagan was essential for the world climate perseverance, the Danish government and the UNFCCC has been putting hard effort in making the meeting in Copenhagan a success for preventing global warming and climate change. But it is considered failed because it did not mention any figures of the emission reductions that the developed countries are to undertake after 2012. This failure at attaining reduction commitments is the biggest failure of the document. Some process seems to have been made, thus. But there is always a scope for more.

Since the Rio Earth Summit, threats to human health and environment quality have continued to grow steadily. These threats are contributed to by many factors including the changing patterns and scale of industrial production and of the use of natural resources. UNEP's work on economic instruments aims to help society to address these threats and to transition to more sustainable patterns of economic development.[38]

The politics have clearly yielded place to political economy. Economic instruments have a number of advantages. If implemented properly and often in combination with command and control approaches – they can help to:

- Increase prices of environmentally damaging goods and services, as well as increase the returns to more sustainable approaches leading to more sustainable production and consumption patterns;
- Reduce compliance costs by providing flexibility to polluters or users of natural resources to choose the most cost-efficient and environmentally effective measures;
- Minimize the overall cost of achieving a given pollution control target;
- Create dynamic incentives for investments to innovate and continually improve environmental technology, generating both environment and financial benefits ("win-win");
- Allocate property rights and responsibilities of firms, groups, or individuals so that they have both the incentive and the power to act in a more environmentally-responsible manner; and
- Raise revenues that can be used for environmental purposes or for social benefits (e.g. decreasing income taxes). The practical strengths of economic instruments have been demonstrated in both developed and developing countries, including through a number of UNEP case studies.[39]

If we have some noble souls guiding us, why not listen to them?

The guidance document on economic instruments, developed by UNEP, will provide a starting point for evaluating better ways to identify and apply economic instruments to environmental problems, especially in the developing world. Additional learning in number of core areas will be essential to improve the understanding and use of economic instruments. These include more detailed analysis of the ways that economic instruments can support poverty reduction and bridge income disparities, ways to improve implementation, monitoring and enforcement and means to build institutional capacity to design and apply them. UNEP will continue to seek guidance from its working group on how to address these issues in its further work programme.[40]

One is heartened to see some developments on the positive side. See the UNEP network.

UNEP is currently setting up a network collaborating institutions which would assume responsibility to:

- Customize the manual, reflecting regional requirements and cases;
- Distribute the manual and support its use for EIA training in the regions;
- Facilitate the launch of regional workshops to introduce the manual; and
- Monitor and report back on development and experience, through the internet. Collaborating instructions so far identified are:
  - Asian Institute of Technology, (AIT), Thailand
  - Centro Agronomico Tropical de Investigaciony Ensenanza (CATIE), Costa Rica
  - Regional Environment Centre for Central and Eastern Europe (REC), Hungary
  - Southern African Institute for Environmental Assessment (SAIFA), Namibia.[41]

UN efforts are praiseworthy but UN seems to have become an exclusive club. Now it seems to be dominated by the only 'Superpower'. The way out could be international stances even outside the framework of the United Nations which at times look like divided nations.

Generally, centralised decision making agencies regarding environment are powerful to impose their will and languages on others. These agencies are obviously dominated by the technocrat industrialized north. The call for community control is a threat to their power and at worst a recipe for indecision and muddling through to ecological disaster. But the evidence is overwhelming those local level institutions in which power is limited and the common right to survival is the preoccupation of all. They are the best means of repairing the 'damage done through enclosure.

Peace and environmental security is indispensable if we watch the ground reality. The formation of geopolitics accompanying the rise of the modern state occurred long prior to the realization that the continuation and extension of industrial civilization in the context of an expanding danger to health and well-being, threatening human survival. In contrast, the perspectives of global civil society that underpin the groping toward humane governance have been formed with a vivid awareness of ecological constraints on human activities, so much so that it is common for citizen pilgrims to emphasize their loyalty to the earth as strongly as their membership in a global community that can be glimpsed at the horizons of human aspiration.[42]

One of the best-known movements to arise in recent times, however, is certainly focused on the global sphere, and that is the amorphous collection of groups which together constitute the 'anti-globalization movement'. In some ways, it can be characterized as a 'movement of movement': the diverse groups that gathered to protest against the WTO, the IMF, the EU summit meetings and the G8 summit meetings represented causes reining from the environment to Third World debt relief, as do the gatherings in various places on May Day each year, the most visible of the groups have been the revolutionary anarchists who invariably use violence in drawing attention to themselves and their cause. The common target of all groups, in one way or another, is 'global capitalism' and the increasing, and uncountable, power of multinational corporations in the current world order. Whether one supports the basic principles of the liberal economic order or not, there is little doubt and that conflict arising from the misdistribution of goods and resources is likely to have serious security implications for world order in the future.[43]

In the age of rapidly globalising world, new approaches, a strategy, re-turning of the minds, hearts and souls are needed. Changes are needed at all levels: local, national, regional, international and the universal levels. The concept of common heritage of mankind beckons as all.

Networks influence discursive positions when they help persuade states and international organizations to support international declarations or to change state domestic policy positions. The role environmental networks played in shaping state positions and conference declarations at the 1992. "Earth Summit" in Rio de Janeiro is an example of this kind of impact. They may also pressure states to make more binding commitments by signing conventions and codes of conduct.[44]

The following few things have to be constantly kept in mind before embarking upon anything new. Reducing our resource consumption is the key to sustainability.

Current economic activities, especially in rich industrialized countries, are not sustainable. The overuse of natural resources by industrialized countries is the main cause for most environment problems and desertification, which nowadays pose a significant threat to humanity.[45] The outdated models have to be discarded.

Under these circumstances the traditional economic model, which aims at first creating wealth in order to fix environmental damages afterwards, is no longer sustainable. This approach is not only very expensive and therefore economically inefficient, it also ignores the ecological limits of the planet. To create wealth, today's industrialized countries have exploited natural resources to a disproportionately great extent over the past 300 years. Proposing this approach to developing countries without radical changes in production systems and lifestyle is irresponsible and will inevitably lead to socially and environmentally caused conflict. Applying the average resource consumption of US citizens to every human would result in a greatly increased strain on the environment with dramatic consequences for the global environment.[46]

The Environment Impact Assessment, it is rightly thought must precede a 'development project'. The state itself has, at times, violated the norms of environment. The biological balances must not be disturbed. The human selfishness itself should motivate us to realise that we cannot harm other species before the other species harm us.

Too much talk of trade and commerce, development is no good. There has to be a balance between material and natural development.

There are many ways of assessing environmental and sustainable development effects of trade policies or trade liberalization. One of the most commonly used approaches is based on the environmental assessment mythology of the OECD (Organization for Economic Cooperation and Development), which has been further developed by other practitioners of assessment, including UNEP. They have identified the following effects.

Product effects: These effects occur when the products themselves have an impact on the environment or development. Some of the products traded may be environmentally friendly, while others may be hazardous to the environment.

Technology effects: Increased trade may lead to the transfer of production across borders. Again, these technologies may be harmful or friendly to the environment. There is a positive technological effect when a trade policy allows the flow of environment friendly technologies and a negative effect when it prompts the transfer of harmful technologies.

Scale effects: Scale effects occur as trade reforms often raise the overall of economic activity. This is usually accompanied by a higher rate of use of natural and environment resources. This could be offset if efficiency is improved, or if higher economic growth makes greater investment in environment projects possible.

Structural effects: Trade liberalization could lead to changes in the composition of a country's economy is. It specializes in the production of goods or services where it has comparative advantage. If the changes favour the less-polluting industries, then positive environment effects could be felt in that country. On the negative side, the products where the country has comparative advantage may have higher pollution intensity, or may require a greater use of the country's natural resources.

Regulatory effects: Trade reforms may have an impact on environment regulations and standards. On the positive side, trade agreements may explicitly include measures to improve environment standards. But it is also possible that particular provisions of trade reforms may impinge on government's ability to set environmental protection standards.[47]

Let us read more of Guru Nanak, Rousseau, Gandhi, Dr. Meredith, Vedas, Wordsworth, John Ruskin, Tolstoy alike. All these philosophers or activists envisioned and realised the importance of 'tilling of soil' by human beings themselves—the value and dignity of manual labour. They earmarked the simple way of living where closeness to mother earth is eternal and essential.

Straight forwardness in thought and action is needed. Hypocrisy in the field of environment won't do. The world mostly agrees that something needs to be done about global warming and climate change. The first stumbling block, however, has been trying to get an agreement on a framework.

North South

North South is used to describe the economic divide between the industrialised countries of the north and the global poor in the south but this divide is not rigidly vertical in geographical terms. In the present time the issue of environment has become more complex between North and

South. The North is blaming South for environmental degradation. But in reality the industrialized countries have been and continues to be a major source of degradation of global commons through the disproportionate use of their own resources and those of developing countries and disproportionate production and consumption. The North is responsible for global warming and excessive use of non-renewable resources of the earth. But North is creating pressure on the South to halt their development which will further degenerate the environment. On the other side, Southern countries needs development and the use of environment friendly technology is not affordable by them. So they have to reach up to a certain level of development earlier the developed countries achieved. Technical and financial assistance from the North is required to enable the South to use its natural resources in an efficient manner compatible with the protection of environment. Similarly, the North has to reduce the excessive use of global commons and to control the industrialisation and urbanization which is highly against the mother earth.

Yet, rich countries have a lot to do themselves. There were agreed reasons why developing countries were exempted from initial greenhouse gas emission targets: it was the emissions from rich counties that accumulated in the atmosphere for so long to trigger climate change.[48]

Scientists believe that global warming will lead to a weaker Ozone layer, because as the surface temperature rises, the stratosphere (the Ozone layer being found in the upper part) will get colder, making the natural repairing of the Ozone slower.[49] Let us try to control population, Malthus had advised that one marry rather late.

The human population of the planet is estimated to now have passed 6 billion people. But are large numbers themselves a problem? Europe for example, has higher population density than Asia. There are more than two sides to the debate on whether population numbers equate to over-population or not.

But a proper management of human resources can be the answer. By ensuring women's rights, and realizing that women play a crucial role in the development of society, many underlying issues which lead to conflict and problems can be talked more effectively. Better care, education and rights for women mean that children will also benefit. This can eventually allow a society to enjoy more rights and the society can be enriched. Yet these very same provisions are being cut back, oftentimes as a result of harsh structural adjustment policies. The woman should be accorded a dignified place in all the concerned environment. The image of a humble woman planting rice jumps to one's mind. The symbolic gestures by mother nature are aplenty.

Are we blind that we cannot see the threats lurking large in the background?[50] Technology and industrialization had challenged the nature. Japan's claims about their high-tech possessiveness seem faulty when it faced the wrath of nature during recent (11 March, 2011) earthquake and the floods. This natural calamity made the humanity to rethink about its model of development including the use of nuclear energy.

A growing concern from developing countries and various NGOs is the need for public participation and the effect on populations and poor countries that global warming negotiations have. The impacts of climate change will be left on the world's poorest countries the most. In some cases, climate changes have already affected some small island nations. Climate justice, equity and sustainable development are all important parts of this debate that are often left out of mainstream discourse. Equal rights to the atmosphere for all beings and equity within and between nations are paramount.

A mechanism suggested for tackling climate change and global warming has been the idea of using carbon sinks to soak up carbon dioxide. To aid in this, reforestation, or planting of new forests, have been suggested. This is a popular strategy for the logging industry and nations with large forests interests. While there may be some potential in this solution, it cannot be effective on its own. This is because it legitimizes continued destruction of old-growth and pristine forests which are rich ecosystems and have an established biodiversity base (albeit shrinking now) that naturally maintain the environment (at no cost). Creating new forest areas would require the creation of entire ecosystems.

It is sad that the Third World has been made a dump. It is also being made a scape goat, being dubbed as the culprit (overpopulation, child labour, etc.). It is true that everything is not goody-goody here too.

Let us get used to the idea of living in harmony with nature. Too many ACs which deplete ozone layer, too many cars (which bellow smoke), too much clothes are not needed. Let us share environment space, food, shelter and affection.[51]

The humanity needs limit its wants. Nature can fulfil your needs not the greed. The affluence and luxurious life style of rich is always at the cost of the share of the poor people and exploitation of natural resources as well. We should follow immediately the sustainable mode of development otherwise nature has started retaliating and devastating the *homo sapiens*.

REFERENCES

1. Pinar Bilgin (2003). "Individual and Societal Dimensions of Security". *International Studies Review*, Vol. 5. No. 2. p. 203.
2. Richard Wyn Jones (1999). *Security, Strategy, and Critical Theory*. Boulder, London: Lynne Rienner. p. 165.
3. Barry Buzan and Ole Waever (2003). *Regions and Powers: The Structure of International Security*. Cambridge: Cambridge University Press. p. 360.
4. David Crystal (ed. 2000). *The Cambridge Paperback Encyclopedia*. New Delhi: Cambridge University Press. p. 288.
5. David Held and Anthony Mcgrew (ed. 2000). *The Global Transformations Reader An Introduction to the Globalization Debate*. UK: Polity Press. p. 381.
6. Robert Jackson and George Sorensen (2003). *Introduction to International Relations*. Oxford: Oxford University Press. p. 251.
7. Kate' O Neil (2009). *The Environment and International Relations*. Cambridge University Press.
8. James Lee Ray and Juliet Kaarbo (2002). *Global Politics*. Boston, New York: Houghton Mifflin Company. p. 437.

9. Andrew Hurrel (1998). "International Politics Theory and Global Environment", in Ken Booth and Steve Smith (eds.). *International Relations Theory Today*. UK: Polity Press. pp. 139-41.
10. *Ibid.* pp. 133-34.
11. *Ibid.*
12. Richard Peet (1999). *Theories of Development*. Jaipur: Rawat. pp. 188-90.
13. Matthew Paterson (1996). "Green Politics", in Scot Burchill and Andrew Linklater. *Theories of International Relations*. New York : Martin Press. p. 253.
14. *Ibid.*, pp. 253-54.
15. M.K. Gandhi (1938, 1958). *Hind Swaraj.* Ahmadabad: Navjivan. p. 96.
16. *Young India* (7-10-26). Ahmadabad: Navjivan. p. 348.
17. *Young India* (18-11-31). *Ibid.* p. 355.
18. *Young India* (7-10-26). *Ibid.* p. 348.
19. Richard W. Mansbach and Edward Rhodes (2006). *Global Politics in a Changing World.* Boston, New York: Houghton Mifflin Company. p. 341.
20. James Lee Ray and Juliet Kaarbo. *Op. cit.* p. 431.
21. Kavita Phillip (2004). "Reflections on the Intersections of Environment, Development, and Human Rights in the Context of Globalization" in Mahmood Monshipouri et al. (eds.). *Constructing Human Rights in the Age of Globalization.* New Delhi: Prentice Hall. p. 68.
22. Ramesh Mishra (2005). "Social Rights as Human Rights", *International Social Work Journal.* Vol. 46. No. 1. p. 18.
23. Ian Clark (1999). *Globalization and International Relations Theory.* Oxford, New York: Oxford University Press. p. 10.
24. Derek Heater and G.R. Berridge (1993). *Introduction to International Politics.* New York, Hampshire: Palgrave, Macmillan. p. 11.
25. James Lee Ray and Juliet Kaarbo. *Op. cit.* p. 429.
26. Alexander L. George (2006). *On Foreign Policy Unfinished Business.* Boulder, London: Paradigm. p. 55.

27. Ronald B. Mitchell (2002). "International Environment", in Walter Carlsnass et al. (eds.). *Handbook of International Relations*. London, Thousand Oaks, New Delhi: Sage. p. 502.
28. Robert Jackson and George Sorensen. *Op. cit.* p. 270.
29. Chris Brown (2001). *Understanding International Relations.* London: Palgrave. p. 240.
30. George W. Schuyler (2004). "Cuba and Venezuela in an Era of Globalization", in Henry Veltmeyer (ed.) *Globalization and Anti-globalization*. Bulington: Astgate. p. 98.
31. Barry Buzan. *Op. cit.* p. 294.
32. Owen Green (2005). "Environmental Issues", John Baylis and Steve Smith (eds.). *Op. cit.* p. 475.
33. Jeffrey Haynes (2005). *Comparative Politics in a Globalizing World*. Cambridge, Malden: Polity. p. 165.
34. *Ibid.*
35. R.P. Pathak (2004). "Environmental Challenges and Gandhian Solution". *The Indian Journal of Political Science.* Vol. LXV. No. 3. p. 371.
36. Anup Shah. "Environmental Issues". http://www.globalisues.org/issue/
37. Keith L. Shimko (2005). *International Relations: Perspectives and Controversies.* Boston, New York: Houghton Mifflin Company. p. 340.
38. "Economic Instrument for Environmental Protection" UNEP. *Briefs on Economics, Trade and Sustainable Development Information and Policy Tools*, from the United Nations Environment Programme, UNEP, July 2002, http///www.unep.ch/edu/publications/unep-econoinst.pdf
39. *Ibid.*
40. *Ibid.*
41. "UNEP's Environmental Impact Assessment Training Resource Manual–Second Edition". *UNEP Briefs.* May 2002. http//eia.unuedu/asout.html
42. Richard Falk (1995). *On Humane Governance Toward a New Global Politics. The World Order Model Project Report of the Global Civilization Initiative.* Cambridge. Oxford: Polity Press. p. 74.
43. Stephanie Lawson (2003). *International Relations.* Cambridge: Polity Press. pp. 109-10.

44. Margaret E. Keck and Kethryn Sikkink (2006). "Transnational Advocacy Networks in International Politics", in Richard Little and Michael Smith (eds.). *Perspectives on World Politics.* London, New York: Routledge. p. 182.
45. "Europe's Global Responsibility Environmental Space, International Trade and Factor X". *SERI*, Sustainable Research Institute. http//www.foeeurope.org/publications/2006/seri-foeen.pdf
46. *Ibid.*
47. UNEP Country Projects – Round II – A Synthesis Report, *UNEP*. pp. 4-5, http//www.unep.org/eou/pqs2/reports/annex-9a-rawanda-country-report.reu.pdf
48. Anup Shah. *Op. cit.*
49. *Ibid.*
50. *Ibid.*
51. *Ibid.*

12

Globalization

Globalization is a process which has transformed all political, economic, social and cultural relations among international community and between community of nations. This is a movement in respect of pace of advancement that has churned the basic web of social relations. This very system is strongly backed by theory of liberalism/neo-liberalism. Presently, it seems that market has been reached at the door of individuals and individual has become helpless particle in the system of market fundamentalism. Many academics identified trends of increasing trade and other links among states during the 1970s. 1980s onward changes transcended mere interconnectedness among the states. International interdependence has been around for centuries and there have been previous periods of globalization. Presently, Globalization is enabling individuals, corporations and nation-states to reach around the world farther, faster and deeper than ever before. It is even not a single process but a complex of processes, sometimes overlapping and interlocking processes. Somewhere and sometimes these processes are complimentary and at the other contradictory and oppositional one.

Relations between different groups of people did not become "global" until technology allow for those who lived in one part of the world to reach those who lived in other parts of the world. It was not until the early fifteenth century when advances in math and engineering made it possible to design ocean-worthy vessels with the capability to sail across far distances that relations become truly international. Prior to this time, relations between groups were isolated with small areas of the globe. The history of these international relations, albeit on a smaller scale, is nevertheless important because it gives an idea of how historical relationships differ from and resemble international politics today. In the eastern Mediterranean in the first to sixth centuries BC, political life was organized within and between small city-states. The ancient Greek city-states, such as Athens, Sparta, and Thebes, consisted of a group of towns or a small city and were governed by a variety of types of political systems, including small oligarchies of the rich, military dictatorships, and limited democracy. The Greek city-state system of international relations is considered a precursor to the modern state system because the city-states related to each other in much the same fashion that countries relate to each other today. From Thucydides account of the Peloponnesian War between Sparta and Athens, we know that the city-states waged war against each other, formed alliances, bargained over peace treaties, and established trading relationships. More important, the city-states were dependent on each other, and there was no overarching authority that governed their relationships. Although the Greeks did not articulate a legal concept of sovereignty, they operated as if the city-states were sovereign: they had ultimate authority over their territory and no higher authority interfered in their internal affairs.[15]

Philosophical ideas about global interconnectedness are centuries old, especially in theories embracing a universalist approach to humankind. The Stoic nation of cosmopolis and the fact that major traditions of religious thought such as Christianity and Islam also conceptualize a community of humankind. These may seem remote from present day discussions of globalization, and were certainly unrelated to theorizing about institutions such as the sovereign state and their place in a global system. It often sees that the states have been connected or interdependent upon each other. Thus, liberalism proposes that the interdependence between states and other actors reached an unprecedental level by the 1970s.[16]

They nonetheless embodied the essential idea of transcending particular political communities. Thus, we can say that the current globalization is not really new, that it is merely a continuation of the trends apparent in the 1970s.

In Europe, exploration and 'discovery' led to knowledge of the finite world and, despite some stiff resistance from ecclesiastical authorities, also to the realization that this world was infact globe-like in shape, not flat. A major practical step in the acquisition of geographical knowledge was taken with the first circumnavigation of the globe in the early sixteenth century. But it was the idea of humanity and the oneness of the human species that became especially important in global thinking although it was hardly the main source of inspiration for explorers, merchants and colonizing agents. Nonetheless, ideas about humanity were embraced by various philosophers of the Enlightenment period, albeit in different ways, and continued to find expression in the universalist ideologies of liberalism and socialism that developed in the wake of the French Revolution.[17]

By the end of Second World War the European colonialism, imperialism and protectionism was replaced by liberal capitalism on the western side and communism on the Eastern.

The transitional period in the wake of the Cold War came to a sudden close by the disintegration of USSR and there was fantastic surge of liberalization or globalization. Post Cold War era and then the forces of globalization also led to the attacks of September 11. This event was seen by many as a turning point in the development of the international system. With the advantage of hindsight, however, one can say that the world did not fundamentally change on, or because of, the events of September 11. Indoubtedly, the timing of the terrorist attacks, the chosen instruments of death the number of casualties, as well as the scale of the physical damage are, indeed, astounding. At the same time, some trends—which had by and large left their imprint on international relations of the 1990s—were generally confirmed. The events of September 11 burned the insecurities of a globalized environment into the consciousness of a public sensitized and shaped by the mass media; galvanized the request for new answers in the process of formulating policy; and accelerated the adaptation process of international institutions and regimes.[18]

The apparent emergence in the late twentieth century of an increasingly tightly interconnected and self conscious global community does not necessarily imply, as some have argued, the arrival of some kind of world society. Whilst the infrastructure of a global social system may be evident, most visibly in the globalization of communications, the media and production. The fact remains that the world is organized into sovereign nation-states. Modern phenomenon also depicts the nation state the supreme territorial, administrative and political unit which defines the 'good community'. National sovereignty and the territorial integrity of the nation-state are jealously guarded, most particularly in the Third World where the struggle to achieve independent statehood is still fresh in the collective consciousness. War and permanent preparation for war, political fragmentation, cultural diversity, and the immense gap between the advanced states and the poorest states remain central features of the contemporary global system. Accordingly, whilst from the vantage point of the affluent West there is a temptation to view the world in terms of intensifying patterns of global interconnectedness, at best this is only a partial and superficial perspective. Nor there is any overwhelming evidence to support the frequently asserted proposition that processes of globalization are precipitating a crisis of the territorial nation-state. On the contrary, the preponderance of the nation-state as the primary unit in world politics is itself a product of globalizing forces.[19]

Global Civil Society

Global civil society refers to the field of action and thought occupied by individual and collective citizens initiatives of a voluntary, nonprofit character both within states and transnationally.[20] Civil society refers to a public space where citizens and groups can engage in political activities independently of the state. NGOs have been assigned a role too. Diverse non-governmental organisations (NGOs) that are strong enough to counterbalance the state and, while not preventing the state from fulfilling its role as peacekeeper and arbitrator between major interests, can nevertheless prevent it from dominating the rest of society. Thus, one of the benefits of a healthy civil society is that it reduces the coercive power of the state and helps it to become more responsible to the needs of its citizens. Developing a strong civil society is often seen as a strategy for overcoming political tyranny and is crucial to the whole process of democratisation. For example, one of the key aims of the Solidarity movement in Poland in the early 1980s was to develop organisations that were outside the control of the state.

The strongest civil societies exist in Western liberal-democratic states, in part because freedom of association and expression are necessary conditions for the existence of a civil society. Over the past two decades, however, constant theme in the literature has been the withering away of civil society. Some observers blame the rise of corporatism, others the dominance of right-wing politics in most of the OECD world. But one of the greatest threats to civil society in the West is the growing tendency towards political apathy and the diminution of communal identity and political participation. As a counter to this, it has been suggested that more people need to get involved in voluntary associations and play an active role in the political life of their communities of civil society is to flourish. [21]

Globalization and Democracy

There is also globalization of democracy as a way of life and the form of government. One of the most important elements in the turbulent transformation of global politics now underway has been the spread of democracy. The end of the Cold War and the political development of the decade that followed have been heralded as great victory for liberal democracy. These developments include the disintegration of Soviet Union, the collapse of communist rule in Russia and nearly everywhere in Eastern Europe, the opening of the Chinese economy, and a return to free locations across Latin America and in an increasing number of states in Africa and Asia. Indeed, the notion that the subjects of a state ought to be able to control that state whatever its claims to sovereignty. No state ought to be able to wield arbitrarily. Unchecked power over the people it rules has in the years since the end of the Cold War become something of a global norm, receiving at least lip service early everywhere in the world. While precise definitions of democracy may be often debated, three of the basic requirements for democracy are widely recognized: that the authority of the state must rest on some sort of explicit or implicit contract between the state and the people it governs, setting limits on what the state can demand in return for the benefits it provides, that within the state the power to pass laws, to judge these laws, and to enforce these laws ought not be concentrated in the same hands lest this lead to abuse of citizens' rights and that procedures need to be established to allow the people to determine who among them will govern, and to remove individuals from office if their decisions are not made with the consent of the people.

Exactly what difference the diffusion of democratic values and the spread of democratic institutions make has been widely debated. One prominent observer, political scientist Francis Fukuyama, argued even before the collapse of the Soviet Union that the imminent spread of democracy would mark an "end of history". In his view, the victory of liberal democracy in the Cold War and humanity's rejection of liberal democracy's last serious ideological challenger, communism, meant that the world's political evolution was reaching an end. While memorable events would still continue to occur, history was at an end in the sense that liberal democracy's triumph represented the final stage in humanity's efforts to create political order. In Fukuyama's view, the remaining opposition to liberal democracy was anachronistic and backward looking and would, in the end, die away. Not all observers are so optimistic about the permanence and finality of liberal democracy, of course, and Fukuyama's proposition remains contentious.[22] Globalization, it has been argued, not only transcends the boundaries of nation-states. Terms such as global civil society, cosmopolitan citizenship and transnational identities are believed to supersede ethic, national and other collective identities. Information technology played a larger role for establishing global civil society.

The Myth of a Borderless World

Kenichi Ohmae claims that if we look at a map of the world indicating flows of trade, investment, and production, we would not be able to redraw the political map. In a nutshell, he is saying that economic flows no longer conform to political boundaries. Interestingly, Ohmae does not actually provide a map that allows us to test his neat idea. For globalization skeptics there is a very good reason he does not, instead of supporting his position, such a map would actually prove him wrong.

In his book *How Much Do National Borders Matter?* John Heliwell take up Ohmae's challenge to see whether economic flows no longer follow political borders. He focuses on the United States and Canada—two of the world's closest trading partners who share one of the most porous borders in the world. If Ohmae is correct, the political border separating these two nations should be nearly unnoticeable if we look at economic statistics. Given the specifics of the U.S.-Canada case, this should be a relatively easy test of the borderless-world thesis. If it does not apply here, one could reasonably wonder if it holds anywhere.

The same pattern is found elsewhere. Despite the creation of a single market under the auspices of the European Union, people in Europe are still six times more likely to trade within their own national boundaries as opposed to across them. Again, there is no denying that the relative importance of trade across national borders is on the rise, but skeptics see this as a far cry from becoming a borderless world.

Universalism or Localism

Excluding the state perception, it has been started calling 'glocalism', meaning closeness of global and local forces either intermingling or reacting (ethnic). Notwithstanding there is universlization of religion and cultures. Strangely, the followers every religion and culture claims that their universalism is supreme—meaning that there is competition of supreme between universalism of different religion and cultures.

In other sense, there is universalization of food, food eating habits, clothing and housing etc. From environment point of view, it is dangerous for the whole humanity. Food, crops, clothing or housing of any geographical area depend on the climatic conditions of the area. Universalization of all those human needs causing environmental and health problems.

In emerging markets, such as China, India, Russia and Brazil, people have changed their eating habits. For example, meat consumption in China, traditionally vegetarian society, has more than doubled since 1980.[23] The universalization of wheat and paddy crops, pizza and burger culture largely affects the consumption pattern in India as well as other TWCs. See for example, people of Punjab had lost the various cereals which were earlier part of their diets. Those were barley, jowar, bazra, etc. On the other side, these crops were less water consuming and environment friendly. Today, people are wholly dependent on wheat and paddy which has high water intake. These crops consume abundant fertilizers and pesticides. This Green Revolution (part of universalization) is one of the major root cause of lowering water level and polluting it. Besides, they are largely responsible for environment degradation in Punjab. Brainard (2009) has pointed out that potential reduction in global food producing after 2050 would raise food prices, create hardships for many poor household; low-latitude poor farmers, especially those dependent on rain-fed agriculture, may face nearer term reductions in productivity; and water could also become scarcer for both in rural and urban poor.[24]

Nation State in Transition

One of the notable features of the contemporary state system is the increasing difficulty for the national economic objectives to be achieved through exclusive national strategies. As a result the political salience of regionalism is enhanced for the realization of goals of political control, policy choices and international business growth. States are, however, not necessarily by-passed in the process of region building. The critical question to ask here is what states are trying to do through regionalism and why. What goals should states pursue? In earlier times, the answer was easy: the state should promote the internal welfare of its citizen, provide for defense against external aggression, and preserve the state's values and way of life. States followed a largely realist script, putting their national interests ahead of global interests. This meant competing with other states for power, position, and prestige, and above all else protecting the state from external attack by acquiring arms for defense. Working with other states on common problems or with many other countries in building multilateral institutions for global governance was secondary—to be considered only after national security was enhanced by acquiring military might and political clout.

Leaders pursue the same goals today, but their domestic and foreign policy options are increasingly limited. Many problems can be resolved only at the risk of worsening others. Under such conditions, the national quest for narrow zero-sum self-advantage and global position often carries prohibitively high costs. The historic tendency towards chauvinism (many countries, right or wrong) in defining national interests can be counterproductive domestically as well as internationally. No country can long afford to pursue its own welfare in ways that reduce its competitor's security and welfare.[25]

Increasing Role of Multinationals in World Politics

One of the roles of the state vis-a-vis today's global economy has been to negotiate the intersection of national law and foreign actors—whether firms, markets or supranational organizations. This raises a question as to whether there are particular conditions that make execution of this role in the current phase distinctive and unlike what it may have been in earlier phase of the world economy. We have, on the one hand, the existence of an enormously elaborate body of law developed mostly over the past hundred years, which secures the exclusive territorial authority of national states to an extent not seen in earlier centuries, and, on the other, the considerable institutionalising, especially in the 1990s, of the "rights" of non-national firms, the deregulation of cross border transactions, and the growing influence/power of some of the supranational organizations. If securing these rights, options, and power entailed an even partial relinquishing of components of state authority as constructed over the past century, then we can posit that this sets up the conditions for a necessary engagement by national states in the process of globalization.

We need to understand more about the nature of this engagement than is represented by concepts such as deregulation. It is becoming clear that the role of the state in the process of deregulation involves the production of new types of regulations, legislative items, court decisions—in brief, the production of a whole series of new "legalities". The background condition here is that the state remains as the ultimate guarantor of the "rights" of global capital, i.e., the protector of contracts and property rights, and, more generally, a major legitimator of claims. In this regard the state can be seen as incorporating the global project of its own shrinking role in regulating economic transactions and giving it operational effectiveness and legitimacy.[26]

There are practical reasons for continuing to make use of 'globalization' and 'antiglobalization' as shorthand reference to the complex dynamics of world developments. For one thing, these terms dominate the theoretical discourse in the field. For another, both terms do make reference to, and allow for a description of, several important dimensions of analysis both in regard to structural change and the force of resistance against this change against the force that drive the system forward. In these terms, globalization has the appearance of a process that is irresistible, inevitable and inescapable—all countries and people having to adjust to it the best way they can, to insert themselves into the process under the most favorable conditions or to make the best deal possible.[27]

The threat perception too is there. The "previously neglected sources of conflict" focused on are environmental threats, threats arising form international migration, and threats emanating from resurgent nationalisms. Nations are slowly changing. Alternative understanding of security in international relations have gained ground and contend that security is linked to something other than, or something in addition to, military force. Building on this idea that the security concept should be 'enlarged', concepts such as 'comprehensive security', 'human security', desecuritization', 'soft power' and 'soft security' flourish in studies of both European and international security. However, do these concepts satisfactorily capture and provide an understanding of the central features of the change to European security? And do they always entail the same understanding of what has actually changed ?[28]

We, in the Third World, have our own hopes, aspirations, doubts and threat perception. The Third World, it seems, is condemned to invisibility, particularly at the centre. In international relations, both as practice and as theory, it resides at the edge. In emergent discourses about 'global culture' and globalization, it becomes mostly incorporated, repressed, homogenized. Some critics even find the 'Third World' of decreasing utility as theoretical and descriptive application in the contemporary world. Yet to the extent that the 'Third World' still carries meaning as a shorthand for the multitude of cultures and identities that remain marginalized, dispossessed and increasingly insignificant in the late modern age, it is useful not only as a sign of discomfort for various global scenarios and projections, but also as a key site of the unfolding of intersubjective identities between North and South (however inadequate some find these terms) within the intersecting parameters of (post) modernity, tradition and globalization. In this sense, the rubric of the Third World remains indispensable to any attempt to understand the global nature of modernity in the contemporary period, if only to remind us that the 'global' does not end at the Tropic of Cancer.

"World politics is changing, but our conceptual paradigms have not kept pace. The classic state centric paradigm assumes that states are the only significant actors in world politics and that they act as units. Diverse domestic interests have effects on international politics only through governmental foreign policy channels. Intersocietal interactions are relegated to a category of secondary importance - the "environment" of interstate politics. As Karl Kaiser has pointed out, the reality of international politics has never totally corresponded to this model. Nevertheless, the models was approximated in the eighteenth century when foreign policy decisions were taken by small groups of persons acting within an environment that was less obtrusive and complex than the present one.

REFERENCES

1. Philip G. Cerny (2010). *Rethinking world Politics: A Theory of Transnational Neopluralism*. Oxford: Oxford University Press. p. 25.
2. John Baylis and Steve Smith (2005). *The Globalisation of World Poltics: An Introduction to International Relations*. Oxford: Oxford University Press. p. 2.
3. Stephine Lawson (2003). *International Relations*. UK: Polity Press. p. 119.
4. John H. Dunning (2003). *Making Globalization Good: The Moral Challenge of Global Capitalism*. US: Oxford University. Press. p. 301.
5. James Lee Ray and Juliet Kaarbo (2002). *Global Politics*. Boston, New York: Houghton Mifflin Company. p. 487.
6. http://www.investowords.com2182/globalization.html
7. John Baylis and Steve Smith (2005). *Op. cit.* p. 2.
8. Philip G. Cerny. *Op. cit.* p. 25.
9. Charles W. Kegley (2011). *World Politics and Transformation*. Belmont: Thomson. p. 419.
10. Achin Vanaik (2004). *Globalization and South Asia*. New Delhi: Nanohar. p. 335.
11. *Ibid.*
12. James Lee Ray and Juliet Kaarbo. *Op. cit.* p. 486.
13. Weigal, David (2002). *International Relations*. London: Arnold. p. 102.
14. James Lee Ray and Juliet Kaarbo. *Op. cit.* p. 487.
15. *Ibid.* pp. 25-26.
16. *Ibid.* p. 487.
17. Stephine Lawson. *Op. cit.* p. 120.
18. Wenger, Andreas & Zimmermann (2006). *International Relations*. p. 337.
19. Mcgrew, Anthony et al. (1992). *Global Politics Globalisation and the Nation State*. Cambridge: Polity Press. p. 2.

20. John H. Dunning. *Op. cit.* p. 301.
21. Grifflths, Martin and Terry O'Callaghan (2004). *Key Concepts in International Relations*. London, New York: Routledge. p. 23.
22. Richard W. Mansbach and Edward Rhodes (2006). *Global Politics in a Changing World*. New York: Houghton Mifflin Company. pp. 98-99.
23. Charles W. Kegley (2011). *Op. cit.* p. 558.
24. *Ibid.*
25. Charles W. Kegley (2007). *World Politics and Transformation*. Belmont: Thomson. p. 584.
26. Mark Kesselman and Joel Krieger (ed., 2006). *Readings in Comparative Politics*. Boston, New York: Houghton Mifflin Company. pp. 90-91.
27. Henry Veltmeyer (2005). *Globalization and antiglobalization*. Burlington: Ashgate. p. 1.
28. Helene Sjursen (2004). *Changes to European Security in a Communicative Perspective*; Vol. 39. No. 2. http//uzdeas.repec.org/p/erp/arenax/p00181.html

13

Role of State and Non State Actors in Global Politics

The modern era starts with the emergence of dominant sovereign nation state system. From the time of treaty of Westphalia (1648) the political system is governed by the states as only dominant actors. Prominent theories of IR more or less also admit the predominance of state. The positivist theoretical inferences still run around the state as most important unit to study. In reality, international relations are highly dynamic. No theory of IR sufficiently predicted the future of world, for example the dismantling of communist bloc. Presently, it seems that a number of forces are actually working and participating in global politics; other than the state.

Prominent neo-liberal thinkers Keohane and Nye viewed three decades ago that the contemporary international relations seems just now to be awakening to the existence and impacts of non-governmental and extra governmental international organizations and interactions, the realm of international behavior labeled transnational relations by Joseph Nye and Robert Keohane.[1] The beginning of the new century has heralded a new era of history of the mankind and accompanied new challenges to man. These challenges, be they social, economic, political, environmental, demographical, are global in nature and made the interdependence among different societies to a newer and a greater level.[2]

The world is rapidly becoming interconnected, linking tighter and tighter into a single integrated community and market. This movement and interaction across frontiers is uniting the world and making national boundaries and governments less important. This process poses both possibilities and problems, creating many winners but also many losers. It is leading to the simultaneous integration and disintegration of states to the growth of some states power and the erosion of the authority of many other states. This transformation is referred throughout the word as globalization.[3]

No nation state can ignore their existence and effectiveness. They are those international actors who are not states, but are instead volunteers drawn from the population of two or more states who form organizations to promote their shared ideals and interests by influencing the policies of national governments and intergovernmental organizations. These non state actors are active in more than one state. Therefore, they can exploit states against each others. Nowadays, non-state actors began to substitute nation states in many areas.[4]

The contemporary state system is challenged by non-state actors like ethno-political groups, religious groups, international terrorists, etc. Before the emergence of the modern nation-state, global structure lacked the territorial divisions among units that characterize a world of sovereign equals. A variety of other actors were generally recognized as constituent parts of the global system and its several subsystems.[5] Non-state actors suddenly have become so powerful because they are able to pose a threat to the entire sovereign nation state world. In the global politics era, non-state actors are acquiring a significant position on the world or global stage in order to solve global problems such as terrorism, human security, environmental degradation, gender, etc.

MNC's, INGO's, NGO's, regional organizations, supranational actors, etc., presently play a regular part in global politics and interact with the governments. Nobody can deny the number of these organizations and the range of their activities. Thus, the transnational actors and international organizations generally are more specialists and involved in a limited range of policy questions. Amnesty International and Greenpeace are central to their own domain. The international relations of the twentieth century have all occurred within complex, pluralist political systems. TNCs (Transnational Corporations) and NGOs have been the main source of economic and political change in global politics.

The state has traditionally been regarded as the central feature of political life. International politics have traditionally concentrated upon the relationships between states. The state, regarded as an actor with purposes and power, is the basic unit of action; its main agents are the diplomats and soldiers. States are by no means the only actors in world politics.[6] Present global politics is posing serious challenge for state or its sovereignty. Intergovernmental organizations (as UN, World Bank, IMF, WTO, OPEC), non-legitimate groups and liberation movements; INGOs (Non Governmental Organizations), as Amnesty International, Red Cross and Green Peace transnational actors like MNCs. These NSAs' activities are changing the concept of sovereignty and nationalism. From the beginning, the discipline of IR has had the analysis of relations among sovereign states as one of its central preoccupations. What are the changes that are sparking a new debate about sovereignty? A growing number of scholars consider this view to be outdated. They argue that sovereignty is increasingly challenged from several sides. Firstly, global market forces more easily penetrate borders and affect national economics in unprecedented ways. Environment concerns, global communication systems, nuclear weapons, terrorism and drug trade are examples of activities that reach across borders. Secondly, the development of norms concerning international protection of human rights and humanitarian law. The core area (of state) of war and control of means violence is not presently under exclusive control of state.[7] All these factors infringe state sovereignty. People band together in many ways as coalitions of private citizens to play influential roles in international affairs. Religions, nationalities based on ethnic and linguistic heritage or MNC's are those non-state actors who push their own agendas and increasingly exert global influence.[8] Thus the role and significance of the state is threatened by developments that came increasingly pronounced in the late twentieth century. The role and function of the nation state in international politics has changed. Although traditional models do not take these non state actors sufficiently into account. Yet, non military and non security issues such as population distribution of food, depletion of natural resources, dependency of Third World countries on the more developed countries, and the use of the oceans and outer space have come to the forefront.[9] War is no longer a major option for foreign policy decision makers, and the more powerful the nation, the less viable war becomes. Weapons of mass destruction have drastically changed the nature of warfare. We are moving to an era dominated by economic power—an era in which war between major states may virtually disappear.

In the post-cold war era the economic performance of the nation-state has been increasingly interdependent in the free market export orientated world. Simultaneously, state primacy has been diluted and the state *per se* has become less effective and relevant with the emergence of a variety of transnational and multinational entities and challenges posed to state primacy by the individual and ubiquitous non-governmental organizations.[10] In the post-cold war era membership of international or regional organizations also have effect of diminishing state sovereignty. Regional blocs as European Union, NAFTA, ASEAN, APEC (Asia Pacific Economic Cooperation) are reducing the governmental control over the national economy. The role of the state in global politics is inherently ambivalent. On the one hand, the state can be seen as the vehicle for the global spread of economy and technological progress, but on the other, it can be presented as source of violence and repression, and as a fundamental barrier to the unification of the world. Equally it can be argued almost in the same breath both that the state is being or has been weakened by the changes related to globalization, and that it has been strengthened by precisely those changes. The forces of technological, economic or military power can be seen both as bursting the bounds of the nation-state as providing it with yet further strength to control its citizens and its social life[11]. According to Ohmae (1995): The Nation-State has become an unnatural, even dysfunctional unit for organizing human activity and managing economic endeavor in a borderless world. It represents no genuine, shared community of economic interests; it defines no meaningful flows of economic activity. In fact, it overlooks the true linkages and synergies that exist among often disparate populations by combining important measures of human activity at the wrong level of analysis.... On the global economic map the lines that now matter are those defining what may be called 'region states'. The boundaries... are drawn by the deft but invisible hand of the global market for goods and services. They follow, rather than precede, real flows of human activity.[12] When we see historically the states have been the most important kind of political organizations in the global system. Their pre-eminence has not gone unchallenged and these are good reasons to believe that these particular organizations may not allow humankind to deal with problems that have become more serious in the twenty-first century. Even so, states are still a very important kind of political entity and are likely to remain significant even if other types of organizations become more influential. So global politics necessarily involves a grasp of essential characteristics of states, including state's power to influence other states[13]. There is increasing role of non-state actors in world politics. The term 'non-state actors' covers an enormously broad range of groups. On the most basic level, not-state entities are associations of individuals or groups that are not established by agreements among states. This broad definition includes such entities as transnational corporations and the business associations, professional associations, ethnic groups, major religious organizations, terrorist groups, and social movements[14]. There is no doubt that non-state actors play a regular part in global politics and each government interacts with a diverse range of non-state actors. Sometimes guerrilla groups challenge the authority of particular governments. In addition, even though they are considered not to be legitimate participants in the system, terrorists and other criminal gangs have an impact, often minor, but sometimes in a major way. Very many more companies and NGOs only operate in a single country, but have the potential to expand into other countries.[15] According to Verbeek since the 1648 Peace of Westphalia, the history of world politics has largely been a chronicle of interactions among states that remain the dominant political organizations in the world. However, the supremacy of the state has been severely challenged in recent years. Increasingly, world affairs are being influenced by intergovernmental organizations such as the European Union (EU). Such international organizations often carry out independent foreign policies and therefore can be considered global actors in their own right.[16] A renown IR thinker Karl W. Deutsch had given warnings in 1989 while taking seriously the vulnerability of mutual relations between states and non-state actors. He said that an introduction to the study of international relations in our time is an introduction to the art and science of the survival of mankind. If the civilization is killed within the next thirty years, it will not be killed by famine or plague, but by foreign policy and international relations. We can cope with hunger and pestilence, but we cannot yet deal with the power of our own weapons and with our behaviour as nation-states. The nation-state holds the power to control most events within its borders, but few events - or even its own actions - beyond them.[17] The dawn of 21st century (Sep/11) justified Deutsch's analysis of international relations.

The realist perspective on the other side still highly portrays international relations as inevitably a realm of conflict and competition for power among states. International politics is fundamentally a struggle for power in which nations must always be wary of the power of other nations. Nations that naively ignore these realities and try to avoid power politics will suffer the consequences of their folly. For realists, state will, and should, jealously guard its sovereign power and seek to increase it when it can. States are expected to oppose any efforts or processes that are a threat to their autonomy. The realist orthodoxy insists that nothing has changed international relations since Thucydides and Machiavelli's advocacy of states' military and economic power determines its fate;

interdependence and international institutions are secondary and fragile phenomena.[18] Anthony G. McGrew viewed that the apparent emergence, in the late twentieth century, of an increasingly tightly interconnected and self-conscious global community does not necessarily imply, as it is argued, the arrival of some kind of world society. Whilst the infrastructure of a global social system may be evident, most visibly in the globalization of communications, the media and production, the fact remains that the world is organized into sovereign nations-states. The nation state is today the supreme territorial, administrative and political unit which defines the 'good community'. From the third world point of view McGrew again argues war and permanent preparation for war, political fragmentation, cultural diversity, and the immense gap between the advanced states and the poorest states remain central features of contemporary global system.[19] For realists, states are the only actors that really 'count'. Transnational corporations, international organizations, and ideology driven terrorist networks, such as Al-Qaeda, rise and fall but the state is the one permanent feature in the landscape of modern global politics.[20] Although realism acknowledges the existence of other actors in the global system such as international organizations, MNC's and individuals, it posits that states are the dominant actors. And if states are the dominant actors, then the political process at the global level involves competition, conflict and cooperation between the representatives of states. States are struggling for power but it does not mean that war and conflict are necessary. Through diplomacy and negotiation, states cooperate to achieve common ends. Furthermore, states have institutionalized cooperative relations, where the national interests dictates, through the vast array of international organizations.[21]

But there are different or opponent views of other schools of thought. To discuss liberal-pluralist paradigm state is no longer the primacy actor on the world stage. Rather, the growth of transnational relations points to the significance of non-state actors, such as multinational corporations, and a myriad of other transnational associations and international organizations. Indeed, the state itself is conceived as a fragmented entity, constituted by an array of bureaucratic organizations and institutions. Therefore, global system is polyarchical or as an agglomeration of different issue areas or policy sectors.[22] Concerning borderless world thesis, John Helliwell in his book *How Much Do National Borders Matter* remarked that economic flows no longer follow political borders. His focus is on United States and Canada - two of the world's closest trading partners who share one of the most porous borders in the world. This should be a relatively easy test of wordless-world thesis.[23] Contemporary liberalism sees great change and emphasizes the transformation of global politics that has arisen from the development of complex interdependence. As the degree and scope of interdependence continue to increase, state will have to coordinate their activities further, non-state and sub-state actors will become increasingly important, traditional matters of security will become less important on international agenda. Global governance will take on more functions once reserved by states.[24] So, in the liberal view, the state enjoys sovereignty but it is not an autonomous actor. There is no explicit or consistent national interest, there are many.[25]

Taking radical view of the present state; radicalists offer two alternative views of the state, each emphasizing the role of capitalism and the capitalist class in the formation and functioning of the state. The instrumental Marxist view sees the state as the executing agent of bourgeoisie. The bourgeoisie reacts to direct societal pressures, especially to pressures from the capitalist class. The structural Marxist view sees the state as operating within the structure of the capitalist system. Within that system state is driven to expand.[26] These Marxist analyses assert that the prevailing world order is the structural differentiation of the world into core, peripheral and semi-peripheral centres of economic power, in simple terms, the division between North, South and Eastern bloc. Prevailing world order is a capitalist order based upon a global structure transnational corporations.[27]

Transnational relations contacts, coalitions, and interaction across state boundaries that are controlled by the central foreign policy organs of government. It treats the reciprocal effects between transnational relations and the interstate system as centrally important to the understanding of contemporary world politics.[28]

Changes in global politics do not deny that governments remain the most important players in the game. Although transnational organizations are vastly more plentiful and significant now than before.[29]

The contemporary study of international politics is plagued by state centrism, conceptions of politics as an autonomous process, an overemphasis on the near term Eurocentrism. As a result, the field is poorly equipped to deal with the issues like globalization, political and economic crises, and systematic instability, or discontinuous change.[30]

National governments are not simply losing autonomy in a globalizing economy. They are sharing powers including political, social, and security roles at the core of sovereignty with international organizations, non-governmental organizations, etc.[31]

The coming era of economic globalization is different, because of changes in the degree of interdependence leading to fundamental transformations or because of information revolution. This fundamental change is mixed with stability. It is hard to draw balance easily. It is true that boundaries are becoming more porous, and some controls more problematic, the future of domestic governance is not so simple. The internet was initially structured by hackers with a libertarian anti governmental culture, but commerce is rapidly changing the net.[32]

The world system of the twenty-first century is not merely a system of unitary states interacting with one another through diplomacy, public international law, and international organizations. States as agents interact, constituting an international system.[33]

There is not to assert that there has been no change in the role of the state, nor to deny important shifts in the range of its powers. The state's identity is undergoing continuous transformation.[34] The state has become just one of several worlds organizational structures. States are increasingly sharing power with non-governmental organizations as state sovereignty weakens. Daniel Bell said, "The nation-state is becoming too small for the big problems of life, and too big for the small problems of life". The nation-state is seen as becoming unable to control the increasingly global problems it (or its people) faces, and unwieldy in dealing with local issues like regional education, regional governance, and regional social matters. In short, the "central paradox of globalization is that rather than creating one big economy or one big polity, it also divides, fragments and polarizes".[35]

The state is not only the unitary actor on the global stage. Therefore, the present day stage of global politics is crowded with countless actors of different types, whose complex interactions substantially determine the intermediate and longer-range course of particular dramas. The state may reshape itself so that certain functions are given up, or delegate to other actors. At the same time, it may acquire responsibilities for new areas of social activity, such as consumer protection, environment management, and the regulation of relationships hitherto deemed to fall within the private sphere.

In the more complex geography the nation state is being supplanted by other private actors. The nation state is the most important actor on the stage of the global politics, but it is not the only important actor. The nation-state will continue to be important indeed that the internal structures of states will be crucial in their ability to adapt to globalization and its effects on them.[36] State responses to the forces of globalism and supplemented by private and non-governmental actors, some of which compete and some of which complement state actions. Transnational corporations may replace legislative functions of state.[37]

The role of non-governmental bodies in drawing attention to human rights abuses, we are enjoyed to recall that international recognized human rights, although held equally by human beings, are held with respect to, and exercised against, the sovereign territorial state. The state remains the central institution for implementation of human rights, even when there are increasingly external constraints upon its freedom of action.[38] The states are still most important. The power of states has been treated as the most important concept in the study of world politics.[39] Although states continue to be key actors in global governance, as Jessica Mathew asserts "National governments are sharing powers - including political, social, and security roles at the core of sovereignty with business, with international organizations, and with the multitude of citizens groups. The steady concentration of power in the hands of states that began in 1648 with the peace of Westphalia is over. Power, indeed, is less concentrated in states and has diffused to the other actors in global governance."[40] State is not a static institution. On the contrary, it is a dynamic institution and it continues to evolve. In the present era, world politics is moving beyond state sovereignty. Martin Shaw pointed out that supranational institutions represent the beginning of new form of 'international state power' or a 'global western state conglomerate'.[41] No doubt non state actors play a significant role on the global stage but nation states are still important in international affairs.

The systems of global and regional governance state now assert their sovereignty less in the form of a legal claim to supreme power than as a bargaining tool, in the context of transnational systems of rule making, with other agencies and social forces. Sovereignty is bartered, shared, and divided amongst the agencies of public power at different levels from the local to global.[42] Therefore, it is acknowledged that in the global power system state is not the sole occupant of power. Power is unevenly distributed among a diverse array of public and private actors and networks. Although sovereignty remains a principle juridical attribute of states but in conclusion we can say that it is increasingly divided and shared between local national, regional and global authorities.[43] Here we can make the inference that there is erosion of role of state in international relations, "but it is not dead".[44] To talk of global politics is to assert that these are processes of globalization at work which in some way contribute to the globalization of political activity. Globalization refers to the multiplicity of linkages and interconnections between the states and societies which make up the modern world system. It describes the process which events, decisions, and activities in one part of the world can come to have significant consequences for individuals and communities in quite distant parts of the globe.[45] There is changing role of the state to play for decreased public services to increased private activities. Consequently, in the international scenario state is not the only player. And competition between the role of state in 'higher politics' and of economy in 'low politics' of economy and other processes, definitely state is losing its conceptualized traditional sovereignty.

The emerging field of global politics is increasingly focused on the study of global governance. Governance can be generally understood as the maintenance of collective order, the achievement of collective goals, and the collective processes of rule through which order and goals are sought.[46] Global governance will come not at the expenses of the state but rather as an expression of the interests that the state embodies. Over the last two decades, though, there has been a terminological shift from the study of international governance to the study of global governance, justified because the purpose of global governance no longer reflect solely the interest of states but now also include other actors, including IOs, transnational corporations, non-governmental organizations, and new kinds of networks. Global governance is produced through networked relations among different kind of actors with different kind of authority and power.[47] The study of global governance reflects these changes in the study of world politics. Whereas this was once limited to how states with pre-existing interests create norms, rules, laws and institutions to regulate their relations, there have been a number of critical additions in the recent past. Global governance thus is a wide-ranging dynamic process of complex interactive decision-making which is subject to continuous development according to the frequently changing circumstances.[48]

Global governance is not the same as world government, and the domestic analogy is not adequate. The world system of the twenty-first century is not merely a system of unitary states interacting with one another through diplomacy, public international law, and international organizations. In that model, states as agents interact, constituting an international system.[49]

Governance is about how actors work together to maintain order and achieve collective goals. The study of global governance is ultimately concerned with how rules are created, produced, sustained, and refined, how these rules help define the purpose of collective action, and how these rules control the activities of international, transnational, and increasingly domestic action.[50] By governance, we mean the process and institutions, both formal and informal, that guide and restrain the collective activities of a group. Government is the subset that acts with authority and creates formal obligations. Governance need not necessarily be conducted exclusively by governments and the international organizations to which they delegate authority. Private firms, associations of firms, non-governmental organizations (NGOs), and association with governmental bodies, create governance, sometimes without governmental authority.[51]

Global governance is equated with multilevel governance, meaning that governance takes place not only at the national and the international level (such as in international governance) but also at the subnational, regional, and local levels. Whereas, in international governance, the addresses and the makers of norms and rules are states and other intergovernmental institutions, non-state actors (in addition to states and intergovernmental institutions) are both the addressees and the makers of norms and rules in global governance.[52]

Global governance is the output of a non-hierarchical network of international and transnational institutions not only IGOs and international regimes but also transnational regimes are regulating actors' behavior. Global governance is characterized by the decreased salience of states and the increased involvement of non-state actors in norm and rule setting processes and compliance monitoring. In addition, global governance is equated with multilevel governance, meaning that governance takes place not only at the national and the international level (such as in international governance) but also at the subnational, regional, and local levels. Whereas, in international governance, the addressees and the makers of norms and rules are states and other intergovernmental institutions, non-state actors (in addition to states and intergovernmental institutions) are both the addressees and the makers of norms and rules in global governance.[53] New actors have entered the world stage and other non-territorial actors, such as international (governmental and non-governmental) organizations, have multiplied. Global threats such as the greenhouse effect, for example, cannot effectively be countered by uncoordinated national policies and thus call for a global climate policy to regulate the behavior of all states as well as non-state actors.

There is a great need of global governance A variety of emerging problems such as HIV/AIDS and other diseases, weapons of mass destruction - nuclear, chemical and biological, ensuring environmental protection, promoting human rights and other issues of global concerns, etc. poses serious challenges which cannot be managed by sovereign states acting alone, even by the sole superpower, the United States. All require cooperation of some sort among governments and the increasing number of non state actors in the world. Globalization is playing a major role in shrinking the planet, proliferating issues, and changing the roles of key actors. In short, there is a wide variety of international policy problems that require governance. Sometimes the need is truly global in scope.[54]

Global governance is not global government, it is not a single world order, it is not top down, hierarchical structure of authority. It is the collection of governance related activities, rules and mechanism, formal and informal, existing at a variety of levels in the world today.[55] The complexity of global governance is function through many actors that are frequently linked in transnational and trans-governmental networks. Such networks have become increasingly dense since the 1970s when Robert Keohane and Joseph Nye (1971) first pointed out the importance of regular interactions across national boundaries of governmental and non-governmental actors.[56] Global governance will come not at the expense of the state but rather as an expression of the interests that the state embodies. As the source of order and basis of governance, the state will remain in the future as effective, and will be as essential, it has ever been.[57]

Globalization impacts upon governance by altering the deeper structures which underlie governance processes and mechanisms, altering various conditions or parameters which affect the likely mix of hierarchy, market and network whether in terms of socio-cultural structures, economic production and consumption, or political processes and institutions.[58]

International Organization

Although the study of international organizations is almost as old as the discipline of international relations, it has fallen in and out of theoretical favor over the decades. After the Second World War there was continuing interest in international organizations because of the experiments in regional integration in Europe. Traditionally, states were established international institutions and the functions that they assign to them. But in the era of global politics the impact of IOs is not limited to the functions assigned to them by states and the regulation of already existing state interests. IOs also construct the social world in which cooperation and choice takes place.[59] These international organizations function effectively to influence the policies of governments and affect the lives and welfare of people in almost every country of the world. Thus international politics is rapidly becoming an ever more important feature of world politics today.

International organizations are not seen as actors in their own right, equivalent to and interacting with states; rather they are institutional channels, obstacles, and aids collectively created by states which modify the traditionally laissez faire character of their relationship.[60]

International organizations are used by states, individually or collectively, as an instrument of foreign policy. They act by their very presence in the system to modify states' behavior. They sometimes achieve a degree of autonomy and influence as political actor in their own right. Nation states will have to coexist with new regional and functional actors. And these actors will gain power and legitimacy at their expense. In such an event, the classic model would begin to look hopelessly outmoded.[61] International organizations have become particularly important authorities in their own right, often working with states and nongovernmental actors in new hybridized forms of authority.[62]

Non-Government Organizations

The rise of multinational corporations and the remarkable growth of other types of non-state actors challenge the traditional state-centric theory of international politics, which holds that nation-states are the primary actors on the world stage. NGOs also play an important role in facilitating a linkage between a global and civil society and thus resolving the global problems. The NGO world is growing and changing in many ways. New functions are performed, new procedures adopted, and more channels of information established. These changes affect the importance of NGOs in the world.[63] NGOs are voluntary associations in the dynamic processes that constitute world politics. They serve as important tools in the construction of a global civil society. The dynamics of global civil society's developmental processes should help to weaken the hold of the state on disciplinary analyses and allows NGOs to assume a more important role in conventionally conceived international relations, or, more specifically, to become more significant actors in the theories and practices of global politics.

Non-Governmental Organizations (NGOs) or more established groups like World Wildlife Fund (WWF) or the International Institute for Environment and Development (IIED) routinely advice governments, and NGOs are now granted observer rights at UN Conferences and some of their members even appear within national delegations. The 'Global Forum' at Rio demonstrated the full range and diversity of NGOs and some have even begun to talk of the emergence, alongside the states system, of a 'global civil society'.[64] NGOs play an important role in facilitating a linkage between a global and civil society and thus resolving the global problems.

Environmental NGOs have played effective roles at UN conferences.

There is growing recognition that non-governmental organizations can have significant effects on state policies and global politics through the creation of international norms although their degree of influence varies across issues and is greater when they enter the international debate at the initial agenda setting point of the process. NGOs also perform a variety of functions in international and state governance. NGOs are increasingly taking up functions that were performed by states.[65]

Transnational/ Multinational Corporations

Transnational relations are not new, although the growth of transnational organization in the twentieth century has been amazing. Transnational relations are a new name for the old phenomenon of imperialism. Transnational relations specifically refer to regular interactions across national boundaries when at least one actor is a non-state agent or does not operate on behalf of a national government or an intergovernmental organization. The study of transnational corporation had an earlier moment in the sun, faded in the shadow of state centrism, and has now returned with a burst of energy. Robert Keohane and Joseph Nye (1972) introduced the study of transnational politics in the early 1970s, but that particular research agenda did not prosper in the short term, with the exception of some increased attention to transnational corporation in world politics. Ernst Hass and John Ruggie explored the role of various kinds of knowledge communities and transnational networks for understanding forms of international change and cooperation.[66]

There are reasons for the increasing emergence of transnational corporation. Two aspects of economic globalization have been central to their recent growth in number and significance: the internationalization of production and the internationalization of financial transactions as a result of freeing of trade barriers and general growth of the global economy.[67] Improved technology has removed many of the imperfections of communications that once helped separate societies. Transnational activity may, paradoxically, have greater effects on interdependence when governments are ambitiously attempting to control their economies than in situations of relative laissez faire.

Changes in world politics do not deny that governments remain the most important players in the game. Although transnational organizations are immensely more plentiful and significant since World War I they not only maintain but also extend their control over outside forces and events. Previously ignored areas of activity have been brought within the regulation and concern of governments. Thus, the sensitivity of governments to changes elsewhere increases as governments become more ambitious. Increased aspirations for control and increased interdependence go hand in hand. Governments have generally not been able to control their environments successfully for long periods of time whenever those environments have changed rapidly as a result of large-scale social forces or advancing technology.

TNCs have the capacity to work through their home governments to seek to influence international policy-making processes.[68] In the era of economic liberalization, and privatization on both the national and the international level, not only the number of TNCs but also their influence in world politics has risen. Today, TNCs control financial capital, technology, employment, and natural resources to an unprecedented extent. Their transnational production has grown in scale, scope, and intensity.[69] TNCs use their power resources in world politics both by trying to influence governmental and intergovernmental policy-making and by cooperating with other market actors: private actors are increasingly involved in authoritative decision making that was previously the prerogative of national governments or intergovernmental institutions.

Multinational corporations can have a powerful influence in local economies, and even in the world economy and play an important role in international relations and globalization. MNC are expanding their presence in more countries and contributing to the interdependence of the world system.

Opportunity for cooperation arises from such interdependence but so too does the risk of conflict. According to Bennett and Oliver, MNCs reflect and contribute to global interdependence.[70]

MNCs are economically important. The most important type of nonstate actor to emerge in the past three decade is the multinational corporations. These corporations that do business in more than one state are not new. Since the early part of the twentieth century many companies among them Singer, Hertz, Nestle etc. have been active in several countries. These multinational corporations are doing business in several countries having headquarter in one state, and all or most of their production is centered there. International commerce is no longer just international trade. Today, if a company wants to sell its products in another country, it may set up a subsidiary for manufacturing there, and indeed, sales of foreign affiliates have recently exceeded world total export.[71] Multinational corporations have become so visible in that they have been spectacularly successful.

However, most of the MNCs have come up in times of change and globalisation. One of the most important motivations for companies to expand their operation internationally is the low-cost factors of production in developing countries.[72] This has had a tremendous influence on the economies of the developing countries, acting as a catalyst in their growth process. Multinational companies can also have significant influence with regard to policy formation in many national governments and in transnational bodies such as the European Union and the World Bank (key actors within the globalization process). They have also profited from privatization and the opening up of services.[73] In recent times, most companies have recognized the need to be responsive to local markets and political needs and the management styles followed by multinationals are gradually shifting towards a trans-national strategy of 'Think global, act local'.

Regional Organizations

Among supranational actors, regional organizations are very correct example which have important reasons for erosion of state sovereignty. International regionalism is a strong force in the present state of world affairs. It is the most important development in world politics in the present state of world relations. The most important development in world politics in the post-World War-II period has been proliferation of regional organizations to bring home the existing reality of global interdependence[74]. Regional organizations too play significant role in the era in the global politics. Globalization encompasses a great variety of tendencies and trends in the economic, social and cultural spheres. The turbulent transformation of global politics now under way is the erosion of borders between national economies and the declining ability of states to ensure the economic well-being of their citizens.[75] With the increasingly interdependent global economy, the purpose and future of state boundaries in the international system come into question. The increasing porosity of borders mean that problems that individual states used to be able to address on their own have now become collective problems that can be solved only through collective action. They are beyond the ability of any single society, acting alone, to solve. States are trying to rearrange political relations by combining their power in national, transnational and supranational or by making regional organizations. Many contemporary states recognize the potential economic benefits of economic integration—the replacement of national economies with larger ones. One of the most striking facts about the modern global political economy is that it is organized strongly on a regional basis. In the regionalism scenario, countries are organized into groupings based on geographic proximity, perhaps following the pattern of current economic groupings like NAFTA, the European Union, and the Asia Pacific Economic Cooperation Forum, SAARC etc. According to Yalem, the growth of regionalism has been more a pragmatic response to the changing dynamics of international politics.[76] Taking into account these regional organizations, particularly the European Union, it seems that international society is not merely an interaction of states as always portrayed. We should think world politics beyond the nation state. Although, except regional organizations other non-state actors as UNO, NGOs (like Green Peace), MNCs are other important actors in international relations. But here emphasis is more on international regionalism.[77] The period since the late 1980s has witnessed a resurgence of regionalism labeled as 'new regionalism' in world politics. Old regionalist organizations have been revived, new organizations formed. Martin Coward argues that the state of the art in international relations needs critical re-evaluation. The state-centric architecture of the cold war system was supposedly replaced by a supranational, transnational networked global order.[78] The basis for regional cooperation professed and practised by regional organizations, lies in the common national interests deriving from propinquity, similarity of socio-political systems, comparable levels of development and complementary of economies, affinition of language, culture, historical tradition and religion. The regional organizations as EU, NAFTA, ASEAN, AU, SAARC, etc. are said to be an alternative model of intraregional relations. EU is a unique and beneficial experience in today's world. It offers new political and institutional experiments, and its uniqueness stands mostly in the fact that it is a process of continuous dialogue and integration. Its most valuable achievement is without doubt the stability that the creation of EU has brought the whole European continent at one platform.[79]

The post cold war era has accelerated the process of European integration and has generated as a search for common security and foreign policies. In this respect, the European Union is the biggest success story of the 20th century.[80] Along with the EU, other such regional organization are emerging as an important factor in international relations causing decline of role of the state. EU is a major factor in establishing peace and stability in Europe. It has activated itself for setting rules to stabilize economy, to control environmental pollution, to form social policy etc. while peace and stability is traditional jurisdiction of the state.

The benefits accruing to the countries resorting to regionalism seems to be more than the loss they are incurring by participating the integration process. Regionalism as both a quantitative and qualitative important factor in global politics has developed over the time. Regionalism as an issue in global politics is a way of taking a perspective on virtually all of the major questions of our time. Thus in the present era, regionalism seems as a primary feature of global order.

The end of the cold war and the changing nature of power and power structures, the increase in the number of democratic political systems and their possible implications for state to state relations, the spread of capitalism and the acceptance of economic liberalism around the globe, the changing nature and significance of international law and international norms of democracy and human rights, and the rise of global environment issues on the international agenda all contribute to, and also stem from, contemporary transnational politics.[81] The international relations of the twentieth century have all occurred within complex, pluralist political systems. The level of interdependence in the world system has risen in the contemporary period as a result of the expanding role of various non state actors and the development of those patterns of interpretation among actors which are characteristics of systems that are heterogeneous with respect to basic type of actors.[82]

TNCs and NGOs have been the main source of economic and political change in global politics. Today the transnational relations affect intergovernmental relations and have themselves become politicalized. This is sometimes referred to as the domesticization of international politics. It might better be called the internationalization of domestic politics. In the era of global politics, there is no an increasing emphasis in contemporary IR on activities that are not centered on the state and infact, operate quite independently of it. Non-state organizations are thriving as international actors in their own right. The global relations of the twentieth century have all occurred within complex, pluralist political systems.[83] The technological revolution, especially in information and communication technologies, not only has been a precondition of globalization but also enables, inter alia, citizens and non-governmental organizations (NGOs) to enter the stage of world politics. Owing to this technological revolution (especially the internet), these new actors can gather and process information more easily and rapidly and are able to formulate more timely and persuasive political appraisals. In addition, the internet is helpful in distributing individuals' and non-state actors' statements instantaneously and inexpensively around the world.[84]

So it is reasonable to think that states need to give way to some extent to these non-governmental political entities. States which dominate an anarchic and politically decentralized global political system seem ill equipped today to deal with the growing variety of problems such as global environmental issues. All emerging issues such as health, education, welfare, development etc. functions have been carried out by nonstate actors. MNC's and NGO's are now also active in law and enforcement and police training, economic and environmental policy making.[85] The global economy and the forces of globalization have become prominent characteristics of the current paradigm of world politics.

At the global level, what we find is not world government but the existence of regimes of norms, rules, and institutions that govern a surprisingly large number of issues in world politics.[86]

Globalization, no doubt expanded the jurisdiction of non states actions in world politics. But it also enhanced the virtual boundaries of states with the help of the technology. Truly, the world needs the decentralized, pluralist actors in world politics who can cater the increasing demand of the people of world communists of different political social, economic and cultural backgrounds. The positive role of NSAs will definitely curtail the role of high power politics which propels the humanity towards war, conflict and destruction.

REFERENCES

1. Ray Nghrori and Bennett Romberg (ed., 1982). *Globalism vs Realism.* US: Westview Press. p. 42.
2. L. Premshekara (2005). "Global Fight against Terrorism – India and United Nation: Issues and Challenges". *Knowledge Society Journal.* No. 2. p. 28.

3. Charles W. Kegley and Eugene R. Wittkopf (1999). *World Politics Trend and Transformation.* New York: St. Martin Press. p. 188.
4. http://www.alternativesjournal.net/ataman2.htm
5. James Field (1971). "Transnationalism and the New Tribe", in Robert O. Keohane and Joseph S. Nye (eds.). *Transnational Relations and World Politics*. Special edition of *International Organization,* Vol. 25. No. 3. p. 355.
6. Joseph Nye and Robert Keohane (1971). "Transnational Relations and World Politics". *International Organization,* Vol. XXV, No. 3. p. xi.
7. Robert Jackson and Georg Sorensen (2003). *Introduction to International Relations*. New Delhi: Oxford. pp. 280-81.
8. Charles W. Kegley. *Op. cit.* pp. 169-207.
9. Michael P. Sullivan (1982). "Transnationalism, Power Politics, and the Realities of the Present System", in Ray Nghrori, and Bennett Romberg (ed.). *Globalism vs Realism.* US: Westview Press. p. 198.
10. James Lee, and Juliet Kaarbo (2002). *Global Politics*. New York: Houghton Mifflin Company. p. 256.
11. Anthony Mcgrew et al. (1992). *Global Politics Globalization and the Nation State*. Cambridge: Polity Press. p. 256.
12. Stephine Lawson (2004). *International Relations*. UK: Polity Press. pp. 134-35.
13. James Lee and Juliet Kaarbo. *Op. cit.* p. 99.
14. Charles W. Kegley. *Op. cit.* p. 175.
15. Peter Willetts (2005). "Transnational actors in international Organizations in global politics", in John, Baylis and Steve Smith (eds.). *The Globalization of World Politics An Introduction to International Relation.* New York: Oxford University Press. p. 427.
16. Charles W. Kegley. *Op. cit.* p. 169.
17. Karl Deutsch (1989). *The Analysis of International Relations.* New Delhi: Prentice Hall of India. p. IX.
18. James Lee and Juliet Kaarbo. *Op. cit.* pp. 515-18.
19. Anthony Mcgrew. *Op. cit.* p. 2.
20. Tim Dunne and Brian C. Schmidt (2005), 'Realism' in John Baylis and Steve Smith. *Op. cit.* p. 175.
21. Anthony Mcgrew. *Op. cit.* pp. 18-19.

22. *Ibid.* p. 20
23. Keith L. Shimko (2005). *International Relations.* Boston, New York: Houghton Miffin Company. p. 204.
24. James Lee Ray, *Op. cit.* p. 515.
25. Karan A Mingst (2004). *Essentials of International Relations.* New York, London: W.W. Norton & Company. p. 105.
26. *Ibid.* p. 106.
27. Anthony G. McGrew. *Op. cit.* p. 515.
28. Joseph Nye and Robert Keohane. *Op. cit.* p. xi.
29. *Ibid.*, p. xxiii.
30. Robert. A Denmark (1999). "World System History: from Traditional International Politics to the study of Global Politics", *International Studies Review.* Vol. 1. p. 43.
31. Yale H. Ferguson and Richard W. Mansbach (1999). "Global Politics at the Turn of the Millennium: Changing Bases of "Us" and "Them"". *International Studies Review.* Vol. 1. p. 88.
32. Robert O. Keohane and Joseph S. Nye, Jr. (2000), "Introduction: In Governance in a Globalizing World", Joseph S. Nye, Jr. & John D. Donahue (eds.). *Governance in a Globalizing World.* Washington, DC: Brookings Institution. p. 18.
33. *Ibid.*
34. Ian Clark (1999). *Globalization and International Relations Theory.* New York: Oxford University Press. p. 68.
35. Daniel Bell (2001). *Globalization.* London: Routledge. p. 123.
36. Robert O. Keohane and Joseph S. Nye, Jr. *Op. cit.* p. 12.
37. *Ibid.*
38. Ian Clark. *Op. cit.* p. 68.
39. Robert. A Denmark. *Op. cit.* p. 88.
40. Karns P. Margaret and Karen A. Minst (2005). *International Organizations The Politics and Processes of Global Governance.* New Delhi: Viva Books. p. 17.
41. Martin Shaw (2000). *Theory of the Global State: Globality as an Unfinished Revolution.* Cambridge: Cambridge University Press. p. 60.
42. A.M. Slughter (2004). *A New World Order.* Princeton: Princeton University Press. p. 33.

43. Anthony Mcgrew (2007). "Globalization and Global Politics", John Baylis and Steve Smith. *Op. cit.* p. 34.
44. E. Kofman and G. Young (1996). *Globalization: Theory and Practice*. London: Printer. p. 136.
45. Anthony G. McGrew. *Op. cit.* p. 23.
46. Michael Barnett and Sikkink Kathryn (2008). "From International Relations To Global Society", Christian Reus and Duncan Snidal. *Handbook of International Relations*. New York: Oxford University Press. p. 63.
47. *Ibid.*
48. Robert O. Keohane and Joseph S. Nye, Jr. *Op. cit.* p. 30.
49. *Ibid.* p. 12.
50. Michael Barnett and Sikkink Kathryn. *Op. cit.* p. 78.
51. Robert O. Keohane and Joseph S. Nye, Jr. *Op. cit.* pp. 30-32.
52. Tanja Bruhl and Volker Rittberger. *From International to Global Governance: Actors, Collective Decision-making, and the United Nations in the World of the Twenty First Century.* http//wsetiabudi.files.wordpress.com/2008/07/globalgovt.pdf.
53. *Ibid.*
54. Karns P. Margaret and Karen A. Minst. *Op. cit.* p. 3.
55. *Ibid.* p. 4.
56. *Ibid.* p. 15.
57. James Lee Ray. *Op. cit.* p. 513.
58. Philip G. Cerny (1999). "Globalization, governance, and complexity", in Aseem Prakash and Jeffrey A. Hart (eds.). *Globalization and Governance*. New York: Routledge. p. 188.
59. Michael Barnett and Sikkink Kathryn. *Op. cit.* p. 23.
60. Richard Little and Michel Smith (1991). *Perspectives on World Politics*. London: Routledge. p. 244.
61. *Ibid.* p. 248.
62. Michael Barnett and Sikkink Kathryn. *Op. cit.* p. 68.
63. Kjell Skjelsbaek (1971). "The Growth of International Nongovernmental Organization in the Twentieth Century", *International Organization*. Special Issue. *Transnational Relations and World Politics*. Vol. xxv. No. 3. p. 70.
64. Brain White, Richard Little and Michael Smith (eds., 2001). *Issues in World Politics*. New York: Palgrave. p. 2.
65. James Lee Ray. *Op. cit.* pp. 459-60.

66. Michael Barnett and Sikkink Kathryn. *Op. cit.* p. 71.
67. Jeffery Haynes (2005). *Comparative Politics in a Globalizing World*. UK: Polity Press. p. 110.
68. *Ibid.* p. 166.
69. Tanja Bru and Volker Rittberger. *Op. cit.* p. 2.
70. Role of MNC's in the 21st century. 15. Dec. 2005. www. globalgophers.com/expatriatestoday/articles
71. James Lee Ray. *Op. cit.* p. 446.
72. http://www.coursework4you.co.uk/sprtbus35.htm 17.06.2006
73. http://wwwinfed.org/biblio/glvbalization.htm
74. B.Mohanan (1992). *The Politics of Regionalism in South Asia*. New Delhi: Mehra Offset Press. p. 11.
75. Richard W. Mansbach and Edward Rhodes (2006). *Global Politics in a Changing World: A Reader*. New York: Houghton Mifflin Company. p. 289.
76. Ronald J. Yalem (1962). *Regionalism and World Order. International Affairs*. London: Blackwell. p. 460.
77. J. Davidson Debra and E. Mitchell Ross (2001). *NAFTA in the New Millenium: Environmental Challenges to International Trade*. Edmonton: University of Alberta. p. 2.
78. Martin Coward (2006). "International Relations in the Post Globalization Era". *Politics*. Vol. 26. No. 1. Glasgow: Blackwell. p. 54.
79. Michel Caillouet (2006). "The European Union in the World Politics", in Rajendra K Jain et al. (eds.). *The European Union in World Politics*. New Delhi: Radiant. pp. 1-2.
80. Catherine Guisan Dickinson (1999). "European Union in a Changing World". *World Affairs*. Vol. 38. No. 4. pp. 26-27.
81. James Lee Ray. *Op. cit.* p. 445.
82. Ray Nghrori and Bennett Romberg. *Op. cit.* p. 21.
83. Michael Barnett and Sikkink Kathryn. *Op. cit.* p. 67.
84. Tanja Bru and Volker Rittberger. *Op. cit.* p. 2.
85. James Lee Ray. *Op. cit.* p. 445.
86. Joseph S. Nye and John D. Donahue (2000). *Governance in a Globalizing World*. Washington D.C: Brooking Institution Press. p. 20.

Bibliography

Aaronson, Susan Ariel (2001). *Taking Trade to the Streets: The Lost History of Public Efforts to Shape Globalization*. Ann Arbor: University of Michigan.

Adler, Emanuel and Micheal Barnett (eds.). "Securing Communities" (Cambridge University Press, Cambridge, 1998), in Little Richard and Micheal Smith (eds., 2006). *Perspectives on World Politics*. New York: Cambridge University Press.

Andreas, Hasencleuor et al. (1997). *Theories of International Regimes*. Cambridge: Cambridge University Press.

Andrew, Vogt (15 Aug. 2010). "Idealism and Liberalism: International Relation and Theory in Brief". (http//www.bukisa.com/articles).

Ashley, R.K. (1996). "The Achievements of Post Structuralism", in Steve Smith et al. (eds.). *International Theory: Positivism and Beyond*. New York and Cambridge: Cambridge University Press.

Ashley, R.K. (1986). "The Poverty of Neorealism" in R.O. Keohane (eds.). *Neo-Realism and Its Critics*. New York: Columbia University Press.

Baldwin, D.A. (ed., 1993). *Neorealism and Neoliberalism: The Contemporary Debate*. New York: Columbia University Press.

Barkin, Samuel. "International Studies Review", No. 5. Part 4, 2003, in Richard Little and Micheal Smith (eds. 2006). *Perspectives on World Politics*. New York: Cambridge University Press.

Barnet, Richard J. and John Cavanagh (1974). *Global Dreams: Imperial Corporations and the New World Order*. New York: Simon & Schuster.

Barnett, Michael N. and Mortha Finnemore. "The Politics, Power and Pathologies of International Organizations", *International Organisation*, Vol. 53. No. 4 (1999), in Little Richard and Micheal Smith (eds., 2006). *Perspectives on World Politics*. New York: Cambridge University Press.

Barnett, Michael and Martha Finnemore (2004). *Rules for the World*. New Delhi. Atlantic.

Barrett, Michele (1980). *Women's Oppression Today: Problems in Marxist Feminist Analysis*. London: Verso.

Barry, Buzan (1996). "The Timeless Wisdom of Realism?", in Steve Smith et al. (eds.) *International Theory: Positivism and Beyond*. New York: Cambridge University Press.

Barry, Buzan. "People, States and Fear: National Security Problem in International Relations" (Harvester Wheatsheaf, Brighton, 1983) in Richard Little and Micheal Smith (eds. 2006). *Perspectives on World Politics*. New York: Cambridge University Press.

Baylis, John, Steve Smith and Patrica Owens (2011). *The Globalization of World Politics: An Introduction to International Relation*. New York: Oxford University Press.

Bergsten, C. Fred (2005). *The United States and the World Economy*. Washington: D.C.: Institute of International Economics.

Booth, Ken (1996). "75 Years on: Rewriting the Subjects Post-Reinventing its Future" in Steve Smith et al. (eds.). *International Theory: Positivism and Beyond*. New York: Cambridge University Press.

Bretherton, Charlotte and Geoffery Ponton (ed., 1996). *Global Politics: An Introduction*. UK: Blackwell.

Brown, Chris (1997). *Understanding International Relations*. London: Macmillan.

Brown, Chris (1992). *International Relations Theory: New Normative Approaches*. New York: Harvester.

Bull, Headley (1995). *The Anarchical Society: A Study of Order in World Politics*. London: Macmillan.

Burchill, Scott and Andrew Linklater et al. (eds., 1996). *Theories of International Relations*. London: Macmillan.

Burchill, Scott and Richard Devetak (eds., 2005). *Theories of International Relations*. New York: Palgrave.

Buzan, Barry and Ole Waever (2003). *Regions and Powers: The Structure of International Security*. New York: Cambridge University Press.

Calvocoressi, Peter (2001). *World Politics 1945-2000*. Singapore: Pearson Education.

Camilleri, J.A. and Falk, J. (1992). *The End of Sovereignty? The Politics of a Shrinking and Fragmenting Worlds*. Aldershot: Elgar.

Carlsnaes, Walter et al. (eds., 2002). *Handbook of International Relations*. New Delhi: Sage.

Carr, E.H. (1964). *The Twenty Years' Crisis*. New York: Harper & Row.

Carter, A. (1993). "Towards a Green Political Theory" in Dobson and P. Lucardie (eds.). *The Politics of Nature: Explorations in Green Political Theory*. London: Routledge.

Catherine, Soanes (ed., 2004). *Compact Oxford Reference Dictionary*. Oxford: Oxford University Press.

Cenry, Philips, E. Kofman and G. Young (1996). *Globalization: Theory and Practice*. London: Pinter.

Chan, Stephen and Jarrod Wiener (1999). *Twentieth Century International History: A Reader*. New York: I.B. Taurs.

Charli, Chandra (ed., 2010). *War, Peace and Hegemony in a Globalized World the Changing Balance of Power in the Twenty First Century*. New York: Routledge.

Chase-Dunn, Christopher and E.N. Anderson (eds., 2005). *The Historical Evolution of World-Systems*. London: Palgrave.

Clark, I. (1999). *The Hierarchy of States: Reform and Resistance in International Order*. Cambridge: Cambridge University Press.

Clark, Ian (1999). *Globalization and International Relations Theory*. New York: Oxford University Press.

Claude, I., Jr. (1962). *Power and International Relations*. New York: Random House.

Cobden, R. (1903). *Political Writings*. 2 Vols. London: Fisher Unwin.

Cooper, R. (1996). *The Post-Modern State and The World Order*. London: Demos.

Cox, Robert W. and Timothy J. Sinclair (1996). *Approaches to World Order*. Cambridge: Cambridge University Press.

Cox, Robert, W. "Millenium: Journal of International Studies", Vol. 10, No. 2 (1981) in Little Richard and Micheal Smith (eds., 2006). *Perspectives on World Politics*. New York: Cambridge University Press.

Czempiel, E.O. and J.N. Rosenau (eds., 1989). *Global Changes and Theoretical Challenges: Approaches to World Politics for the 1990s*. Lexington: Lexington Books.

D. Smith, Steve (1996). "Positivism and Beyond" in Steve Smith et al. (eds.). *International Theory: Positivism and Beyond*. New York: Cambridge University Press.

Darby, Phillip (ed. 1997). *At the Edge of International Relations*. London and New York: Continuum.

Das, Tania (2004). *Beyond Cold War: Security Council and International Politics*. Kolkata: Minerva Association.

Debra, J. Davidson and E. Mitchell Ross (2001). *NAFTA in the New Millenium: Environmental Challenges to International Trade*. Edmonton: University of Alberta.

Destler, I.M. (2006). *American Trade Politics*. New Delhi: Viva Books.

Deutsch, K.W. et al. (1957). *Political Community and the North Atlantic Area*. Princeton: Princeton University Press.

Devtak, Richard (1996). "Critical Theory" in Scott Burchill and Andrew Linklater (eds.). *Theories of International Relations*. New York: Macmillan Press.

Diehl, Paul F. (ed., 2005). *The Politics of Global Governance*. Boulder, Colo: Lynne Rienner.

Discson, Anna K. (1997). *Development and International Relations*. Cambridge: Polity Press.

Dobson, A. and P. Lucardie (eds., 1993). *The Politics of Future: Explorations in Green Political Theory*. London: Routledge.

Dougherty, J.E. and Pfaltzgraff, R.L. (1971). *Contending Theories of International Relations*. New York: Lippincott.

Doyle, M.W. (Dec. 1986). "Liberalism and World Politics". *American Political Science Review*, Vol. 80, No. 4.

Doyle, M.W. (Summer, 1983), "Kant, Liberal Legacies and Foreign Affairs". *Philosophy and Public Affairs*. Vol. 12, No. 3-4.

Doyle, Michael W. and G. John lkenbery (eds., 1997). *New Thinking in International Relations Theory*. Boulder, Colo: Westview.

Duffield, Mark, "The Global Governance and New Wars: The Merging of Development and Securing" (Zed Books, London, 2001) in Little Richard and Micheal Smith (eds., 2006). *Perspectives on World Politics*. New York: Cambridge University Press.

Dunne, Tim (2005). "Liberalism, in John Baylis and Steve Smith". *The Globalisation of World Politics*. Oxford and New Delhi: Oxford.

Dunne, Timothy, Milia Kurki, Steve Smith (2007). *International Relations Theories*. Oxford: Oxford University Press.

Dunning, John H. (2003). *Making Globalization Good: The Moral Challenge of Global Capitalism*. Oxford: Oxford University Press.

Dwivedi, Dhirendre (2005). *Collective Security Under United Nations*. New Delhi: Kanishaka.

Elshtain, Jean Bethke (1985). "Political Theory", Vol. 13. No. 1 in Little Richard and Micheal Smith (eds., 2006).

Perspectives on World Politics. New York: Cambridge University Press.

Enloe, Cynthia (1996). "Margins, Silence and Bottom Sungs: How to Overcome the Underestimation of Power in the Study of International Relations", in Steve Smith et al. (eds.). *International Theory: Positivism and Beyond*. New York: Cambridge University Press.

Erikrson, Johan and Giampiero Giacomello (eds., 2010). *International Relations and Security in the Digital Age*. New York: Routledge.

Exkersly, R. (1992). *Environmentalism and Political Theory: Towards an Ecocentric Approach*. London: UCL Press.

Falk, Richard A. and Saul H. Mendlovitz (eds., 1973). *Regional Politics and World Order*. San Francisco: W.H. Freeman.

Falk, Richard and Andrew Strauss (Jan-Feb., 2001). "Toward Global Parliament." *Foreign Affairs*. Vol. 80, Issue 1.

Ferguson, Yale H. and Richard W. Mansbach (2008). *A World of Polities Essays on Global Politics*. New York: Routledge.

Fierke, K.M. (2007). *Critical Approaches to International Security*. Cambridge: Polity Press.

Fierke, K. and K.E. Jorgensen (eds., 2001). *Constructing International Relations: The Next Generation*. London: M.E. Sharpe.

Finifter, A.W. (eds., 1993). *Political Science: The State of Discipline*. Washington, DC: American Political Science Association.

Finlayson, Alan (ed., 2003). *Contemporary Political Thought: A Reader and Guide*. Edinburgh: Edinburgh University Press.

Frank, A.G. (1980). *Crisis in the World Economy*. London: Heinemann.

Friden, Jeffrey A. and David A. Lake (eds., 2000). *International Political Economy*. Boston: Dedford/St. Martins Press.

Fukuyama, Franchis (1996). *The End of History and the Last Man*. New York: The Free Press.

Gadzey, T.K. (1994). *The Political Economy of Power: Hegemony and Economic Liberalism*. New York: St. Martin's Press.

Galtung, Johan. "Journal of Peace Research", Vol. 13. No. 2 (1971) in Little Richard and Micheal Smith (eds., 2006). *Perspectives on World Politics*. New York: Cambridge University Press.

George, Alexander (2006). *On Foreign Policy: Unfurnished Business*. Boulder London: Paradigm.

Gill, Stephen (ed., 1993). *Gramsci, Historical Materialism and International Relations*. New York: Cambridge University Press.

Gilpin, R. (1981). *War and Change in World Politics*. Cambridge: Cambridge University Press.

Gilpin, Robert. "Global Political Economy: Understanding the International Economic Order" (Princeton University Press, Princeton, 2001) in Richard Little and Micheal Smith (eds., 2006). *Perspectives on World Politics*. New York: Cambridge University Press.

Goodin, R. (1992). *Green Political Theory*. Cambridge: Polity Press.

Goodin, R. (Dec. 2, 1990). "International Ethics and Environment Crisis". *Ethics and International Affairs*, Vol. 4. No. 1.

Goodin, Robert E. (1996). *A New Handbook of Political Science*. New York: Oxford University Press.

Gooneskere, Savitri (ed., 2004). *Violence, Law and Women's Rights in South Asia*. New Delhi and London: Sage.

Gray, Johan (1998). *Liberalism*. Delhi: Book Land.

Griffith, Martin (ed., 2007). *International Relations Theory for the Twenty First Century*. New York: Routledge.

Grifflths, Martin and Terry O'Callaghan (2004). *Key Concepts in International Relations*. New York: Routledge.

Gulin, Robert, "The Political Economy of International Relations" (Princeton University Press, Princeton, 1987), in Little Richard and Micheal Smith (eds., 2006). *Perspectives on World Politics*. New York: Cambridge University Press.

Haas, E.B. (1958). *The Uniting of Europe: Political, Social and Economic Forces 1950-1957*. Stanford: Stanford University Press.

Haas, E.B. (1975). *The Obsolescence of Regional Integration Theory*. Berkeley: Institute of International Studies.

Haas, E.B. (March, 1976). "Turbulent Fields and the Theory of Regional Integration". *International Organization*, Vol. 30. Issue 2.

Hadjor, Kafi Duenor (1993). *Dictionary of Third World Terms*. London: Pengium.

Hans, J. Morgenthau (1985). *Politics Among Nations: The Struggle for Power and Place*. New York: Knopf.

Hansenclever, Andieas and Peter Mayer (1997). *Theories of International Regimes*. Cambridge: Cambridge University Press.

Haq, Nisar-ul (Jan-March 2005). "The United Nations and Elimination of Discrimination against Women", *The Indian Journal of Political Science*. Vol. LXVI, No. 1.

Harris, Paul G. (ed., 2009). *Climate Change and Foreign Policy Case Studies from East to West*. New York: Routledge.

Harris, Paul G. (ed., 2009). *Environmental Change and Foreign Policy Theory and Practice*. New York: Routledge.

Harry, Howe Ransom (May 2, 1968). "International Relations". *Journals of Politics*, Vol. 30. No. 2.

Hayden, Patrick (2005). *Cosmopolitan Global Politics. Burlington*, Ver: Ashtaate.

Haynes, Jeffery (2005). *Comparative Politics in a Globalizing World*. UK: Polity Press.

Heater, Derek and G.R. Berridge (1993). *Introduction to International Politics*. New York: Palgrave Macmillan.

Held, David. "Review of International Studies", Vol. 29, 2003, in Little Richard and Micheal Smith (eds., 2006). *Perspectives on World Politics*. New York: Cambridge University Press.

Herz, J. (1951). *Political Realism and Political Idealism*. Chicago: University of Chicago.

Heywood, Andrew (2002). *Politics*. New York: Palgrave.

Heywood, Andrew (2003). *Political Ideologies—An Introduction*. New York: Palgrave Macmillan.

Hill, Christopher (2003). *The Changing Politics of Foreign Policy*. New York: Palgrave Macmillan.

Hoffman, John and Pual Graham (2010). *Introduction to Political Ideologies*. Dorling Kindersley (Indian edition) Pearson Education.

Hollis, M. and Smith, S. (1990). *Explaining and Understanding International Relations*. Oxford: Clarendon.

Hollis, Martin and Steve Smith (1990). *Explaining and Understanding International Relations*. New York: Oxford University Press.

Holmes, Mary (2007). *What is Gender? Sociological Approaches*. New Delhi: Sage.

Holsti, K.J. (1988). *International Politics: A Framework for Analysis*. Englewood Cliffs: Prentice Hall.

Holsti, K.J. (1996). *The State, War, and the State War*. Cambridge: Cambridge University Press.

Holsti, K.J. "Taming the Sovereigns: Institutional Change in International Politics" (Cambridge University Press, Cambridge, 2004), in Richard Little and Micheal Smith (eds., 2006). *Perspectives on World Politics*. New York: Cambridge University Press.

Hooper, Charlotle. "Review of International Studies", Vol. 25, 1999, in Little Richard and Micheal Smith (eds., 2006).

Perspectives on World Politics. New York: Cambridge University Press.

Hughes, B.B. (1991). *Continuity and Change in World Politics: The Clash of Perspectives*. Englewood Cliffs: Prentice Hall.

Immanuel, Wallerstein (1996). "The Inter-State Structure of the Modern World System", in Steve Smith et al. (eds.). International Theory: Positivism and Beyond. Cambridge: Cambridge University Press. *International Political Science Review*. Vol. 31. No. 4.

Ivison, Duncan (2002). *Post Calonial Liberalism*. Cambridge: Cambridge University Press.

Jackson, Robert and George Sorenson (2003). *Introduction to International Relations Theories and Approaches*. New York: Oxford University Press.

Jackson, Robert (1996). "Is There a Classical International Theory?", in Steve Smith et al. (eds.) *International Theory: Positivism and Beyond*. New York: Cambridge University Press.

Jackson, Robert H. and Alan James (eds.). "State in a Changing World" (Clarendon, Oxford, 1993), in Richard Little and Michael Smith (eds., 2006). *Perspectives on World Politics*. New York: Cambridge University Press.

James, Patrick (1993). "Neorealism as a Research Enterprise". *International Political Science Review*. Vol. 14. No. 2.

Jilani, Hina and Eman M. Ahmad (2004). "Violence against Women: The Legal System and Institutional Responses in Pakistan", in Savitri Goonesekere (ed.). *Violence, Law and Women's Right in South Asia*. New Delhi, London: Sage.

Jones, Richard Wyn (1999). *Security, Strategy and Critical Theory*. London, Boulder: Lynne Rienner.

Kaplan, M. (1964). *System and Process in International Politics*. New York: Wiley.

Karns, Margaret P. and Karen A. Mingst (2005). *International Organizations: The Politics and Processes of Global Governance*. New Delhi: Viva Books.

Keck, Margaret E. and Kathryn Sikkink. "Activities beyond Borders: Transnational Advocacy Networks in International Politics" (Cornell University Press, Ithaca, New York 1998), in Little Richard and Michael Smith (eds., 2006). *Perspectives on World Politics*. New York: Cambridge University Press.

Kegley, Charles W. (2007). *World Politics Trend and Transformation*. Belmont (USA): Thomson Wadsworth.

Kegley, Charles W. Jr. and Eugence R. Wittkopf (1993). *World Politics Trend and Transformation*. New York: St. Martin Press.

Kegley, Charles W. Jr. (ed., 1995). *Controversies in International Relations Theory*. New York: St. Martins Press.

Kegley, Charles W. Jr. and Shannon L. Blanton (2011). *World Politics Trend and Transformation*. New York: Wadsworth.

Keohance, Robert O. and Joseph S. Nye (2001). *Power and Interdependence*. New York: Addison Wesley-Longman.

Keohane, R.O. (1975). "International Interdependence and Integration", in F. Greenstein and N. Polsby (eds.). *Handbook of Political Science*. MA: Addison-Wesley.

Keohane, R.O. (1977). *Power and Interdependence: World Politics in Transition*. Boston: Little Brown and Company.

Keohane, R.O. (1984). *After Hegemony: Cooperation and Discord in the World Political Economy*. Princeton: Princeton University Press.

Keohane, R.O. (May, 1987). "Power and Interdependence Revisited". *International Organization*. Vol. 41. Issue 4.

Keohane, R.O. (Summer, 1989). "International Relations Theory: Contributions of a Feminist Standpoint". *Millennium: Journal of International Studies*. Vol. 18. Issue 2.

Keohane, R.O. and Hoffmann, S. (eds., 1993). *After the Cold War: International Institutions and State Strategies in Europe, 1989-1991*. Cambridge: Harvard University Press.

Keohane, R.O. and Nye, J.S. (eds. 1971). *Transnational Relations and World Politics*. Cambridge: Harvard University Press.

Keohane, Robert O. and Joseph S. Nye, Jr. "Power and Independence", 3rd Edition (Little, Brown, Boston, 2001), in Little Richard and Michael Smith (eds., 2006). *Perspectives on World Politics*. New York: Cambridge University Press.

Kesselman, Mark and Joel Krieger (eds., 2006). *Readings in Comparative Politics*. Boston, New York: Houghton Mifflin Company.

Kim, Hyung Min (Sep. 2010). "Comparing Measures of National Power". *American Political Science Review*. Vol. 94. No. 3.

Kirasner, Stephen D. "World Politics" Vol. XXVIII. No. 3, in Richard Little and Micheal Smith (eds., 2006). *Perspectives on World Politics*. New York: Cambridge University Press.

Kissinger, Henry (1995). *Diplomacy*. London: Simon and Schuster.

Krasner, Stephen (1996). "The Accomplishments International Political Economy", in Steve Smith et al. (eds.). *International Theory: Positivism and Beyond*. New York: Cambridge University Press.

Lawson, Stephine (2004). *International Relations*. UK: Polity Press.

Linklater, A. (1989). *Beyond Realism and Marxism*. New York: St. Martin's Press.

Linklater, A. and Burchill, S. (eds., 1996). *Theories of International Relations*. London: Macmillan.

Linklater, Andrew (1996). "The Achievements of Critical Theory", in Steve Smith et al. (eds.). *International Theory:*

Positivism and Beyond. New York: Cambridge University Press.

Little, Richard and Micheal Smith (ed., 2006). *Perspectives on World Politics*. New York: Routledge.

Little, Richard (1996). "The Growing Relevance of Pluralism?", in Steve Smith et al. (eds.). *International Theory: Positivism and Beyond*. New York: Cambridge University Press.

Long, David (1996). *Towards a New Liberal Internationalism*. Cambridge: Cambridge University Press.

Mansbach, Richard W. and Edward Rhodes (2006). *Global Politics in Changing World*. Boston, New York: Houghton Mifflin Company.

Mcgrew, Anthony et al. (1992). *Global Politics Globalization and the Nation State*. Cambridge: Polity Press.

Mclean, Iain and Alistair Mamilian (eds., 2005). *Oxford Concise Dictionary of Politics*. Oxford: Oxford University Press.

Mearsheimer, Johan H. "The Tragedy of Great Power Politics" (WW. Norton & Co., New York, 2001), in Richard Little and Micheal Smith (eds., 2006). *Perspectives on World Politics*. New York: Cambridge University Press.

Micheal, O'Neil and Dennis Austin (eds., 2000). *Democracy and Cultural Diversity*. Oxford: Oxford University Press.

Mingst, Karen (1999). *Essential of International Relations*. New York: W.W. Norton and Company.

Modelski, Geogre (1987). *Principles of World Politics*. New York: The Free Press.

Moller, Jorgen Svend-Erik Skaaning (June, 2010). "Beyond the Radical. Delusion: Conceptualizing and Measuring Democracy and Non-Democracy". *International Political Science Review*. Vol. 31. No. 3.

Monshipouri, Mahmood et al. (eds., 2004). *Constructing Human Rights in the Age of Globalization*. New Delhi: Prentice Hall.

Preface

Everything in this world, being or the matter is dynamic: the change might be gradual or swift. International relations are highly dynamic, in constant flux, unpredictable and complex. Shifting from state-centred international politics to multi-actors-centred global politics, there have been tremendous changes. Present global politics is moving through the path of political, economic and cultural flux. There are constant mutations in our world and in the study of international relations. The world is refashioned, particularly, after the end of Cold War and the demise of Soviet Bloc. The Cold War era was considered the 'hard borders', or 'high politics' era. It reassured the predominance of neo realism, bipolar international power structure and domination of nation's state system.

Post Cold War era implies a revolutionary restructuring of global politics. However, the cascade of globalization strengthened the liberalism—its interdependence, institutionalism and market fundamentalism. Yet there has been an emergence of fourth major debate and this is called post-positivism. The events of past two decades in world politics and its unpredictable nature have challenged the metanarratives, their 'objective truths' and existentialism. Post-positivism is a broader theoretical outlook. It has posed different methodological challenges to positivism. Post modernism, critical and normative theories rejected the logic of positivism which separate facts from values, and testify claims in the form of hypotheses. Critical theorists and postmodernists assume that in social science facts cannot be vertically separated from values. The existing truths are historically constructed and they are subjective. For example, the objective truth of social relations accepts men are powerful, logical, genius and women are weak, emotional and dependent. Feminist IR would call it historically constructed. This gender bias phenomenon is privileged for men. All these observations are men made and stem from human agency. Hence, postpositivism rejects the foundation of metanarriatives that there are 'objective truth' of social relations and they cannot be changed. If we accept this notion of positivism, then there is no scope for change and the world will be unequal and a constant play of power politics that justifies war as an instrument to achieve power and national interest.

The present world is undergoing a process of structural transformation in multiple dimensions: technological economic, cultural or institutional. The prevalence of global economy is in terms of global interdependence of financial markets. There is universalisatisation of production, management, distribution of goods, cereals and crop patterns, eating and dressing, music and dance. It is largely the result of international trade and technology. With advancing globalisation, new issues such as human security, gender, environment, non-state actors represent the widening scope of global politics.

Presently, human security is one of the most fundamental needs of humanity. This concept of security consists of social, economic, cultural, political, environmental and physical security of humans. Where people would be safe having economic assurance, sociality and order, and life free without fear. Hence, introducing gender to IR means to highlight the inequalities between men and women where women are a disadvantaged group. J. Ann Tickner (1988) has rightfully remarked, "International politics is a man's world, a world of power and conflict in which warfare is a privileged activity. Traditionally, diplomacy, military service, and the science of international politics have been largely male domains." Hence, gender issues have received increasing attention in IR. Global environmental change has the potential to have serious impacts on human security. Ecological problems threaten the globe as such. One aspect of this problem is that more and more production, consumerism, luxury and comfort are visibly

Mooney, Annabelle and Betsy Evans (eds., 2007). *Globalization: The Key Concepts*. London and New York: Routledge.

Moore, John Allphin, Jr. and Jerry Pubantz (2008). *The New United Nations*. Singapore: Pearson Education.

Moravesik, Andrew. "The Choice for Europe: Social Purpose and State Power from Messina to Maastrieht" (Cornell University Press, Ithaca No. 4, 1998), in Little Richard and Micheal Smith (eds., 2006). *Perspectives on World Politics*. New York: Cambridge University Press.

Nardin, T. (1983). *Law, Morality and the Relations of State*. Princeton: Princeton University Press.

Naunihal Singh (2002). *Dynamics of International Relations*. New Delhi: Mittal.

Neumann, Iver B. and Ole Weaver (1997). *The Future of International Relations Masters in the Making*. New York: Routledge.

Nicholson, Michael (1997). *International Relations: A Concise Introduction*. New York: Palgrave.

Norman J. Padelford et al. (1976). *The Dynamics of International Politics*. New York, London: Macmillan.

Nye, Joseph and Robert Keohane (June 3. 1971). Transnational Relations and World Politics. *International Organization*. Vol. XXV. No. 3.

Oatley, Thomas (2009). *International Political Economy*. Singapore: Pearson Education.

Paolini, Slbert and Phillip Darby (eds., 1997). *At the Edge of International Relations*. New York: Continuum.

Peterson, M. (1996). "Green Politics", in Scott Burchill and Andrew Linklater (eds.,). *Theories of International Relations*. London: Macmillan.

Peterson, Matthew (Nov. 2007). "Environmental Polities: Sustainability and the Politics of Transformation", *International Political Science Review*. Vol. 28. No. 5.

Peterson, V.S. and Runyan, A.S. (1993). *Global Gender Issues*. Boulder: Westview.

Petras, James and Henry Veltmeyer. "System in Crisis: The Dynamics of Free Market Captalism" (Zed Books, London, 2003), in Little Richard and Micheal Smith (eds., 2006). *Perspectives on World Politics*. New York: Cambridge University Press.

Petras, James and Henry Veltmeyer (2004). *A System in Crisis: The Dynamics of Free Market Capitalism*. London: Palgrave.

Piven, Frances Fox, "Socialist Register", 1995, in Little Richard and Micheal Smith (eds., 2006). *Perspectives on World Politics*. New York: Cambridge University Press.

Randhir Singh (2006). *Crisis of Socialism*. Delhi: Ajanta Books International.

Ravenhill, John (ed., 2005). *Global Political Economy*. New York: Oxford University Press.

Ray, James and Lee Juliet Kaarbo (2002). *Global Politics*. New York: Houghton Mifflin Company.

Risse, Thomas and Beth Simmons (eds., 2002). *Handbook of International Relations*. London: Stage.

Rosamond, Ben (2000). *Theories of European Integration*. New York: Palgrave.

Rosenau, J.N. (1990). *Turbulence in World Politics: A Theory of Change and Continuity*. Princeton: Princeton University Press.

Rosenau, J.N. and E.D. Czemmiel (eds., 1992). *Governance without Government: Order and Change in World Politics*. Cambridge: Cambridge University Press.

Rosenau, James (1996). "Probing Puzzles Persistently: A Desirable but Improbable Future for IR Theory", in Steve Smith et al. (eds.). *International Theory: Positivism and Beyond*. New York: Cambridge University Press.

Rosentha, Elisabeth (Sep. 13, 2005). "Global Warming: Adapting to a New Reality". *The New York Times* (www.nytimes.com).

Rothstein Robert L. (2006). "On the costs of Realism", in Richard Little and Micheal Smith (eds.). *Perspective on World Politics*. New York: Routledge.

Rudolph, Christopher (March 2005). "Sovereignty and Territorial Borders in a Global Age." *International Studies Review*. Vol. 7. No. 1-20.

Saul, John Ralston (2005). *The Collapse of Globalism and the Reinvention of the World*. New Delhi: Pengium.

Scholte, Jan Aart, "Global Civil Society", Ngaire Woods (eds., 2000). *The Political Economy of Globalization*. London: Macmillan.

Scott, Shirley V. (2004). *International Law in World Politics*. New Delhi: Viva Books.

Seidman, Steven and Jeffrey C. Alexander (2001). *The New Social Theory Reader*. London and New York: Routledge.

Shamasastry, R. (1951). (Translated) *Kautilya's Arthasasted*. Mysore: Shri Raghuveer.

Sharma, Urmila and S.K. Sharma (2000). *International Relations: Theory and History*. Delhi: Atlantic.

Shaw, Martin (1999). "The Global Revolution and the Twenty-First Century: From International Relations to Global Politics". Stephen Chan and Jarrod Wiener (eds.). *Twentieth Century International History: A Reader*. New York: I.B. Tauris.

Shaw, Martin (2000). *Theory of Global State: Globalist as Unfinished Revolution*. U.K.: Cambridge University Press.

Shaw, Martin, "Review of International Political Economy", Vol. 4. No. 3 (1997), in Little Richard and Micheal Smith (eds., 2006). *Perspectives on World Politics*. New York: Cambridge University Press.

Shimko, Keith L. (2005). *International Relations—Perspectives and Controversies*. Boston and New York: Houghton Mifflin Company.

Smith, S., Booth K. and Zalewski, M. (eds., 1996). *International Theory: Positivism and Beyond*. Cambridge: Cambridge University Press.

Smith, Steve and Amelia Hadified (2008). *Foreign Policy: Theories, Actors, Cases*. Oxford: Oxford University Press.

Snarr, Michael and D. Neil Snarr (eds., 1998). *Introducing Global Issues*. London: Lynne Rienner.

Spiro, Herbert J. (1966). *World Politics the Global System*. Illinois: The Dorsey.

Stean, Jill et. al. (2010). *An Introduction to International Theory Prespective and Themes*. .Singapore: Pearson Education.

Stephen, Hobden and Richard Wyn Jones (2005), "Marxist Theories of International Relations", in John Baylis et al. (eds.). *The Globalization of World Politics*. Delhi. Oxford: Oxford University Press.

Steven L. Lamy (2005). "Contemporary Mainstream Approaches: Neo-Realism and Neo-Liberalism", in John Baylis et al. (eds.). *The Globalization of World Politics*. Oxford: Oxford University Press.

Stoeva, Preslana (2009). New Norms and Knowledge in World Politics. London: Routledge.

Strange, Susan. "Journal of International Affairs", Vol. 42. No. I (1988), in Little Richard and Micheal Smith (eds., 2006). *Perspectives on World Politics*. New York: Cambridge University Press.

Sulliva, Michael P. (1982). "Transnationalism, Power Politics, and the Realities of the Present System". Nghrori, Ray and Bennett Romberg (eds.). *Globalism vs Realism*. US: Westview.

Sushil, Kumar (ed., 1993). *Gorbachev's Reforms and International Change*. New Delhi: Lancers Books.

Sutch, Peter and Juanita Elias (2007). *Basics International Relations*. London, New York: Routledge.

Sylvesta, Christine (1996). "The Contributions of Feminist Theory to International Relations", in Steve Smith et al. (eds.). *International Theory: Positivism and Beyond*. New York: Cambridge University Press.

Sylvester, C. (1994). *Feminist Theory and International Relations in a Postmodern Era*. Cambridge: Cambridge University Press.

Tansey, Stephen D. (2006). *Politics: The Basics*. London, New York: Routledge.

Thompson, J.E., and Krasner, S.D. (1989). "Global Transactions and the Consolidation of Sovereignty", in E.O. Czempiel and J.N. Rosenau (eds.). *Global Changes and Theoretical Challenges: Approaches to World Politics for the 1990s*. Lexington: Lexington Books.

Tickner, J. Ann (1988). "Hans Morgenthau's Principles Political Realism: A Feminist Reformulation" in James Der Derian (1995, ed.) *International Theory Critical Investigations*. New York: Macmillan.

True, J. (1996). "Feminism", in S. Burchill and A. Linklater (eds.), *Theories of International Relations*. London: Macmillan.

United Nations Environment Programme (UNEP) (2002). *Global Environment Outlook*. New York: Oxford University Press.

University Ellen M. Freebery (2004). "Translating a Liberal Feminism Revisiting Susan Okin on Freedom, Culture and Women's Rights", in Mahmood Monshipouri et al. (eds.). *Constructing Human Rights in the Age of Globalization*. New Delhi: Prentice Hall Press.

Vanaik, Achin (ed., 2004). *Globalization and South Asia*. New Delhi: Manohar.

Veltmeyer, Henry (ed., 2005). *Globalization and Anti-globalization*. Burlington: Ashgate.

Viotti, Paul R. and Mark V. Kauppi (2007). *International Relations and World Politics Security, Economy, Identity*. New Delhi: Pearson Education.

Waever, Ore (1996). "The Rise and Fall of the Inter-paradigm Debate", in Steve Smith et al. (eds.). *International Theory: Positivism and Beyond*. New York: Cambridge University Press.

Wallerstein, Immanuel (1996). "The Inter-state Structure of the Modern World System", in Steve Smith et al. (eds.). *International Theory: Positivism and Beyond*. New York: Cambridge University Press.

Wallerstein, Immanuel, "Comparative Studies in Society and History", Vol. 16. No. 4 (1974), in Little Richard and Micheal Smith (eds., 2006). *Perspectives on World Politics*. New York: Cambridge University Press.

Walter, R.B.J. (1993). *Inside/Outside: International Relations as Political Theory*. New York: Cambridge University Press.

Waltz, Kenneth (1979). *Theory of International Relations*. London: Addison-Wesley.

Waltz, Kenneth N. "International Security", Vol. 25. No. 1 (2000), in Little Richard and Micheal Smith (eds., 2006). *Perspectives on World Politics*. New York: Cambridge University Press.

Weber, Cynthia (2010). *International Relations Theory: A Critical Introduction*. USA, Canada: Routledge.

Weigal, David (2002). *International Relations*. London: Arnold.

Wendt, Alexander. "Social Theory of International Politics", Cambridge University Press, Cambridge, 1999, in Richard Little and Micheal Smith (eds., 2006). *Perspectives on World Politics*. New York: Cambridge University Press.

Wever, Ole (1996). "The Rise and Fall on the Inter-paradigm Debate," in Steve Smith and Ken Booth (eds.). *International Theory: Positivism and Beyond*. Cambridge University Press.

Williams, Howard (1996). *International Relations and the Limits of Political Theory*. London: Macmillan.

Yunus, Mohammed (2003). *Foreign Policy: A Theoretical Introduction*. UK: Oxford University Press.

Yurdusev, A. Nuri (2003). *International Relations and Philosophy of History: A Civilization Approach*. New York: Cambridge University Press.

Zalewski, Marysia (1996). "All These Theories Yet the Bodies Keep Piling up: Theories, Theorists, Theorizing", in Steve Smith et al. (eds.). *International Theory: Positivism and Beyond*. New York: Cambridge University Press.

Zeits, Johan L. (2003). *Global Issue: An Introduction*. UK: Blackwell.

WEBLINKS

http:www.yale.edu/lawweb/avalon/westphal.htm

http:www.jeanmonnetprogram.org/papers/00/00f0801.html

http:www.geocities.com/Athens/2391/

http:www.mtholyoke.edu/acad/intrel/carr.htm

http:www.globalpolicy.org/globaliz/econ/histneol.htm

http:www.ukc.ac.uk/politics/englishschool/

http:www.revise.it/reviseit/EssayLab/Undergraduate/Politics/e3 13.htm

http://europa.eu.int/

http:www.westga.edu/~escott/history/mercan.html

http:www.marxists.org/

http:www.usip.org/

http:www.assets.cambridge.org/0521808707/sample/0521808 707WS.pdf

http:www.uta.edu/huma/illuminations/

http:www.ukc.ac.uk/politics/publications/journals/kentpapers/ webb4html

http:www.addc.vt.edu/feminism/enin/html

http:www.globalpolicy.org/nationas/sovereign/sover/index3 htm

http:www.investowords.com2182/globalization.html

http:www.okusi.net/garydean/works/globalization

http:www.cpogg.org/paper%20/amerang/kourad/20spalth.pdf

http:www.alternativesjournal.net/ataman2htm

http//onlinelibrary.willey.com

http//ips.cap.anu.edu.au/ir/Pubs/Work-papers/02-1.pdf

http//mil.sagepub.com/content/extract

http//www.curstan.edu/honors/document/journals/sounding/Ruiz.pdf

htt//www.wastonistitute.org/bjwa/archieve/feminist_theory/wibben.pdf

htt//www.tulane.edu/dnerson/papers/IPE.pdf.

http//www.globaleconomigovernance.org./wp/content/upholds/IPE/globalizaton

http//www.interpapes.ca/en/publications/feminist_political_economy.pdf

http//www.2.UPS.edu/ipe/whatis.pdf

http//scholar.harvard.edu/jfriend/publications/international-Political_economy-global and domestic_interactions

http//www.amazon.com/international-political-economy-intellectual-history

http//www.rautledge.com

http//www.polis.leads.ac.UK

http//www.ehow.com

http//www.asrudiancenter.worldpress.com/critical_theory_ar_an_international_relations

http//plato.standford.edu/entries/critical_theroy

http//ideas.repec.org/P/erp/conweb/html

http//www.e-ir.info

http//www.cba.unomahia.edu./faculty/web/diamond.pdf. Hayak constructivism.pdf

http//www.colorado.edu.philosophy/center/some/papers/buckley-poster-facts and-principal-constructivism.pdf

http//www.digitalarchive.gsu.edu/philosophy-theses

http//www.amazon.com/international-relations-theory-twenty-first-century.pdf

http//www.in_spire.org./reviews/previus/hso1072004/Pdf

http//www.buskisa.com/articles

http//www.isn.ethz.ch/isn/Digital-Library/Publications/Details

http//www.nla/gov/au/openpublish/index.php/imd/aticle/news

leading to exploitation of the non-renewable resources of our mother Earth. It has not only threatened its very existence, but also created a distance between humans and nature. Presently, globalisation is the most important process affecting relations between states as well as non state actors. The world is rapidly becoming interconnected and becoming single integrated community. This movement and vibrant interactions are uniting the world and making national boundaries 'soft' and less important. A number of non state actors are making this process more successful. No nation state can ignore their existence and effectiveness. Consequently, the contemporary state system is challenged by non state actors. However, information communication technologies have widened the jurisdiction of the state and also made it virtual.

Keeping all these dimensions in view, this book is divided into three parts: History, Theory and Issues. The history part contains the history of international relations, particularly, the Cold War and post Cold War era. The Second Part examines the theory of international relations. All major conventional theories, Idealism, Realism/Neorealism, Liberalism/ Neoliberalism, and Dependency theories have been analysed. Along with it one alternative theory, International Political Economy has also been studied due to its present relevance in global politics. The post positivist theories such as Post Modernism, Critical Theory and Constructivism have been sufficiently explained. The Third Part consists of various important issues and processes. This section is divided into Five Chapters: Human Security; Gender Sensitization of World Politics; Environment: Contrasting Conceptions and Global Responsibility; Globalization; and Role of State and Non State Actors in Global Politics.

I take this opportunity to thank all those who have helped us to complete this task. I am highly grateful to Harjodh for his continuous inspiration. He has emboldened me to initiate this difficult objective. I always feel lucky enough, possessing precious friends Baljinder, Shashi and Surinder who have always been my source of inspiration. Shashi and her loving daughter Aastha made sincere effort to beautify this work. Ajit

Pal and Sukhdev also deserves appreciation for their sincere help. Lastly, my co-outhor Sheveta Sehgal, and I are highly thankful to Atlantic Publishers and Distributors (P) Ltd. for the interest evinced in publishing this book.

Parmjit Kaur Gill

http//www.impra.ub.uni_muenchen.de/2478/pdf

http//www:waterdorn.org/pub/23

JOURNALS

- *American Political Science Review* (Quarterly). New York: Columbia University Press.
- *Ethics and International Affairs* (Quarterly). New York, Wiley: Carnegic Council.
- *Harijan* (10-2-1946). Ahmedabad: Nav Jivan Publishing House.
- *India Quarterly*. Delhi: Sage.
- *Indian Journal of Political Science* (Quarterly). Jaipur. Indian Political Science Association.
- *International Organization* (Quarterly). Cambridge: Cambridge University Press.
- *International Science Review* (Quarterly). New Delhi: Sage.
- *International Social Work* (Bi-monthly) London: Sage.
- *International Study Review* (Quarterly) New York, Wiley: Blackwell.
- *Journal of International Politics and Development* (Twice Yearly). Kokomo: Indiana University.
- *Journals of International Affairs* (Quarterly). New York: Columbia University Press.
- *Millennium: International Studies* (Try-Yearly). London: Sage.
- *Philosophy and Public Affairs* (Quarterly). New York: Sage.
- *Theory and Society* (Quarterly). New York: Springer.
- *Young India* (18-6-25). Ahmedabad: Nav Jivan Publishing House.